Contents

Series Note ix
Preface xi

Section I: Ideas and Ideologies

Introduction 3
  Samir Kumar Das
1. Shefali 9
  Ranabir Samaddar
2. Security, Gender and Conflict Prevention: 20
  Perceptions from South Asia
  Sumona DasGupta
3. Ethnicity and Democracy Meet When Mothers Protest 54
  Samir Kumar Das
4. Afterword 78
  Stree Shakti Sanghatana
5. Islam, Feminism and the Women's 97
  Movement in Pakistan: 1981–1991
  Fauzia Gardezi
6. Women, Nationalism and War: "Make Love Not War" 112
  Rada Ivecovic

Section II: Movements

Introduction 133
  Kalpana Kannabiran
7. Women in Sri Lankan Peace Politics 138
  Saro Thiruppathy and Nirekha De Silva
8. Motherhood as a Space of Protest: Women's Political 152
  Participation in Contemporary Sri Lanka
  Malathi de Alwis

9. Negotiating Peace: Feminist Reflections
   Kalpana Kannabiran, Volga and
   Vasantha Kannabiran
	175

10. The Space between: Women's Negotiations with Democracy *Paula Banerjee*	201
11. Minorities, Women and Peace: A South Asian Perspective *Meghna Guhathakurta*	218

SECTION III: VOICES

Introduction *Anuradha Bhasin Jamwal*	233
12. Shed No More Blood: Mothers for Peace	238
13. WAF to Continue Protest against Discriminatory Laws	240
14. The Way of the World *Josiane Racine and Jean Luc Racine*	243
15. Chadur aur Diwari *Fehmida Riyaz*	272
16. Drawing Lines, Erasing Lines: Feminism as a Resource in Opposing Xenophobia and Separatism *Cynthia Cockburn*	274
17. In Conversation with Dr Hanan Ashrawi *Aditi Bhaduri*	289
Further Readings on Themes in Peace Studies	301
About the Editor and Contributors	311
Index	315

Women in Peace Politics

SOUTH ASIAN PEACE STUDIES

Series Editor: Ranabir Samaddar

OTHER TITLES IN THE SERIES

Volume 1: Peace Studies: An Introduction to the Concept, Scope, and Themes (edited by Ranabir Samaddar)
Volume 2: Peace Processes and Peace Accords (edited by Samir Kumar Das)
Volume 4: Human Rights, Human Rights Institutions and Humanitarian Crisis (edited by Ujjwal Kumar Singh)

EDITORIAL ADVISORY BOARD

Daya Varma, Professor, McGill University, Montreal, President CERAS, Montreal, Canada
Ghislaine Glasson Deschaumes, Founder and Director of the international journal of critical thought *Transeuropéennes*, Paris, France
Itty Abraham, East–West Center, Washington DC, USA
Jyrki Kakonen, Jean Monnet Professor, Department of Political Science and International Relations, University of Tampere, Finland
Oren Yiftachel, Professor, Department of Geography, Ben Gurion University, Beer Sheva, Israel
Paul Joseph, Professor of Sociology, and Peace and Justice Studies, Tufts University, MA, USA
Rada Ivekovic, Professor, Department of Sociology, Jean Monnet University, Saint Etienne, France
Shree Mulay, Director, McGill Centre for Research & Teaching on Women, McGill University, Montreal, Canada
Stefano Bianchini, Director, Europe and the Balkans International Network, University of Bologna-Forli Campus, Forli, Italy

EDITORIAL BOARD FOR THIS VOLUME

Paula Banerjee
Samir Kumar Das
Kalpana Kannabiran
Anuradha Bhasin Jamwal

SOUTH ASIAN PEACE STUDIES: VOLUME 3

WOMEN IN PEACE POLITICS

Edited by Paula Banerjee

SAGE
Los Angeles • London • New Delhi • Singapore
www.sagepublications.com

Copyright © Mahanirban Calcutta Research Group (MCRG), 2008

All rights reserved. No part of this book may be reproduced or utilized in any form or by any means, electronic or mechanical, including photocopying, recording or by any information storage or retrieval system, without permission in writing from the publisher.

First published in 2008 by

SAGE Publications India Pvt Ltd
B 1/I-1 Mohan Cooperative Industrial Area
Mathura Road, New Delhi 110 044, India
www.sagepub.in

SAGE Publications Inc
2455 Teller Road
Thousand Oaks, California 91320, USA

SAGE Publications Ltd
1 Oliver's Yard, 55 City Road
London EC1Y 1SP, United Kingdom

SAGE Publications Asia-Pacific Pte Ltd
33 Pekin Street
#02-01 Far East Square
Singapore 048763

Published by Vivek Mehra for SAGE Publications India Pvt Ltd, typeset in 10/12pt Century Schoolbook by Star Compugraphics Private Limited, Delhi and printed at Chaman Enterprises, New Delhi.

Library of Congress Cataloging-in-Publication Data

Women in peace politics/edited by Paula Banerjee.
 p. cm. — (South Asian peace studies; v. 3)
 Includes bibliographical references and index.
 1. Women and peace—South Asia. I. Banerjee, Paula.

JZ5597.2.S64W66   303.6'6092254—dc22   2008   2008020035

ISBN: 978-0-7619-3570-4 (PB)

The SAGE Team: Elina Majumdar, Anushree Tiwari, Mamta Singh and Trinankur Banerjee

TO FLAVIA AGNES

MOTHERHOOD AND DEMOCRATIC POLITICS

Feminist writings seem to be divided on the question of what could be the possible outline of women's agenda that aims at bringing them to the centre of democratic politics in the region. Most of the feminists, for example, seem to have set the agenda in the backdrop of a binary between ethnicity/nation and democracy in which ethnicity/nation is viewed as the bastion of patriarchy. According to this line of argument, it is by way of decisively breaking away from the confines of ethnicity or nationhood that a transition could be made towards democracy and a more democratic form of politics. Any struggle against patriarchy, therefore, will have, first of all, to be a struggle against ethnicity/nation that, almost as a rule, subjects women to patriarchy. Similarly, a democratic struggle is to be firmly ensconced in a feminist agenda. Men will certainly have a vested interest in the perpetuation of both ethnicity and nation on the one hand and patriarchy on the other. Cynthia Enloe for example, looks upon "the making of nations" and ethnicities as "a process of struggle between women and men" (Enloe 1993: 250). While men will always tie them down to their national and ethnic affiliations and thereby subject them to all varieties of patriarchal pressures, women's struggle against any of these affiliations will first of all have to be a struggle against men *within* their communities. The gendered nature of the struggle against one's ethnicity and nation, according to them, is only obvious. The point, as we will see, is also borne out by many an empirical study—albeit sporadically conducted—from time to time on the women's movements in different parts of the northeast. Thus, Dolly Kikon's study referring to the women in Naga society warns us:

> Every Naga woman has experienced humiliation and insults from men on the basis of her womanhood. These men are not outsiders or strangers. They are their "respected" uncles, cousins and in some cases, fathers and brothers who never fail to remind them about the "predestined inferior" roles that have been already slated out for them (Kikon in Fernandes and Barbora [eds] 2002: 179).

Sukalpa Bhattacharjee in another interesting study designates the women within the ethnic communities of the northeast as "internal minorities" and highlights the agenda of reforms that such women's organizations as Mizo Women's Federation (MWF or Mizoram Hmeichhe Insuihkhawn Pawl) have brought to the forefront of their political struggles while interrogating patriarchy (Bhattacharjee in Dhamala and Bhattacharjee [eds] 2002: 133). Their reforms agenda touches upon almost every sector of human life, ranging from the abolition of dowry, enactment and implementation of the Christian Marriage Bill and Christian Marriage and Adoption Bill in place of the prevailing Mizo customary laws to women's entitlement to inheritance and succession. Conversely, wherever women's politics has been governed by the traditional and ethnic norms, as in the case of the Naga Mothers' Association, they have imposed—in the words of Bhattacharjee—"a limit on the woman's self". In another interesting study on the Meitei women of Manipur, N. Vijayalakshmi Brara draws our attention to "their reluctance to touch the norms of the society" and initiate radical social reforms (Brara in Fernandes and Barbora [eds] 2002: 195). Elsewhere, she observes that Meira Paibis[1] "have not questioned the power of patriarchy" (quoted in Banerjee 2002: 15). They do not have, for instance, any policy or ideology towards domestic violence and polygamous liaisons, etc., which are widely prevalent in the Meitei society. "These organizations" as Brara tells us, are "*of* women and not necessarily *for* women". An autonomous women's agenda—unaffected by the ethnic and nationalist ones—is regarded as the key to success of the women's movements in the region (Mahanta in Banerjee 2002: 27).

Feminist agenda, according to this line of argument, has to be pure and clinically sanitized as it were so as to be completely autonomous from that of ethnic movements. Such a purist view, as we will see, fails to appreciate the fact that the relation between ethnicity and democracy is far more complex than what it would have us believe. Women's democratic struggles in the region are in many ways embedded in ethnicity and ethnic movements and the success of their struggle depends not so much on their ability to stand alone (for that is what seldom happens in any society), but very much on how they steer and negotiate their way through the conflict between their gender identities as women and as members of some particular ethnic communities: "... we are always not just a woman but a woman who has to deal one way or another with 'being' a Serb, an English woman, or Indian" (Cockburn 2004). This view impels us to appreciate that democratic politics does not have to be necessarily anti-ethnic as much as ethnic politics does not have to be necessarily anti-democratic. Indeed, as we argue, there is no way by which we can erect a wall of separation between them. The prospects of democracy in the region are likely to be determined by the contingent and specific nature of these struggles. Feminism in India's northeast cannot simply thrive on pursuing any pure and autonomous project of emancipating the women from their ethnicity and ethnic movements.

Motherhood in recent years has acquired so much of metaphorical importance that it has been responsible for inspiring many a women's movement throughout the world. This illustrates how democratic struggles in India's northeast are interspersed with, what is now called, "the maternal frame" and vice versa. The "maternal frame", which centres women's activism on the metaphor of motherhood, is by now fairly widespread. Some of the most well known instances of the "maternal frame" were Chile, Argentina, El Salvador and Guatemala during the 1970s and 1980s. Groups such as *Co-Madres* in El Salvador, *Madres de la Plaza de Mayo* in Argentina and *Grupo Apoyo Mutuo* (GAM) in Guatemala demanded information from the government about the disappearances of their loved ones on the basis of their identities as mothers and wives. Because of the patriarchal attitude of the nation-states, the hallowed status of mother also protected these women from the extreme violent repression that was prevalent against the dissidents in those countries at that time. During the anti-pass campaign of the 1950s, the Federation of South African Women capitalized on the prescribed collective identity as "mother" shared by women to justify their involvement in the anti-apartheid and national liberation movement. In Jaffna (Sri Lanka) the Mothers' Front came into existence in 1984 at the peak of ethnic violence and played a great role in carrying forward the peace agenda in the country.

Invocation and use of the metaphor of mother is not new to Indian politics. It dates back to the days of the first partition of Bengal in 1905, when there was intense furor against "splitting the mother" and anti-partition popular mobilization, particularly of "the poor and the obscure", centred on the presumed indivisibility of mother (Bose in Bose & Jalal (eds) 1997: 51). The nation that is represented by this indivisible motherhood is also indivisible: Hindus and Muslims are not born of two different mothers. This presumption, according to Bose, still holds true in our age when community-based politics threatens to "slice mother into two" and the metaphor of motherland accordingly shapes many of our responses to ethnic conflicts in contemporary India. In more recent times, the Association of Parents of Disappeared Persons (APDP) came into existence in Kashmir under the leadership of Pervez Imroz in 1994. But, Mothers' Union of Tura (Meghalaya) formed in November 1941 is perhaps the oldest surviving mothers' organization in the northeast.

As democratic politics, in its pure and unadulterated form, is a rarity in the region, these kinds of mothers' movements will have to be distinguished from the paradigm of *pure motherhood* that deliberately avoids any kind of political commitment or intervention on their part and insists only on some form of emotional communion with their children "long absent", "disappeared" or simply "missing" from homes, irrespective of the political cause they have been fighting for. The mother, according to this paradigm, makes a clear distinction between her biological and emotional bonding with children and her children's political and ideological commitments. She expects only the return of her children whom she has been missing for long, whether the political cause they have been fighting for is fulfilled or not. The examples of such pure motherhood are not by any means rare. In June 2002, families of 210 United Liberation Front of Assam (ULFA) militants including Pranati Deka—its then "cultural secretary", submitted a petition to the Assam Human Rights Commission and accused the ULFA "commander-in-chief" of forcing their wards into illegal activities. ULFA, however, interpreted it as a forcible way of collecting signatures from the families and thereby "maligning the leadership as a violator of individual human rights". The mother of Paresh Baruah, ULFA's "Commander-in-Chief", in an informal interview with Indira Raisom Goswami, for example, entreated her to "bring back her son" (Ved 2004). In both these instances, motherhood or mothers' relationship to their children, appears to be pure in the sense of being unsullied by the political movements and struggles their sons and daughters have been waging for years and it is the theme of reunion that comes back and forth in their interviews and memoirs, petitions and entreaties, etc. When the mothers supposedly accuse the ULFA Chief of forcing their wards into "illegal" activities, they seem to go a step further in repudiating the legitimacy of these movements. Motherhood in this instance is not only blind but also an antonym of these struggles. Many scholars and journalists have a tendency to romanticize and dramatize pure motherhood but in political terms such actions are of little value. Pure motherhood is characterized by the pain and anxiety of the loss of sons and daughters in times of prolonged and acute wars and war-like situations and the constant longing for reunion with the "erring" and "misguided" children. The image of a mother, according to this paradigm, is a suffering one and she is, at least theoretically, least bothered about the cause her children are fighting for and the paradigm is premised on the "expectancy" of return of her "missing" children. The suffering mother is alone and isolated;[2] she cannot share her agonizing experiences with others. She thinks she is the only one in the society who has been subjected to such sufferance and there is none else with whom she can establish social bonds and solidarities to eventually make a political intervention of sorts. Pure motherhood is always of a stand-alone type. Bereft of any social and political mooring, it anxiously waits for the moment of reunion.

We, however, see in women's role as mothers the key mediating point where democratic politics and ethnicity/nation meet and affect each other in many unexpected ways. Of course, motherhood is not the only way by which women situate themselves as democratic subjects. There are many other ways too and certainly pure democratic politics conducted through "rational deliberations" by equally "rational" and self-interested individuals a la Habermas is perhaps only one of them. But the metaphor of motherhood, currently in circulation in the northeast, seems to have consciously stayed away from the paradigm of pure motherhood by way of committing the mothers to the *justness* of the cause their children have been fighting for, organizing them accordingly and thereby constituting them as equal and democratic subjects. It is this commitment to the cause that not only makes motherhood political but also critically connects ethnicity to democracy in altogether unexpected ways.

Mothers Crossing Lines

On being asked "how anyone has war without soldiers", Mother Courage, in the famous Brecht play of the same name, answers: "No need for it to be my kids". While this had the potential of becoming the voice of universal motherhood, unifying within its ambit all the suffering mothers, the sentiment remains very personal to her and its universal promise was never actualized in course of this brief play. *Mother Courage* in the ultimate analysis is the story of a hapless mother's solitary battle—not so much against war—but very much against the forcible conscription of her kid into the war army.

Much of mothers' politics today draws on its organized nature. Mothers' solidarities have been gaining in their political importance by way of implicitly preparing a critique of what we earlier called pure motherhood. The politics of Naga Mothers' Association (NMA) may serve as a case in point. The NMA was formed on 14 January 1984 in Kohima as a voluntary organization open to all Naga women with a "clear objective of combating all social evils confronting the society at that time in various forms, to provide a common platform for women's issues and interests and to uphold the dignity of motherhood". The organization does not have any rigid structure of rules and procedures. In fact it operates through various, already existing, local level tribal women's organizations. By contrast, Naga Women's Union Manipur (NWUM) functions more like an association in the modern sense of the term—with its own constitution and explicitly defined hierarchies and rules. Unlike NMA, it holds more regular assemblies, brings out reports and publications and is involved in formal and organized politics of the region. The NMA's motto is "human integrity" and its early focus was to counter the social evils of alcohol abuse, drug addiction and the spread of HIV/AIDS. It is interesting to see how mothers' organizations like the NMA and, to a certain extent, Mothers' Union of Meghalaya, mentioned earlier, focus on predominantly social issues like substance abuse and alcoholism, etc., and eventually bring them to the political arena, which enables them to situate themselves right between the warring groups. It is the concern for their sons and daughters that has inspired them to oppose midnight combing operations by the army and paramilitary personnel, unlawful detention and arrests, rape and other sex-related crimes, black and draconian laws and the unnecessary delay and derailment caused to the "Indo-Naga" peace process, etc. Their entry into the political arena springs from the realization that any concern for their sons and daughters also demands from them some kind of political action and intervention.[3] Unless the larger issues are addressed, their society cannot be cured of these evils.

In 1987, a beginning was made in the history of the Mothers' Union of Meghalaya when there was a firing by the Central Reserve Police Force (CRPF) on the people of Tura town and a combined emergency meeting of the All-India Garo Union, consisting of the representatives of Garo Students' Union, and Mothers' Union was held. The meeting condemned "the unprovoked and illegal firing" and demanded strong administrative action in order to bring the culprits to book. It is interesting to see how the NMA's anti-drug and anti-alcohol campaign brought them to the core of ethnic and "nationalist" agenda. Its concern for addressing social evils brought it gradually to the world of politics and made it realize their "indivisibility" (Chenoy 2002: 135) and inseparable connection. For the NMA, the changeover came in 1994 when it transformed itself into a group poised for making peace interventions. In the same year, the NMA initiated an inquiry into the massacre of many civilians in Mokokchung and submitted a memorandum to the National Human Rights Commission. The NMA also opposed the imposition of Armed Forces (Special Powers) Act (AFSPA) of 1958 on Nagaland. Unless the causes of these social evils are properly addressed and taken care of, the cases of drug addiction, substance abuse, alcoholism and such other things are bound to shoot up. The NMA does not believe in preserving the status quo for fear of peace being disrupted by it. But it subscribes to peace being established through justice.[4] It views such apparent social evils as alcoholism, drug and substance abuse and sex-related crimes not so much as single and isolated cases, but as offshoots of larger social and political problems. NMA's three successively elected Presidents Sano Vamuzo, Neidonuo Angami and Khesilie Chisi have located these social evils in the political problems facing the Naga society (Manchanda 2004: 25). The NMA, with the help of Kripa Foundation and other charities, set up a Drug

Rehabilitation Centre and an AIDS Care Hospice. After ceasefire was declared in 1997, the NMA with the NWUM went to speak to the Nationalist Socialist Council of Nagaland–Issac Muivah faction (NSCN [I-M]) leaders and then to Khaplang—the leader of the other faction—to appeal to them to meet and talk over their differences. The factional killings continue, although the intensity has been substantially reduced. The NMA's language of mobilization revolves around motherhood and it may have held it back from enunciating a pure and unalloyed gender rights agenda. A resolution of the seventh NMA assembly stresses the need for social reform among the Naga women. The NMA does not agitate for women's representation in *Naga Hoho* (the traditional apex representative body of the Nagas). It actually reproduces the same gendered division of labour—"we have our role to play as mothers and they theirs"—Neidonuo Angami explained.

Why does motherhood become the governing, if not the indispensable, metaphor of women's politics in today's northeast? One explanation, of course, is the hallowed status that a mother enjoys in every society, especially in the traditional ones. Speaking of the role of mothers in the general context of the region, N. Vijayalakshmi Brara observes: "They are the only ones who can dare to warn and scold the people in underground movement ... When they speak, society listens" (quoted in Das and Banerjee [eds] 2001: 37). Although this sounds somewhat exaggerated, there is no denying the truth that the mothers have of late become a viable democratic constituency in the northeast.

But it will be wrong to say that by playing the role of mother, women in these societies remain bound by their families and traditions that otherwise perpetuate patriarchy, for while playing it, they also fill it up with newer and hitherto unknown understandings. It is the everyday performance of their role as mothers that is responsible for introducing a certain difference to the traditional role that the women are supposed to play. This is what involves inevitable politicization of motherhood. Besides, their invocation of motherhood as a metaphor should not be seen only as a continuation and reproduction of their traditional role but more as a political strategy. In a society ridden with conflicts that invariably reduce women to abject victimhood, there are "not many entry points" left for them to organize and assert themselves (Banerjee 2002: 5). Motherhood is probably one of those few "entry points" still left for them to make effective peace interventions. In a society where institutions of democratic politics have either not come into being or have been severely undermined, where the forces of patriarchy confine women to their socially designated roles and stereotypes, it is impossible to think of the institutions and idioms of modern democratic politics to strike roots and inform women's politics in the region.

Thus, the politics that secretes out of the metaphor of motherhood turns pure motherhood, as it were, on its head. It disentangles motherhood from any given mother–child relationship and thereby de-contextualizes itself. Every woman is a mother—potential or real—and there is a mother in every woman. It does not matter whether a Naga dies or a Kuki; it is important that a mother has lost her child. The NMA's shift towards universal motherhood thus marks a departure from the established paradigm of ethnic politics in the region. As Neidonuo Angami observed in 2001 when the Bangkok declaration was made, extending Indo-Naga ceasefire "beyond territorial limits":

> We welcome the recent ceasefire without territorial limits to all Naga-inhabited areas. But to our surprise our sister states (Manipur, Assam, Arunachal Pradesh) have started to oppose it. We feel sorry for the unnecessary loss of lives in Imphal and the properties destroyed. We feel sorry there are differences in perspectives on the ceasefire. To us the ceasefire means cessation of armed confrontation, the creation of space for people to people dialogue, free movement of peoples, a time and space for consultation to find a permanent solution to the conflict. But to others it is threatening. In what way has it become a threat is not clear. We hope that we can explain what we mean by ceasefire. We are confident that they will understand. We appeal to them as Mothers that we should all work for peace because if a child dies, it touches us, it grieves us. Because for a mother anybody's child is our child (quoted in Manchanda 2004: 62).

She has been persistently making the point. In a civil society dialogue organized in 2002, she, for example, pointed out that "as mothers we do not care just for our children but other children too who are victims of atrocities and violence" (quoted in Banerjee 2002: 16). The NMA, in fact, keeps one day each year for mourning the dead—irrespective of the community he or she belongs to, for it means somebody has lost her son or daughter. It is this metaphor of a universal mother (that is very unlike the traditional motherhood that remains confined to the four walls of the particular family, clan or community) that also drives them to listen to the experiences of mothers who do not belong to the same community, open dialogues and build bridges with them. In 2002, for example, she asserted that "the only way to build relationships is to have an understanding of others' problems" (quoted in Banerjee 2002: 16). Pure motherhood remains obsessed with only one's own biological children and is oblivious to what happens to the children of others, who may have been killed by one's own children. Even an aggressor's mother is bound to shed tears for the mother of the victim and vice versa. Concern for all victims implies transcendence of the narrow ethnic boundaries and collective concern for all people whose lives have similarly been blighted by rape, torture and intimidation—irrespective of one's ethnicity and nation.

While class as a trans-ethnic or transnational solidarity has lost much of its pertinence in recent years, particularly in the region, this paper within its short span traces the role mothers play in societies mired by prolonged spells of ethnic wars and violence. The existence of voluntary groups like the All-Tribal Women's Organization (ATWO) in Manipur helped in bringing such conflicting communities as the Nagas, the Kukis and the Meiteis together and encouraging habits of cooperation and trust. The three communities mentioned above are presently caught in a tangled web in which everyone is making the homeland claim over the largely overlapping and, in some cases, over the same territory. Naga Women's Union, Manipur (NWUM) has taken the initiative of organizing workshops and seminars that have promoted Inter-Group Dialogue and Mediation Skills. ATWO's mandate covers both Naga and Kuki women. Given the high levels of tension and suspicion between the communities, its Kuki President in 2004—M. Hechin Haokip tried an experiment in social integration by organizing inter-community volleyball matches. At the peak of the Naga–Kuki war in the early 1990s, Amita Tushimi and T Shangnu of NWUM went to Kuki villages and appealed to the women and elders to try and stop the killings. They facilitated the meeting between the Nagas and the Kukis. In the run-up to the 1999 Parliamentary elections, NWUM records that it had intervened eight times to stop violence from exploding. During the Manipur Assembly elections in 2000, NWUM women intervened at least on 10 occasions to defuse tensions between rival factions of Naga rebels, the public and the armed groups and between different communities.

It is interesting to note that in times of heightened ethnic and intercommunity conflicts, it is mostly women who are seen to cross the ethnic lines. In fact *Athwass* (a Kashmiri word which means handshake or holding of hands as an extension of solidarity or trust) is the name of an initiative conceptualized at the Women in Security, Conflict Management and Peace (WISCOMP) roundtable held in 2000, that brought together women from Kashmiri Pundit, Muslim and Sikh communities for the first time in almost a decade since the conflict in its renewed form started in the Valley. Its main objective is to familiarize themselves with "contrasting realities and narratives" they hold and harbour about each other and this is expected to ensure their transparency in our dealings with others and dissolve the boundaries (Gopinath and Sewak 2003). In Kashmir, we know of other initiatives too. But still there is what Urvashi Butalia calls, "considerable reluctance" to involve wives of the men in army and the security forces who too are victims of conflict (Butalia 2002: xix). Building bridges is not going to be easy and will be a long haul. In simple terms, there is no way we can celebrate the women's role in crossing the lines.

CARE AND RESISTANCE

While motherhood is a universal category, it is obvious that the pure mother is a suffering person, standing alone and constantly appealing to our compassion and sympathy instead of bonding herself with others. The universal mother, freed from the specific context of the biological mother–child relationship and the obligations particular to the context, is the agent of social resistance. Sufferance does not numb her to inaction and passivity. She strips herself, bangs on the stately gates of Kangla Fort and dares the assailants to rape her. The social acceptability of mothers lies in the fact that they can reveal their softness and plasticity. The men are unable to cross the ethnic lines because they are very much public persons and they are often held back by the hard public positions they are called upon to take.

Thirty-two year old Thangjam Manorama alias Henthoi was picked up by the jawans of 17 Assam Rifles from her home at *Baman Kampu Mayai Leikei* village on the outskirts of Imphal, Manipur around midnight on 10 July 2004 for her alleged link with People's Liberation Army or PLA (her arrest memo describes her as "a suspect of PLA") and her bullet-ridden and badly mutilated body was recovered next morning by the villagers about three kilometres away from where she was arrested. The members of her family refused to accept her body on the allegation that she was raped before being murdered. At about noon, when the residents of her village staged a sit-in demonstration in the locality and completely jammed the traffic flow on an arterial national highway, few could realize that it was not just another incident of rape and murder that usually evokes only impromptu and momentary protest but fizzles out with the passing of time and is easily forgotten before the next incident occurs.[5] The incidents otherwise look isolated, having no visible connection between them. The public memory is rekindled each time such an incident takes place and does not seem to leave any lasting impression on the public life of the region. Public memory in the region thus follows a predictable pattern: it reaches a climax each time an incident takes place but fades out as one incident replaces another. Manorama's killing, however, was not an ordinary death of this nature that could fade from people's memory. It was not simply an incident that could be easily forgotten and turned into the brittle pages of history. Such incidents of protest that followed the murder of Manorama are by no means uncommon in the northeast and are organized with fair regularity the moment violations take place. But, protest against Manorama's rape and murder became an integral part of people's sustained struggle for the repeal of a draconian law viz. the Armed Forces (Special Powers) Act, 1958 that is emblematic of how democratic norms are violated and how rights and liberties enshrined in and guaranteed by the Constitution of India do not seem to apply to the people of the state.[6] As Surajit Sharma, reporting from Imphal, observes:

> Merely punishing the men involved in the killing of Manorama will not pacify the people they say. They are demanding the complete

revocation of the AFSPA so that the excesses of the security personnel can be put to a final stop (Sharma 2004: 15).

The greatest challenge that democratic struggles all over the world face, is to weave the apparently finite and the everyday struggles into a sustained one and to make it part of a larger democratic struggle, considered as indispensable to the functioning of a democracy. Indeed, the local women's protest marked just the beginning. By the evening of 11 July the protest spread like wildfire and turned into a movement against the Armed Forces (Special Powers) Act of 1958 organized by the local women's organizations viz. *Meira Paibis* (torchbearers) and *Nupi Marups* (women's organizations). On 15 July, the movement took an unprecedented turn when about a dozen of women protesters of All-Manipur Social Reformation and Development Samaj bared themselves in front of the historic Kangla Fort, the headquarter of 17 Assam Rifles (AR), banged on the doors of the stately gate and asked the "Indian Army" to "rape them" in full public view. On 16 July, a large number of women defied curfew and prohibitory orders and came out on the streets, battling the rubber bullets and tear gas shells lobbed by the security forces, and submitted a memorandum demanding (1) immediate arrest and prosecution of the personnel of 17 AR responsible for the rape and brutal killing of Kumari (Miss) Thangjam Manorama, (2) immediate stop to the systematic and genocidal killing of the Manipuri people, (3) the immediate withdrawal of 17 AR in particular and the army in general who have been committing genocidal killings against the people of Manipur and (4) the removal of "draconian Armed Forces (Special Powers) Act of 1958 with the immediate revocation of Disturbed Areas status for the whole of Manipur". A committee ("Committee Against the Brutal Killing of Thangjam Manorama Devi By 17 AR") set up for coordinating and organizing protests firmly maintained that Manorama was an innocent civilian who did not have any connection with any of the underground organizations operating in the state.

It is interesting to see that the brutal rape and murder of Kumari Thangjam Manorama reflect not just another incident of "stripping" of an individual woman's dignity but what Monalisa Chankija calls, "stripping of all our human dignity". More than anything else, the protesters in front of the historic Kangla Fort demanded women's right to *human* dignity by emphasizing the "superfluity" of their clothes. Their clothes are only incidental to their human dignity. If that is gone, then the clothes they cover themselves with become superfluous. It is equally interesting to note whether the protest against the brutality and savagery of the army and paramilitary forces gradually merged into some form of an all-encompassing *civil* protest against the Armed Forces (Special Powers) Act of 1958, that also cut across the narrow ethnic boundaries and could encompass other communities as well, particularly the Nagas of the Hills of Manipur. While the protesters were of Meitei origin, we will do well to remember that Naga Peoples' Movement for Human Rights (NPMHR) was probably the first in the region to voice its protest against the Act and took it to the apex court, albeit with little success. This paper only sheds some light on how women in the region are caught in the tangled web of ethnicity, patriarchy and democratic resistance and continuously renegotiate and realign them in their struggle for democratic rights and justice.

The Manipuri women's protest against the rape and murder of Thangjam Manorama both deploys and deconstructs the metaphor of mother circulating in our society. We have already pointed out that the unique protest against the rape and murder (might not have occurred in that order) of Thangjam Manorama was not an isolated incident. In fact, it triggered off a series of public protests that opened up the arena of a wider democratic struggle. But in what sense does the "naked protest" of about a dozen Manipuri mothers, banging on the stately gates of historic Kangla Fort (turned into the headquarters of 17 AR[7]) and urging the "*Indian* army" to rape them, mark a paradigmatic shift from the everyday language of shame and victimhood? Each of them, baring herself, claimed to be Manorama's mother ("We are all Manorama's mother"—said a banner held by them) although none happened to be her biological mother. All of them represent the universal mother who eternally cares for her sons and daughters. The mothers who took off their clothes are reported to have "raised a number of slogans questioning, how long they have to suffer, while their sons and daughters are being trampled, tortured, raped and killed by the security personnel" ("Women give vent to naked fury..." *The Sangai Express*, 2004). One, of about three hundred women assembled outside Manorama's house, raised her voice of protest roared amidst massive applause: "We are all Manorama's mothers" and Geeta Pandey—the BBC correspondent covering the story—noted that "not one eye in the gathering is dry".

Monalisa Chankija—the editor of *Nagaland Post* and a Naga herself—observes: "We have been stripped of all our human dignity and the clothes we cover ourselves (with) have become superfluous to our reality". As she makes this observation, she, at one level, finds no difficulty in identifying herself as a Naga with the Meitei mothers and, at another, returns to patriarchy the shame that it has inflicted on them for centuries. Mothers were not just making their *symbolic* stripping *literal* by way of actually stripping themselves, as Chankija would have us believe. In a society where women's dignity is being violated every now and then, covering their bodies has already become superfluous. If patriarchy inflicts shame on them, then protest against patriarchy can be voiced only by way of overcoming it and giving the shame back to it. The jawans of the 17 Assam Rifles, as reports point out, looked "helplessly" at these women and a senior officer came running to them with folded palms apologizing on behalf of the unit. This is perhaps the way of shaming the aggressors.

Most importantly, protesting elderly women were also claiming themselves as mothers. Motherhood is incompatible with "stripping". If the protesting women were asserting their motherhood, their protest also involved its subversion. It was not typical of the paradigm of pure motherhood. This kind of subversion is very uncommon in the history of motherhood in the region. Mothers are never seen in their nakedness. Every culture has to evolve its ways of excising sexuality of the mothers from public discourse and acknowledges it only at great pain.[8] Discussing the sexuality of one's mother is always held as a taboo. Every culture has its ways of desexualizing motherhood. Much of our culture revolves around the problem of desexualizing the mothers. While mother is everywhere perceived as embodying the nation and is therefore central to the nationalist discourse, the latter finds it difficult to contain the Oedipus complex that flows in the society it addresses. The mother represented in the nationalist discourse cannot be an object of sexuality and sexual attraction. Accordingly, the ethnic or nationalist discourse has to appropriately redesign itself in a manner that it renders her finally unavailable for sexual gratification.[9] Their stripping is unusual and unacceptable. Seeing a mother naked is as much a child's sin.[10] But a Manipuri mother is also a political mother whose very act of caring is simultaneously an act of protest. Maternal care is therefore political. This required a deliberate act of breach and transgression of motherhood in its very language. It was basically intended to turn the shame on the rapists and a "drama" was required to be enacted to get across the message.[11] The "drama" gave the protesters a handle to throw off the everyday language of shame and victimhood. But what a drama it was! *The Sangai Express*—a local English-language daily for example reports: "A number of women fainted at the site of protest and they were taken to the hospital for necessary treatment." Unaccustomed as they are, with "the naked protest" by the mothers, it was such a great shock to them. The drama that turns the shame on the rapist throws a gauntlet to the existing patriarchy—a patriarchy that is responsible for investing female body with honour and shame and finds "naked fury" of elderly mothers insufferable. Patriarchy has the anxiety of keeping women's body under control and is haunted by the chronic fear of women breaking the barriers of shame imposed on them.[12] The greatest challenge to patriarchy is the uncontrollable sexuality of mothers that is expressed precisely through the "naked fury" in Manipur.

Interestingly it is their abiding obeisance to motherhood that instantly catapults the region's women into the whirlpool of resistance. For it is, after all, the sense of care for their children that simultaneously propels them to fulfill their obligation towards a daughter being harassed, raped, molested or murdered and a son being tortured, killed, incarcerated or mutilated. As Sara Ruddick puts it:

> A woman's politics of *resistance* is composed of women who take responsibility for the tasks of caring labor and then find themselves confronted with policies or actions that interfere with their right or capacity to do their work. In the name of womanly duties that they have assumed and that their communities expect of them, they resist" (Ruddick 1989: 223–224).

Maternal care in other words is the "entry point" of their involvement in an extraordinarily violent and militarized society that chokes almost all other avenues to political resistance by women. The language these women speak is the stereotypical "woman's language"—the language of love, loyalty, care and affection—but this they speak with a public anger in a public place in ways they never meant to do.

THE POLITICS OF GRATITUDE

As the famous line of Subodh Sengupta's Bengali poem on "The mother of Manipur" (*Manipurer maa*) poignantly asks: "How do you feel (if) your own mother strips herself?" It almost instinctively angers the sons and daughters and fires up their emotions. The sons, in particular, are under an obligation to protect and defend their mothers. The bodies of the sons are viewed by the nationalist discourse in India as healthy and virile bodies—capable of protecting and defending their mothers.[13] A worthy son is one who is capable of fulfilling this obligation or one who can avenge any insult and humiliation meted out to his mother. In any form of nationalistic or ethnic mobilization, it is the proud mother who silently calls upon her son to stand up and asks for gratitude to be shown to her. While summing up the Tamil nationalist literature, Sumathi Ramaswamy points out how the Tamil mother (*Tamilttaay*) is "typically featured as an endangered mother, frail, pitiful, and in desperate need of help from her sons" (Ramaswamy 1999: 39). While the sense of gratitude should itself be strong enough to work up children's emotions, cursed is the mother who has to ask for it. Mother is the archetype of a silent sufferer—who will suffer quietly but never approach her son to return it (honour).

In this connection, we may briefly refer back to the language controversy in Assam. Bengali, as we know, replaced Assamese as the language of "law courts and educational institutions of Assam" by the colonial authorities way back in 1836. Assamese was reinstated in 1873. The period between 1836 and 1873 is described in Assamese circles as "the dark age of the Assamese language". It was during this period that some eminent Assamese intellectual and a few organizations, based both in Calcutta and Guwahati, petitioned the British for bringing back the Assamese language. In 1854, *Anandaram Dhekiyal-Phukan* (Dhekiyal-Phukan in Neog [ed.] 1983/1854: 168), under the pseudonym of "a man of this world" (*ei sansarar ejan lok*), penned an imaginary conversation between two mothers represented by the Assamese and Bengali languages respectively. The Assamese mother regrets that the language that brought the Assamese people up "is now being hated by them and they are enthusiastically adopting your language". Mothers, in simple terms, want their children to feel obliged to them and honour the obligations they incur by virtue of being born to their wombs and learn the mother tongues. If mothers are caring, sons need to be grateful too. The reciprocity of a mother's care and the son's gratitude is what forms the nucleus of mothers' politics in the region. Patriarchy assigns this monopoly role to the son. The "naked protest" not only breaks but also makes the patriarchal image. It is the ambivalent nature of the act that makes it so remarkable and promises to carry forward the democratic struggle on a sustainable basis.

Pebam Chittaranjan's is the story of a worthy son who, by his own account, might have failed in avenging the mother's humiliation but was never short of remorse for having failed in showing gratitude to the mother—the motherland. On 15 August 2004, Chittaranjan—an adviser of the Bishenpur unit of Manipur Students' Federation (MSF) took upon himself the task of defending and protecting the mother. He wrote his suicide note in cold blood, amply doused his body with petrol and immolated himself in full public view in an Imphal street. All this took quite sometime and was filmed by many cameramen present at that time. On being asked why they did not make any attempt to stop him, one of my respondents pointed out: "Why should I? He is doing a noble act and an act to be followed by a million others".[14] He was admitted to the Regional Institute of Medical Sciences, Imphal with 85 per cent burns and died the very next day. His suicide note has been translated into several languages including Bengali. One part of it expresses his resentment against the Armed Forces (Special Powers) Act of 1958: "It is better to self-immolate than die in the hands of the security forces under this ... Act." But the other part re-invokes the nationalist rhetoric. In fact it begins with these words: "First I bow down to my motherland. My mother—chained by the colonial power, the mother of the hills and plains—who have been sacrificing many of her children! Give me strength, so that I can embrace death for the (good of the) next generation of my beloved motherland".

Chittaranjan's remains were never returned to the family, but were instead forcefully cremated by the army. People however held a "royal cremation" along with a "spear-salutation" (traditionally reserved for the members of the royal family) in which he was accorded the title of *athoba* (warrior). But Pebam Chittaranjan was not the only one. There were many others who were reportedly preparing themselves to lay down their lives. A three-member CPI (M–L) delegation consisting of Jayanta Rongpi, Rubul Sharma and Kavita Krishnan that visited Manipur on 6–8 October 2004 reported:

> The Regional Engineering College (REC) students told us that when they were prevented from immolating themselves by the police, they were not brought immediately to the Hospital. Instead, the police brutally beat them after arresting them, and when they came to the Hospital, they had severe injuries. Sanjay, an M.Sc. from Manipur University, spoke to us at length, asking us to ask the Central Government at Delhi, why AFSPA was being imposed on the North East when POTA was being repealed. Another student on the next bed, Gautam, was being visited by his parents, who also spoke to us. One other student, Ranjan, was so badly burnt that he had been taken to Safdarjang Hospital, Delhi. And, most memorably, I went to the women's hostel, where the Warden and many of the students, who also held posts in the Union, spoke to me. Most of them had participated in the mass protests, and been severely injured. Several of them had had broken limbs, as well as other injuries. They were proud of those who had been more severely hurt, pushing them forward, saying, "She is a heroine". And all of them were eager to go to future protests.

The sons and daughters, therefore, have no regrets. They remain ever grateful to their mother. They owe their birth to her and she has made them what they are—the worthy sons and daughters of their mother. The mother has imbibed in them the virtue of gratitude. She is the key agency of their socialization.

Democratic struggles, gender and maternal politics, in other words, are caught up in an intricate web so much so that it is impossible to separate one from the other. Much of the democratic struggle in the northeast is cited in the politics of motherhood as much of women's assertion today invoking the metaphor of motherhood is also cited in these democratic struggles. The sites are not mutually exclusive.

Notes

1. Meira Paibis are literally known as "torchbearers" in Manipur. Born on 29 December 1980, Meira Paibis are the numerous locally-based, highly decentralized women's organizations of the numerically dominant Meiteis, comprising women bearing torches in their hands, patrolling their respective neighbourhoods (*leikeis*) at night against widespread alcoholism, substance abuse, rampant army atrocities, combing operations and illegal detentions by them.
2. Many mothers who lose their husbands and children in violent conflicts live in some kind of social isolation—whether self-imposed or not. In many examples, the traditional support networks for the widows do not seem to work—particularly for fear of reprisal from the state or the militant groups.
3. The initial campaign against substance abuse and drug trafficking also brought the Centre for Social Development (CSD), Imphal to a political campaign for peace in the state (I interviewed Nobo Kishore Singh, one of the leaders of CSD in March 2003 in Shillong, Meghalaya).
4. Anuradha M. Chenoy describes it as "feminist understanding of peace" (Chenoy 2002: 135).
5. A timeline of such individual incidents of protest against the imposition of Armed Forces (Special Powers) Act (1958) is available in Bengali at the APDR (2004).
6. Armed Forces (Special Powers) Act 1958 gives the armed forces almost a free run and authorises even a non-commissioned officer "to open fire or use force even to the causing of death" without any necessary order from any higher authority. Article 4(a) of the Act for example states:

> Any commissioned officer, warrant officer, non-commissioned officer or any other person of equivalent rank in the armed forces may, in a disturbed area—if he is of opinion that it is necessary to do so for the maintenance of public order, after giving such due warning as he may consider necessary fire upon or otherwise use force, even to the causing of death, against any person who is acting in contravention of any law or order for the time being in force in the disturbed area prohibiting the assembly of five or more persons or the carrying of weapons or of things capable of being used as weapons or of fire-arms, ammunition or explosive substances.

Article 6 of the Act also deprives the victim or anyone the right to legal remedies except in certain circumstances:

> No prosecution, suit or other legal proceeding shall be instituted, except with the previous sanction of the Central Government, against any person

in respect of anything done or purported to be done in exercise of the powers conferred by this Act.

The United Nations Human Rights Commission (UNHRC) in its 60th session, held in Geneva in September 1997, scathingly criticized the Act on the ground that it was contradictory to the democratic norms and principles.
7. But now this has been returned to the people of Manipur by the Prime Minister of India.
8. Indeed, the most widely practiced way of insulting one in India is to "swear" to outrage the modesty of one's mother. Most of the invectives and abuses in Indian languages involve imagining another's mother as an object of sexual desire.
9. Sumathi Ramaswamy shows how the beautiful "Tamil mother" (*Tamilttaay*) portrayed in the works of Tamil poets and litterateurs gets transformed from a sensuous object of sexual desire and passion into a "sexually unavailable" entity—"passive, undesiring female herself, erasing all traces of active sexuality from her being" (Ramaswamy in Rajan 1999: 28). Elsewhere in the same essay, she describes her portrayal as "the compassionate image of desexualized, spiritualized, motherhood" constantly invoking only the "filial bonds" (ibid.: 47). Conversely, the mother represented in the "Bharat Mata" (Mother India) temple of Varanasi through the geographical map of India was held as convenient, "precise" and "scientific"-capable of addressing these ambiguities (Gupta 2001: 203).
10. By contrast, in Russia for example, "soldiers' mothers movement' is predicated on "essentialist interpretation of motherhood" (Zdravomyslova in Patomaki [ed.] 2000: 40).
11. The word "drama" was used by Kalpana Sharma who notes: "Even the women's protests would have gone unreported had it not been so dramatic. Perhaps that is why they were forced to resort to this unique form of protest despite their fairly conservative society" (Sharma 2004).
12. In the words of Joane Nagel: "While female fecundity is viewed in the mothers of the nation, unruly female sexuality threatens to discredit the nation" (Nagel in Spencer and Wollman eds, 2005: 123).
13. Ironically, the nationalist discourse linked the issue of children's "health and hygiene" with the "health of the nation" (Whitehead in Uberoi [ed.] 1996: 187–209).
14. E. Shyamachandra, a witness to the entire incident, interviewed by me in September 2004.

REFERENCES

All translations from non-English sources are by the author, Samir Kumar Das.

APDR (Association for Protection of democratic Rights) 2004. *Prasanga Manipur: Pathore pathore nache aagun* (in Bengali) [The context of Manipur: Fire dances in the stones]. Kolkata: Association for the Protection of Democratic Rights.

Banerjee, Paula. 2002. *Second Civil Society Dialogue on Peace*. Kolkata: Calcutta Research Group.

Bhattacharjee, Sukalpa 2002. "State, insurgency and (wo)men's human rights" in Ranju R Dhamala and Sukalpa Bhattacharjee (eds), *Human Rights and Insurgency: The North East India*. Delhi: Shipra Publications.

Bose, Sugata. 1997. "Nation as mother: Representations and contestations of 'India' in Bengali culture" in Sugata Bose and Ayesha Jalal (eds), *Nationalism, Democracy and Development: States and Politics in India*. Delhi: OUP.

Brara N. Vijayalakshmi. 2002. "Breaking the myth: The social status of Meitei women" in Walter Fernandes and Sanjay Barbora (eds), *Changing Women's Status in India: Focus on the Northeast*. Guwahati: North East Social Research Centre.

Butalia, Urvashi. 2002. (ed.). *Speaking Peace: Women's Voices from Kashmir*. London: Zed Books.

Chenoy, Anuradha Mitra. 2002. *Militarization and Women in South Asia*. New Delhi: Kali For Women.

Cockburn, Cynthia. 2004. "Drawing lines, erasing lines: Feminism as a resource in opposing xenophobia and separatism" (mimeo).

Das, Samir Kumar and Banerjee, Paula (eds). 2001. *Civil Society Dialogue on Human Rights and Peace in the Northeast*. Calcutta: Calcutta Research Group.

Ei Sansarar Ejan Lok. 1983/1854. "Asomiya aru Bongali bhashar kathopakathan" (*in Assamese*) [A conversation between Assamese and Bengali languages] in Maheswar Neog (ed.), *Orunodoi 1846–1854*. Guwahati: Asom Prakashan Parishad.

Enloe, Cynthia. 1993. *The Morning After: Politics at the End of Cold War*. Berkeley: University of California Press.

Gopinath, Meenakshi and Manjrika Sewak. 2003. *Transcending Conflict: A resource Book on Conflict Resolution*. New Delhi: WISCOMP/FUR.

Gupta, Charu. 2001. *Sexuality, Obscenity, Community: Women, Muslims and the Hindu Public in Colonial India*. New Delhi: Permanent Black.

Kikon, Dolly. 2002. "Political mobilisation of women in Nagaland: A sociological background" in Walter Fernandes and Sanjay Barbora (eds), *Changing Women's Status in India: Focus on the Northeast*. Guwahati: Northeastern Social Research Centre.

Mahanta, Aparna. 2002. "Women's initiatives for peace and gender in North East India" in Paula Banerjee (ed.), *Second Civil Society Dialogue on Peace*. Kolkata: Calcutta Research Group.

Manchanda, Rita. 2004. *We Do More Because We Can: Naga Women in the Peace Process*. Kathmandu: South Asia Forum for Human Rights.

Nagel, Joane. 2005. "Masculinity and nationalism—Gender and sexuality in the making of nations" in Philip Spencer and Howard Wollman (eds), *Nations and Nationalism: A Reader*. Edinburgh: Edinburgh University Press.

Ramaswamy, Sumathi. 1999. "Virgin mother, beloved mother: The erotics of Tamil nationalism in colonial and post-colonial India" in Rajeswari Sunder Rajan (ed.), *Signposts: Gender Issues in Post-Independence India*. New Delhi: Kali for Women.

Ruddick, Sara. 1989. *Maternal Thinking: Toward a Politics of Peace*. New York: Ballantine Books.

Sharma, Kalpana. 2004. "Manipuri women's dramatic protest". *The Hindu*, 25 July.
Sharma, Surajit. 2004. "Who is bothered about Manipur?" in *The North East Frontier Magazine*, September.
The Sangai Express. 2004. "Women give vent to naked fury in front of 17 AR at Kangla". *The Sangai Express* (Imphal), 15 July.
Ved, Mahendra. 2004. "Quest for peace", interview with Indira Goswami. *The Times of India*, 20 November.
Whitehead, Judy. 1996. "Modernising the motherhood archetype: Public health models and the Child Marriage Restrain Act of 1929" in Patricia Uberoi (ed.), *Social Reform, Sexuality and the State*. New Delhi: Sage.
Zdravomyslova, Elena. 2000. "Civic initiatives: Soldiers' mothers movement in Russia" in Heikki Patomaki (ed.), *Politics of Civil Society: A Critical Perspective on Democratisation*. Helsinki: Network Institute for Global Democratisation.

4

AFTERWORD[*]

Stree Shakti Sanghatana

> We Were Making History...
> Life stories of Women in the
> Telangana People's Struggle

When we began these interviews what struck us about each of them was the excitement and the release that this period held for the women who participated in the Telengana movement. During the interviews we shared their sense of immense possibility, of a new horizon opening up for them. What also affected us deeply was the openness and trust with which we were received. It was almost as if the simple fact of recognizing their experience, seeing it as valuable and worth recording, entitled us to share a part of that experience. Their past history constituted, as it were, the basis of our attempt to recover for ourselves a tradition of struggle. It was as if this attempt of ours had revived the significance of their own struggle after a long period of silence. Kamalamma said, "They told me your story will also be history, but until you came, who asked for our story?" Swarajyam said, "Who wrote our history? Who interviewed us? When you are doing this, shouldn't we at least tell you [what happened]?"

They welcomed us like long lost friends, spent time with us ungrudgingly, and asked us to come again. They saw our project as significant and felt duty bound to contribute. We were fed, looked after, and even given small sums of money for our expenses. Their confidence in our capacity to carry this project through added an even greater responsibility to this task.

---

[*]Previously published in *We Were Making History: Life Stories of Women in the Telengana People's Struggle*, pp. 258–274. New Delhi: Kali for Women, 1989.

Who were these women? Where did they come from? Why did they pour into the movement in such large numbers?

There were women of all kinds from different backgrounds and with different experiences. Some from peasant, and some from middle class families. Some even from landlord families. One was brought up in an orphanage and took up a teaching job to support her mother; another belonged to a tradition of devadasis; one had walked out of a violent and disastrous marriage, yet another was from a traditional Brahmin family and was married at the age of five. Many were women from the middle class, forced to observe one form or other of purdah; women whose lives were circumscribed by the kitchen and the household. These women suddenly discovered the opportunity of experiencing something other than producing for the family.

To understand a little more about the status of women in that period, it may be useful to look briefly at the "areas" and "boundaries" within which they were confined. Hitherto the distinction between the private world of the family, domestic labour, sexuality and reproduction, and the public world of production, politics and war, had been maintained clearly. Women were relegated to the private world. It is necessary to see how clearly the two are private world. It is necessary to see how clearly the two are interlinked although they seem apparently unconnected. It is not as if women had total control over the private world. The actual control of the private world lay in the hands of men who moved fairly easily between the two. This private world, apparently the world of women, is also designed to cater to the needs of men. The wall dividing the private world from the public world, however, had been impenetrable for these women. They had not even peeped beyond its confines. Dayani Kausalya tells us that, before the struggle, they had never stepped outside the four walls of the home, not even into their own fields. But purdah was not just the visible and outward symbol of that separation of the two worlds. It was an ideological barrier that controlled their vision, thought and personality. It is the *laxman rekha* which a woman crosses risking her very existence, the point beyond which her personal virtue, her chastity is no longer any protection.

Although the peasant women were not confined to domestic production and seemed to move freely into the public sphere of production; war and political action were outside their reach. For these peasant women the distinction between the public and private spheres was not as rigidly and clearly demarcated. They moved fairly easily between the two. It was they who built up the struggle in the villages against the repression of the *Nizam* and the *Razakars*. Faced with *vetti*, the sexual bondage of the devadasi system, the assumption that they were sexually available to the landlords, the forced levies and the grinding poverty, it was the peasant women who bore the brunt of the oppression, and later, during the struggle, of the repression. After 1944, when the repression increased, many of the men moved to the forests while the women remained behind, holding together what was left in the village. The women formed the backbone of the resistance. They drew on group support. They realized that their strength lay in numbers, used traditional ritual occasions like childbirth, death, or a girl reaching puberty to stay together and foil attempts of rape and torture. They drew on the skills they had and the everyday objects around them to defend themselves. Chilli power, slings and pestles formed their weapons. The majority of the women who participated in the Telangana Struggle were like this. Unlike the few heroines of the movement, these were the countless ones who belonged, as it were, to the prehistory of the movement. It is conventional to pay tribute to the masses who fought any war, but it took us some time to recognize and accept the real importance of these women: what they meant, more so, what they could have meant to the movement. The simplicity with which they articulated their experience,—"we left our pots and ran into the jungle"—the inability to speak of the details of their personal lives made their tales seem repetitive. Ailamma tells us time and again how her crops and grain were laid waste, and her daughter raped. Many said: "Was it a single trouble we suffered. For us to tell you? What is there to tell?" And yet the pain, even the bitterness that was so clear in their voices as they talked, could not be ignored. The starkness with which they described how their families and households were destroyed, how they were beaten and tortured, was clear and totally unsentimental. And yet as they spoke of this period there was nostalgia, which revealed how significant it was to them personally. The stimulation, the support and excitement of working with a resistance movement came through clearly.

For them it seemed as if the walls of the household had suddenly fallen apart. The time was such, and the hope of a new society so near, that the men in the struggle realized that they could never achieve it without their women and without a newer, freer woman.

During the period of struggle women were drawn in the large numbers, partly out of the conviction that they had a role to play as half the human race and partly out of necessity. In times of severe repression the presence of women and their active involvement has been indispensable. They are invariably the providers of the movement and lent credibility to the squad among the villages. It was their presence, which lent the semblance of a family and thus provided cover to the dens. There was also the feeling that if women were also involved they would not stand in the way of their men joining the struggle. The presence of women created trust among the villagers and added a sense of respectability.

Moving into the struggle did mean a tremendous liberation for these women, who believed that it was possible to break with custom to travel alone, travel at night, carry guns, act as couriers, fight in squads—all of which they did. Kondapalli Koteswarmma describes how they pawned their jewels, went to the bank, and sold newspapers on the streets.

There can be no question of the fact that their involvement with the Communist party provided a significant growth in consciousness for the women. Reading, writing, discussing political questions, attending classes, addressing public meetings and organizing women gave them a very positive sense of their role. Priyamvada says: "We gained the confidence to speak at public meetings. We spoke so well that people would come and ask us if we were B.As. or M.As. In one way if we had no connection with the Party we would have been ordinary women who knew nothing." Talk to Kamalamma and she tells us she grasped the meaning of her experience and was able to respond meaningfully only because she came into the struggle. "It's because of the Communist Party that my learning stood me in good stead. But my sister has forgotten everything and it's all wasted now," she says.

It was as if the Party gave them a chance to make practical sense of whatever learning they had. It gave them the tools to understand their social reality and was a source of enormous strength and clarity. They felt that the struggle brought them wisdom, knowledge, clarity and enormous physical stamina. Acchamamba says: "I don't know how I did it—it was just the magic of that time." Kondapalli Koteswaramma says: "It was the Party that said to us: come, and gave us encouragement to come out." Dudala Salamma tells of that time and says: "I don't know how I got the wisdom out of all that ... at least you learnt the letters but I've lived grazing buffaloes. All these details are at the tip of my tongue." Dronavalli Anasuya says: "It was the Party that made us all human beings." Women described to us vividly the liberating effect the movement had on their lives and on their growing consciousness. Let us look briefly, however, at what the Party had to say about the women in the movement and their contribution to it. Devalapalli Venkateswara Rao says: "In public meetings women would form fifty percent of those present. In Nalgonda for instance we had to reserve half of the seats for women. This condition during public gatherings lasted until 1951" (Peter Custers: unpublished interview).

Women evidently flocked to public meetings and also came forward to join the movement in large numbers. They came leaving home and family behind, without thought or care for their personal safety or the risk involved. Ravi Narayana Reddy says:

> Everywhere resistance was put up by our local volunteers. Here women were a supplementary force. People moved out to confront it with slings and stones. Women carrying the stones for the slings ... In Mallareddygudem for example the fighting lasted for eight hours. Here a female stone-cutter was killed called Nagamma. Her name is never mentioned but she was very heroic.

From the interviews with the peasant women who took part in the resistance, as well as statements, such as these by leaders, it is evident that women came not only into the movement but also to join the Party in considerable strength. Given this fact, can we see any consistent policy about motivating women or recruiting them into the Party? Kota Venkata Reddy says:

> For the first time in history the feeling [existed] that women and men are equal. Apart from the economic struggle, propaganda in favour of women's equality [was conducted]. People [were engaged]

in a complete struggle, there was no need to have a separate struggle for women (Peter Custers: unpublished interview).

He goes on to add that the Party took up a programme to fight rape by *Razakars*, and instructed the women to fight collectively to protect themselves when the Union Army came. It also took up a campaign against wife beating, child marriages and encouraged divorce where necessary. They campaigned against the derogatory phrases generally used for women in cultural propaganda. He adds:

> In the Communist Party the percentage of female members was ten. Aside from that many women sympathized. There was no discrimination against women becoming members but the low percentage is because of women's backwardness in traditional society.

This suggests that the leadership believed that there was no conscious discrimination against women but it was their traditional backwardness which prevented their coming into the Party. Priyamvada seems to feel differently:

> They [women] probably felt that if they came to the Party where men and women worked together freely, their lives would change for the better. They could not say all this very clearly but they felt that they could experience another life, live as they chose to. But the Party could not support them as it did not have a clear idea of how to tackle the problem of women who left their husbands and came away. They were also not sure whether it was the correct thing to take such women away from their husbands. They were afraid that the Party would lose its reputation. It would have been good to support these women. After all, the Party had a base. These women wanted to come away because they found their situation unbearable. So many women came willingly in those days. There was a context then.

This feeling of equality between men and women, the possibility of a better life where men and women would work freely together the promise of a different experience evidently brought women flocking to the struggle. It is as if their backwardness in traditional society, instead of holding them back as suggested, actually impelled them towards the alternative that the Party seemed to provide. But the Party found it very difficult to absorb these women into its ranks, risking its reputation and, in the process, alienating public sympathy. Women thus were not seen as people possessed of will and determination but as separate, embarrassing and burdensome. There was also a deliberate and malicious propaganda outside that there was no morality or principle in the Communist Part.

It is also a fact that in times of upheaval, when in reality social norms are being broken and old values begin to crumble, a stronger effort is made to visibly and vocally reiterate faith in the old morality. And so we find what appears to be a reinforcement of traditional ideologies. This could be the basis for the fear that it may not be the correct thing for the Party to "take women away from their husbands." So, women had to fight against traditional beliefs and a feudal outlook, even to become a part of the political struggle. That supporting the women in these personal struggles and politicizing the context of that struggle could have brought a new and progressive philosophy into existence was apparently a possibility that the Party did not realize. For us, the fact that such a Party, given its progressive ideals and structure, did not realize the significance of the connection between ideology and everyday life, especially for women, is a matter of real regret. Exploitation and oppression do not disappear automatically after any struggle. A conscious analysis of every step one takes, of one's day to day thoughts and actions is necessary to establish a new philosophy for a new life. The Party's capacity to understand their struggles and support the women was crucial to their political survival.

Given the backwardness of women in traditional society and the power of the ideology of the family it is not surprising that their presence was seen as a source of problems:

> Yet although there were few female squad members, bars to women's participation were absent, generally [their coming] was not preferred because of technical difficulties.

We can see how confusing this would have been for the women. On the one hand there was no bar on their coming and yet there was the feeling that their coming would cause difficulties! These difficulties were of course related partly to the belief in the physical weakness of women and partly to the problem of sexual relationships, unwanted pregnancies, and small children, all questions traditionally associated with women. Given the time and social norms dominant then, it was probably extremely difficult for the Party to evolve a rational policy for the recruitment of women.

What were these "technical difficulties" as they actually manifested themselves? Mainly the sense that women were *physically* inferior. But women in squads moved with the same speed as men. There are also many instances of women showing far more courage and initiative than the men. Swarajyam recalls an incident of how a woman in the squad fired at the police, when the squad leader—who was also her husband—did not give the order to fire on time. Later she was actually reprimanded for indiscipline although her prompt action saved the squad. Acchamamba talks of carrying a comrade who was wounded by a bullet on her shoulder for miles through the forests until she realized that he had died. Dudala Salamma proudly told us that she leapt five feet with big leaders like Badam Ella Reddy and Nalla Narasimhulu. Dronavalli Anasuyamma says:

> There was a strong argument in the Party that women should not be taken into the squads that it is physically difficult for them. When I wanted to join they said the same thing. I argued saying that nowhere in the world could a revolution succeed without women participating in it., ... Initially though they were doubtful of my strength, later they acknowledged it. Once, while walking from one village to another, the police approached from the opposite side. We escaped and I ran away but the courier got arrested. Then the party changed its attitude. ... While they could run in three minutes, we would take five minutes. After all we have some physical handicaps, in such times the difference was obvious. But then in practical terms our squad leaders realized that it did not matter.

These were women who insisted on their right to fight beside the men, proved, that given a chance of action, every handicap would recede, and demonstrated that courage had little to do with mere physical strength. But it was not so easy to convince everyone. Ch. Rajeswar Rao says that the demand that women should come in large numbers and that they should be taken into the squads came from the women themselves. The Party did not encourage it. He admits that the number that actually came in might be small, but they worked with a lot of courage. The other problem was that of pregnancy and childbirth Kamalamma says:

> I was pregnant again. I kept moving around with them, it was time for the child to be born. ... We had no protection there. No hope of getting a midwife. I was very troubled by the thought of delivering the child. There was an old midwife there and they fetched her. I delivered under a cluster of bushes in the night and after the old woman had done her work they drove her away before day break.

After the child was born she moved around again with the squad, but in six months she was forced to give the child away. She talks of how difficult it was when she was asked to give the child away. She describes the event:

> We begged him to take this child and he agreed. I placed the child in his hands and left. After that, neither my body, nor my mind, nor my eyes stayed in my control. There was one torrent of tears from eyes to earth.

The fact that the Party was not in a position to take up the whole question of birth control and unwanted pregnancies led to a situation like Kamalamma's. A consistent policy would have prevented a situation as painful as this. Kamalamma herself did not question the wisdom or necessity of the decision, but she does not deny her pain. Taking up the problem of the child as a problem of the Party organization within a guerrilla squad, indeed considering the question of reproduction politically, rather than Kamalamma's personal problem which was endangering the squad, would have made the decision more bearable. Not even permitting her to wait until her husband returned to sup-port her, left her feeling totally isolated and broken. She was given the choice of returning to the village to be chopped into pieces or of remaining with the squad and giving away the child. Even in such a situation, she was pained by the accusation that she did not have a correct proletarian consciousness. While the fact that birth control methods were not as freely available then and the exigencies of underground life could explain away such instances that occurred, it is necessary to understand the limitations of these attitudes as they continue to this day. Some women told us that they had used creams and had themselves operated on.

If only the Party had placed the same emphasis on training in birth control methods as it had on first aid, healthy cooking and training "model housewives", the situation may have been different. When these questions are not taken up seriously and earnestly as political questions even today, we must look back and see the consequences of such attitudes towards women. Only then does the possibility of understanding and placing the roots of women's oppression as something, which is almost parallel to class exploitation, and which must be taken up simultaneously, emerge.

The other "technical difficulty" that women posed was of course the problem of sexual relationships. The constraints that are placed on a woman's sexuality in any given society are often an index of her real status. While women during the movement were freely allowed to enter the public sphere of production and political action, the moral code by which they were measured was still the code of the private domain—the domain of the family, household, domestic labour and reproduction. Not only was her virtue watched and judged, the responsibility of maintaining the moral tone of the entire group often rested with the women.

Narasamma, a Party member, raises important questions about political education and guidance to women in her letter to the Party. She speaks of the old outlook continuing. Sundarayya quotes excerpts from this in his book:

> You must coach up cadres properly, even if it means a few more days' delay, so that they can go to the villages with a clear understanding. Especially, with regard to cadre protection, enough precaution and care is not being taken. You must give us books which we can understand. You must take more pains to find such material for us. We women are still being looked upon with the old outlook that we are inferior. Any slip or mistake we commit, our leaders come down very heavily on us. It becomes a scandal. We must be guided and improved not derided. If we move a little freely, we are watched with suspicion. Why have you not allowed any women to participate in actual guerrilla raids on the enemy?

For a perfect instance of how women experienced this continued discrimination, there is Acchamamba's story:

> They started a story about me. They said I was having an affair with one of them. I said it was not true. I was prepared to lose my life, but

I was not that kind of woman. They said I was guilty. I said I would stand there, and they could shoot me if they wanted to. I asked them to prove it. I was not afraid of dying. If I was I would not have come into the movement.

She was expelled and a pamphlet issued saying she was expelled. Later they took her back into the Party. Thus, a woman who was doing all the medical work in the squad, who was invaluable to the movement, was expelled for what was seen as a moral lapse. Her word did not stand against the suspicion, against the accusation of the man himself. She was checked, searched, and sent out.

Often, as a result of such actions, women received dual messages from the Party. On the one hand when they were anxious or worried about sexual advances they were probably given to understand that one should adjust to such situations instead of making an issue of trivialities. On the other, there was the emphasis on morality and discipline in the Party. There were instances of some men being tried, even executed for womanizing or raping women who gave them shelter or helped them. There were strict instructions that men in the squads should not develop relationships with tribal *koya* women.

The underground existence of the Party, the stage of the struggle would have made all these questions even more problematic and fraught with danger. This could be one of the reasons for the ambiguity and for what appears to be ad hoc action. On the one hand we find manifestations of puritanical anger, as in Acchamamba's case; and on the other we hear of how women, who got pregnant when their husbands were away in jail, were helped to secure abortions and attempts were made to reconcile the husband to accepting the fact. But what made it perhaps even more difficult for the women was probably the fact that they have always been held traditionally responsible for the desires they excite, and the realization that attitudes within the Party had not changed all that much. That they somehow felt responsible. Efforts were undoubtedly made to deal with the problem as sympathetically as possible. But still the contradictions remained. The contradiction between the fact that while officially there were "no bars" to women being recruited, the uneasy feeling remained that their presence would

Afterword 89

cause "technical difficulty"! These women, who were constantly confronted with the contradictory messages that kept coming through simultaneously, and with the gap that yawned between what was overtly stated and covertly felt, must have found their positions precarious and uncertain to say the least. Sugunamma says:

> When we were underground some marriages took place. After all everyone in the dens was not the same. There were some unmarried men, some who had left their wives behind. ... Before that call it innocence or call it ignorance we thought they were all brothers. Two or three of them wanted to use me. Some were married. I felt troubled that even in the Party people could be like this. After developing the faith that the Party was pure, nothing like this could happen, when it did happen I felt that the only protection I could get would be through marriage. There was no one for me to talk it over with. ...

The difficulty women felt was inherent in the inadequacy of the situation itself. On the one hand, the Party had to scrupulously maintain an image of purity and dedication, on the other it had to cope with the reality of a situation where men and women thrown together were working under conditions of great stress, where relationships that sprang up could not be dealt with in strict accordance with theoretical assumptions or preconceived notions of correctness.

Given the situation, had it been possible to face the contradiction squarely, or attempt to deal with it openly, a lot of the assumptions about women would have perhaps changed perceptibly. But the traditional assumption that prevailed in feudal society, that woman was the bearer of virtue and tradition, was too deeply rooted in the Party to be questioned radically.

As a result, we see that regardless of what the Party would have liked in all earnestness to achieve, the actual conditions were such that women found that the only protection against sexual advances was marriage; further when relationships sprang up, they found the gossip and the blame was always focused on women. While individual cases were taken up and personal solutions found, the situation did not seem to allow for any possibility of taking up questions of birth control, sexuality, and reproduction politically.

Today we see that it is only when these questions are dealt with as political questions, when they are not relegated to the private sphere as merely women's problems, that a fuller participation of women in any movement becomes possible. A context existed to take up issues of reform like child marriages, widow marriage, wife beating, rape and divorce. But historical experience has demonstrated that while these issues do alleviate the condition of women, they are ineffective in changing their status. The real measure of this status is the extent of the constraints exercised on her sexuality and reproduction. Comprehending this fully involves a radical questioning of the very structure of the family and the nature of its oppression for women. It would also involve the recognition of the woman's right to choose between the family and political life; it would question the assumption that the onus of maintaining the family intact rested with the women or indeed that the family had to be kept intact at any cost. There would have been no place for the fear that it was not correct to "take women away from their husbands."

The metaphor of the family constantly used to describe the Party reinforced aspects of a feudal culture that continued to assert itself within the organization and perhaps served to keep women in roles which were extensions of their roles in the private sphere. The natural consequence of this was to marginalize their contribution. To understand this marginalization more fully, a closer look at the roles that were actually assigned to women in the struggle, their own self-conception, and the Party's attitude to women's work as it emerges in the statements of individual leaders may be useful. Women, we can see, resisted being confined to traditional roles and insisted on coming into the squads and facing danger. They also managed the dens, supplied food to the squads, acted as couriers and nursed the sick—all of which they did with efficiency and pride. They perceived it as significant and necessary work and they performed it with a sense of dignity.

Brij Rani Gour says:

> Those days we had work here in the dens ... looking after our comrades and giving them medicines ... There was no such thing as women's work and men's work. There was no such thing as looking down on women in the Party. Our comrades doing all the work ... they did not see it as secondary or unimportant.

Dronavalli Anasuya says: "But in the dens women did all the work". When we actually questioned women about the nature and division of work in the dens and centres, they always replied that it was shared equally. But what emerges during the narration is the fact that women were doing most of the work.

We can thus see a discrepancy between what they claimed and what actually happened. It was as if they accepted unquestioningly the ideal of equality without actually looking at the extent of its existence in practice. What we find especially disturbing today, is that in the interviews the emphasis is always on the problems of interpersonal relationships and the responsibilities of sustenance and nature, rarely on the significant work that they did. Acchamamba's story illustrates this. Here was a woman who at sixteen was perhaps one of the first barefoot doctors in India. With a background like hers one would expect a great deal of detail about her medical experience and some discussion of medical policy or the problems she faced. The emphasis instead is on the adulation she received, the adventures she had and her narrow escapes. Her professional skill becomes secondary, as it were, to her role as a woman. Acchamamba, who recognized the public importance of the work she was doing, does not seem to have realized the value of the knowledge she had gained. The result is that there is barely any space in her narrative for her medical skill, which retreats into the background before her numerous problems and adventures. The texture of her experience as a doctor eludes us somehow and we are left with her experience as a woman. The emphasis even for her is on the gratitude and admiration that was showered on her for her skills rather than on the revolutionary dimensions of her practice. We do not need to emphasize the political loss involved in this. "Where else would they get another person like me?" she asks And she simply lost these hard-earned skills once the struggle ended. We must ask the question "Why?"

It is easy enough for us to understand why it was possible for women to take up all kinds of supportive work with such a positive sense of it, if we look at some of their dreams. Speaking of an ideal society, Priyamvada says:

> We dreamt that in families there would be no such thing as women bending before men. We dreamt that we would live so freely and happily. But since repression came so soon we never had time to

question whether equality was there in the Party itself. Everybody went underground very soon. The men did not really share the work in the house then.

We have gained some idea of the perception the women had of their won work. Now let us look at some of the trends in the Party. Ravi Narayan Reddy says:

> Some of the women have fought with guns also. Not many, but generally they were helpful in other ways. For instance, cooking food for the squads and then taking messages from one part of the country to another, from one district to another. And then, when the squad is fighting, carrying food for them—and all this. They were nurses also, to treat wounded people and all that.

He then adds that women were emancipated as far as the struggle was concerned. Then answering a question about why they were not recruited to the Communist Party, he says:

> I mean, not that way emancipated, in the sense that they did not have the consciousness to fight with rifles and all that. After all they are women is it not? After all they are women; we did not like that women should be taken into the battlefields.

These statements hardly need any further explanation. They are a fair sample of the confusion that results when traditional assumptions are interwoven with programmes of emancipation. And while in a movement there may be a conscious and honest attempt to demonstrate that women are equal, the underlying feeling that "after all they are women, is it not?"—that women's consciousness is low, so low that they cannot serve on committees, will only serve to put them back into their kitchens when the need for them in the public domain is over. Mallu Swarajyam who commanded a guerrilla squad and was a living legend in the Telangana Movement says:

> In the Party they will see only what the movement needs. Questions concerning women are often suppressed. ... Their (women's) use is that. So when the struggle was withdrawn they told us to go and marry ... We fought with them. We said that even if the forms of struggle had changed we should be given some work.

What happened to the women who had to go back when the struggle was called off? What did it mean to be sent back to the kitchen, to domesticity? Priyamvada says that she often felt like committing suicide. Sugunamma describes how ten years later, she asked Swarajyam's husband what Swarajyam was doing, he retorted, "she is cooking and she is eating. What else?" She was horror-struck and amazed. If this was how *someone like Swarajyam could be described*, who would bother about someone like her? She also described how when they demanded work, in his typical manner Basavapunniah said, "What will you do? We are ourselves doing nothing. Go home and stay there". She says:

> They have used us so long and now they say go stay at home. How could they even understand what the situation was at home? How could one ever tell them? What mental torture I was really upset. That was my first taste of suffering.

It was this lack of awareness of what it meant for them to go back and the complacency of the assumption that the home was their place after all that really hurt the women. It was then that the degree to which they had been marginalized really struck them. It was because their work in the struggle was at some level always considered secondary that it was so simple to ask them to go back to the kitchens.

All the knowledge, the wisdom and courage gained in the course of the struggle was eventually useful to sustain the family, after the struggle was called off. Kamalamma begged in her village to feed her children, Acchamamba worked on her farm. Lalitha took up a job as a teacher after taking a series of Hindi examinations, Tai worked as a teacher to support her mother and her husband's family. Salamma carried liquor and worked as a wage labourer to bring up her sons, and so it went on ... The four walls of the family which had so recently fallen apart releasing the women into the public domain had been propped up more strongly and securely than before. The skills gained at such cost in the public world were eventually used to strengthen and prop up the pillars of the private world.

Priyamvada says that after the parliament elections and Police Action 'these dreams were smashed crushed like an egg.

What a blow it was. After the elections, do you know where we were? Like the proverbial rug ... lying exactly where it was thrown.

If it had only been possible for the women to discuss their problems together, so that they knew what to expect or demand when they faced similar situations, they would perhaps have been less bewildered and mustered some confidence and strength. As things were, most of the women had to turn to a husband, brother, or sister to confide in. What the younger women felt however was the unrelenting pressure to be "strong", not to give in to weakness or emotion. That is why even as Kamalamma grieved over the loss of her child, her anguish at being chided for not having a correct proletarian consciousness was even greater. This experience has not changed over time. Even today women are manipulated into denying their anger over what they perceive as unjust for fear of being accused of being emotional, subjective or irrational. There is nothing strange about the fact that the Party organization actually came in the way, prevented women coming together and exchanging experiences, and proved an obstacle in their seeking solutions to their problems. Dronavalli Anasuya tells us how she was warned not to support Swarajyam on some issue. Similarly Swarajyam was warned on another occasion not to support Nagamma, out of sympathy or partiality, because she was a woman. What is apparent here is a certain trepidation that if women began to support each other on the basis of sisterly solidarity, it would seriously erode the discipline in the Party.

Women were able to tell us of the contradictions that they faced in those days. Unfortunately, a consciousness which was aware of the power relations between men and women, and its connections with power relations in society as a whole, which could understand analyse and resolve these contradictions on the basis of that knowledge was not yet available to them at that time.

Let us look for instance at the kind of political education that was imparted at that time. Dronavalli Anasuya says:

> The Party had no great clarity on how to raise women's consciousness. If they are not given political training how can they rise to leadership

positions? Although women left their traditional roles and came into the struggle, there was no great change in their awareness of issues that were specific to women. If that had happened then they would have questioned their situation. The reason for that in my opinion is the failure of the Party to prepare women politically.

Kondapalli Koteswaramma, speaking of this same matter, says humourously, "In the *Bharatiya Mahila Mandali Club*, every year they used to hold classes. That political education—without seeing how much they had understood perhaps they went ahead too fast, that is what we feel today ... It was like feeding an infant *avakai* on his *annaprasan* day." They would tell us about all kinds of politics. "*The politics were like boiled iron pellets we were barely able to swallow!*"

As we have mentioned earlier, Narasamma's letter to the Party on political education is another good example. Women repeatedly talked about their problems. The fact was that the political education they were given was not easy to grasp. It is also evident that they were aware of the enormous gap that yawned between their own experiences and the political ideological positions that were apparently located so "far above" them. But how far was the Party in a position to perceive this chasm? And, if it did, did it attribute it to the *backwardness of the women or did it perceive it as a shortcoming in its own political training*?

If the women simply could not understand what was being taught, then is it not logical to question the value of such training? One thing seems certain: that if political education and training is to be relevant to women, then it has to leave behind the boundaries of the public sphere and enter and assimilate even the normally invisible aspects of the private sphere. We would even argue that an adequate understanding, of the "private" will demand a recasting of our sense of the public.

What are the questions that arise as a result of the women's movement today? Are women's issues being recognized as political issues? Is it possible for us to move towards a "new society" without confronting the problems that relate to the private sphere? If the experiences and problems that constantly come up in our day-to-day lives are not linked to our politics, how can there be an increased awareness of these issues? Without such an increased awareness, it seems inevitable that woman will move back after each struggle into their traditional roles. Until we begin to formulate a new politics which goes beyond the boundaries that confine the politics of today.

5

ISLAM, FEMINISM AND THE WOMEN'S MOVEMENT IN PAKISTAN: 1981–1991[*]

Fauzia Gardezi

It can be said that the women's movement in Pakistan began with the Women's Action Forum (WAF) in 1981.[1] This organization began as an urgent effort to unite women and women's organizations to combat the attack on women launched by General Zia-ul-Haq's martial law government. No doubt feminist struggle in Pakistan pre-dates the formation of WAF. However, the regular incidence of women taking collective action specifically against their oppression as women and the level of awareness created of the need for change in this regard, was new to this period.

Roughly ten years later, WAF is still active and action and awareness by women overall, continue to grow. In addition, Pakistani women are still fighting state action against them. With the 1990-return to a government which includes right-wing Islamic parties, new battles will ensue. The threat posed to women by the recently-passed *Shariat Bill* and plans for a separate women's university, both legacies of the Zia period, are among the issues confronting the Pakistani women's movement today.[2]

It would be useful then, to look back on this important decade of women's history in order to take stock of the women's movement, the problems it has encountered and the changes that may

---

[*] Previously published in a volume by the Pakistan India People's Forum for Peace and Democracy entitled *Other Voices From Pakistan: A Collection of Essays, News Reports and Literary Writings*. 1995, pp. 57–70. New Delhi: New Age International Limited. Also reproduced from *South Asia Bulletin*, Vol. X, No. 2, 1990.

be needed to fight the ongoing struggle. This article attempts to make a partial contribution toward this end. The focus here is not on the measures taken by Zia's government, or the specific issues women were fighting against during this period, as this is well documented elsewhere.[3] Nor will the organizational dilemmas of WAF be discussed. Rather, it is believed that there is a need now to take a broader look at some of the more theoretical problems and debates that have emerged within the movement during the last two years. After a period of what was often of necessity, quickly-planned, reactive responses to issues set by the martial law government,[4] the need to develop frameworks to guide action and provide direction to the movement becomes apparent. Of the small amount of writing done on the women's movement in Pakistan, the most detailed analysis is provided by Khawar Mumtaz and Farida Shaheed in their book, *"Women of Pakistan: Two Steps Forward, One Step Back?"* Therefore, this article will primarily address issues raised in it. In particular, it is argued here that two of the main problems encountered by the women's movement in Pakistan involve: 1) trying to work within an Islamic framework and 2) not incorporating feminism sufficiently into the movement. This refers primarily to the activities of WAF.[5] However, as this is a discussion of the women's movement in Pakistan during the last ten years, it is necessary to provide a brief profile of the different types of women's movement in the country, focusing on some of the underlying principles, assumptions and philosophies of the movement, and their implications.

A Women's Movement from Above

WAF is the organization most often associated with the women's movement in Pakistan, but this movement also exists in other organizations. Maria Mies talks of two kinds of women's movements in Third World countries,[6] both of which are evident in Pakistan. The first is a grassroots movement of groups and organizations of women coming together on their own. In Pakistan, this includes, but is not restricted to, the WAF.[7] A second type of women's movement, as described by Mies, is a "movement from above", involving, for example, the efforts by various organizations to integrate women into development, the establishment of women's study centres or departments and official programmes geared toward women.

It is important to draw a distinction between the two types of women's movements as they differ in their agenda. While the grassroots movement encompasses a wide range of viewpoints on what sort of change is needed, it includes among these, the demand for an end to patriarchal relations in all spheres of society. The second, more bureaucratic type of movement, however, often falls short of feminist demands and focuses on working within the existing social order rather than transcending it.[8] Many of the activities of the second stem from a genuine concern to bring women in, where in the past, they have been left out, such as government administration, academic study and development programmes. In addition, they serve to increase awareness of problems faced by women. For these reasons they can be considered part of women's movement. However, it is usually simply not possible to pursue a feminist line within these organizations as they are premised on seeking solutions within the existing order, or they are controlled by those who will not allow any attempt at or discussion of real change.

A clear example of this is outlined by Nighat Said Khan in her discussion of the Women's Division and the National Commission on the Status of Women set up by the Zia government as well as the Sixth Five Year Plan (1983–1988).[9] These and other measures were taken by the government to give the impression of addressing the socio-economic problems of women, women's rights and women in development. However, these organizations were given little real power, often their recommendations, demands and protests were ignored, and members were often not selected for their ability to represent women. Thus, apparently, the real purpose behind their establishment was to make it seem that the government was advancing the position of women.

This conservative strain in the bureaucratic women's movement is evident in women's studies departments in Pakistani universities which avoid using the term "feminism". Even much of the writing on women in Pakistan is prefaced with statements distancing the work from "radical" "western" feminism. The foreword in one book on women criticizes the "wild" and "unrealistic" demands of western women.[10] The author of the foreword in another book commends Pakistani women for advocating gradual change and being dedicated to their families, which are "a great protector of women's social position".[11]

Whatever is meant by this, it is clear that the idea of a sheltered and protected housewife is a myth. To know this, one need only look at the daily reports in Pakistani newspapers of women attacked or murdered by husbands, brothers, sons or other male relatives for "doubts on their character". The idea that family and home are non-patriarchal, non-political spheres is evident even in the writings of some women activists themselves. For example, two of the reasons suggested by Mumtaz and Shaheed for WAF's inability to mobilize many housewives are: 1) that "housewives who do not leave their homes or go to work, may not be exposed to the type of backlash currently being faced by working women and, therefore, may not be as motivated to resist the current trend" and 2) that they are "less articulate".[12] The argument that women felt this backlash less in the home is at odds with the frequency with which Zia's *Hudood laws* were used against women by husbands or other male relatives.[13]

Feminism is a movement which points out the oppressive and exploitative relations between men and women in all aspects of society, including the family. It is not surprising then that there will be attempts to incorporate part of the mainstream feminist movement in order to lessen the more fundamental threat to the existing order that feminism poses. Elsewhere, Antonio Gramsci's concept of "passive revolution" has been used to explain state action with regard to women.[14] This concept is used to describe how ruling groups, to retain their dominance, will attempt to absorb parts of subordinate groups or movements demanding change, including some of their ideas, platforms and even their members, in order to weaken the movement and the larger threat it poses. Some components of the women's movement from above, in Pakistan, can be seen as examples of this. Passive revolution is clear in steps taken by the Zia government, ostensibly to benefit women. Some women activists were even included in the bodies set up by the government.[15] WAF members complained though, that these were really attempts at "pacifying and defusing women" rather than actually meeting their demands.[16] In another example, one male director of a Pakistani development research institute, in fact, writes that there is need to support non-radical women's groups and give women some rights to prevent the emergence of a militant women's movement in Pakistan[17]—this is essentially the logic of passive revolution.

This women's movement from above is based on a certain understanding of women's oppression, what it is, and what is needed to change it. Thus, the political goals of this movement may differ or conflict with those of a grassroots movement. There is a need for analysis of this branch of the women's movement, particularly its implications in terms of passive revolution, so that some of the tendencies within it do not end up weakening the overall women's movement and determining its course. It is to an examination of some of the recent political and theoretical debates within WAF, the most prominent organization of the grassroots women's movement in Pakistan, that we now turn.

FEMINISM FROM WITHIN ISLAM

Perhaps the major debate within WAF today and during the past decade is whether or not a struggle against patriarchy should be waged from within the framework of Islam. In part, the need to work within Islam stemmed from the fact that the anti-women legislation and actions taken by Zia's government were proclaimed to be part of an Islamization programme. Various Islamic laws were proposed or enacted such as the Hudood Ordinances, the Law of Evidence and the law on QISAS and DIYAT. These laws, among other things, made it difficult to prove the crime of rape, put rape victims at risk of being charged with adultery and reduced the worth of a woman, and her testimony in some cases, to half that of a man. Islam was also used to justify various government directives on women's dress, a plan to create a separate women's university and an unwritten ban on women's participation in spectator sports.

Thus, there was a need to show that opposition to these laws and measures was not opposition to Islam. Yet there are conflicting views on the wisdom of continuing to work within Islam. One side of this debate is presented by Shahnaz Rouse who argues that what is needed is "a movement that poses resolution of its problem in opposition to Islamic discourse. The point is not to reject Islam, but to clearly state that the issue of women's rights is a secular issue of human rights."[18] On the other hand,

Mumtaz and Shaheed argue that Islam is part of Pakistan's culture, in order not to be perceived as alien, there is a need to operate within Pakistani culture and, therefore, within Islam.[19] In addition, they state that, while upper and upper-middle class women may prefer a secular women's movement, a discussion of women's rights within Islam is needed to appeal to lower-middle class and working class women.[20]

The Women's Action Forum, particularly the Lahore chapter, has often subscribed to the latter position with regard to Islam in the last ten years. There are, however, problems with this approach. While working within Islam may win the support of some women, this does not mean that women cannot alternatively be mobilized around a discourse based on a strong critique of patriarchal social relations and social structures. More importantly, working within an Islamic discourse in many ways threatens the struggle against women's oppression.

For one thing it gives power to Islamic fundamentalists, those who have championed the cause of women's oppression and subordination. The framing of discourse in terms of Islam, and the impression this creates— that all dialogue must be in these terms—is stated by the Islamic right-wing itself to be its greatest source of power. For example, one member of the *Jamaat-e-Islami*, when asked what success they felt they had, given their poor showing in elections, responded that "they had changed the way people spoke: people were now forced to speak in Islamic terms."[21] Some, in the women's movement, believe that there is a need to counter fundamentalist interpretations of Islam with more progressive interpretations.[22] But there are innumerable different interpretations of what Islam is all about among the "experts" themselves. The women's movement will simply be adding its voice to the fray. And on this terrain of the fundamentalists, a victory for progressive forces is not likely. As stated by Shahnaz Rouse this will also contribute to "thwarting a return to democratic norms and secular discussion."[23] The women's movement will defeat itself if it contributes to creating such a climate.

There is also a danger that focusing too much on Islam and what it says about women will detract from a discussion of an attempt to address women's real problems. One active WAF member, interviewed by the author, expressed the concern that

Islam was not an important issue in the minds of the majority of poor women and that the entire debate over whether to follow a secular or an Islamic approach was sidetracking the struggle to address basic problems of existence faced by women in Pakistan.[24] Mumtaz and Shaheed describe how the Lahore chapter of WAF has used Islam to appeal to women, yet it has always felt the need to appeal to women by taking up their problems of everyday existence. In one instance, WAF failed to help a group of women who lost their jobs because of their involvement in union activities.[25] (It was felt that this was not a strictly feminist issue, a statement which is very problematic and will be taken up shortly.) Through such actions and the general focus on working within Islam, WAF runs the risk of giving people more religion while neglecting their material problems, a tendency which runs counter to feminism and progress.

Finally, the view that one must work within Islam because it is part of the culture of Pakistan and one does not want to be perceived as "alien", in itself subordinates women and undermines the feminist struggle through some of its implications. Patriarchy itself is part of the culture; one cannot challenge patriarchal relations while obeying the dictates of the dominant culture. This argument is also tantamount to saying that one cannot pursue women's rights *on their own merit* because the culture does not permit it. This subordinates women's rights and the women's movement to cultural factors and weakens them. And, while this argument only suggests that those who do not work within Islam will be *perceived* as alien, one does not want to lend any credence to the often expressed view that they, in fact, are alien.

In addition to the dangers of working within an Islamic framework, one must also question the need to do so. Do those who want to take away women's rights in the name of Islam derive their power from the support of the people? Have the anti-women laws enacted in the name of Islam been passed by governments with popular mandates? The answers to such questions are clearly related to the issue of whether or not the women's movement needs to give primacy to challenging the Islamic character of these laws and other attacks on women. WAF has had success in mobilizing some women, from a particular class or income group, by pointing out how the laws were un-Islamic.[26] The point here is not to deny this, but to suggest that an alternative discourse may also mobilize large numbers of women, from this class and others, without the inherent dangers discussed earlier.

Also, the argument that an appeal to Pakistani cultural norms and Islam is of central importance in gaining people's support implies a particular theory of human consciousness. It suggests that a woman's perception of the world and her behaviour will be influenced more by ideal factors than her own concrete life experiences and an appeal based on these. A belief that consciousness is determined by material factors, or simply an understanding of the extent of exploitation and oppression under which the majority of Pakistani women live, must lead one to question whether a woman will assign greater importance to factors relating to ideas and beliefs (which she may or may not hold) than to factors relating to her material experiences.

One cannot, of course, ignore the role of hegemonic discourses in influencing people's outlook and behaviour. But in a country in which the majority of people, particularly women, are illiterate, are not exposed to the state-controlled television broadcasts and do not go through extensive years of schooling, it will be difficult to recruit people to the world view of the ruling group. And, while Islam may be an important part of many people's lives, it is not the same Islam as that of the fundamentalists. The poor showing of fundamentalist parties in elections shows that when Pakistanis are presented with this type of discourse, emphasizing a repressive sort of Islam, they reject it.

BRINGING FEMINISM INTO THE MOVEMENT

While the question of working within Islam may have been the main source of disagreement within WAF during the last ten years, women disagreed as well over the issue of feminism and the movement. By and large the Pakistani women's movement avoids the use of the term feminism.[27] As already discussed, at times the women's movement in Pakistan is even portrayed as being in opposition to feminism, which is seen as "western" and "alien". One has to question the real reasons behind such allegations, especially since they are not made against other philosophies, theories or movements originating in the West. In addition, it is simply not the case that the feminist struggle in Pakistan has been imported from the West, it is rooted in Pakistani women's own experiences.

Apart from the ulterior motives of some of those who attack feminism, much of the avoidance of feminism comes out of a misconception of what it actually is. Feminism is a struggle, in particular, against the oppression and exploitation of women. But it also has to involve a broader critique of the entire society because gender-based oppression does not merely exist at the same time as other systems of oppression—they are interconnected. As an example, the reason women in Pakistan are overwhelmingly confined to casual, part time, low wage labour in the informal sector of the economy is not only because they are being discriminated against as women, but also because it is part of an attempt to create a cheap labour force for the capitalist class.[28] Thus, one cannot struggle against or overcome either patriarchal or class oppression in isolation from the other.

There may be a narrow strain within feminism which views the struggle as simply a matter of achieving equal rights with men, while not calling for any broader restructuring of society. But, increasingly, there is a realization that feminism cannot be reduced solely to a concern with sexual inequality. In part, this is because it ignores the inequality that exists among men themselves. But also, women have different experiences based on characteristics other than gender. To struggle around gender alone is to downgrade this diversity and generalize the experiences of women who may not face other forms of oppression. Feminism is and must be every woman's movement and the only way it can be this is to bring into its fold every woman's experiences.

This is not to say that what women experience, specifically based on the fact that they are women, is a lesser form of oppression than, for example, class. Mumtaz and Shaheed rightly point out that for upper class women in Pakistan, gender-based oppression is one of the few types of oppression they experience, while for other women it is one of many.[29] But this does not diminish the importance of gender-related experiences for poorer women. It does not mean that "the women's issue does not have the same immediacy for working class women as it does for upper class women."[30] It must be understood that gender issues include violence against women by men, and degradation of women's economic dependence, and male control over women's lives. These are not luxuries that only more privileged women can afford to address. They are bread and butter issues, often they are life and death issues. Therefore, one must not minimize the impact that they will have on the lives of poor or working class women, or subordinate them to other issues when talking of women of oppressed classes. A gender-based struggle must not be waged alone, but it also must not be compromised.

The lack of a clear feminist framework of the type discussed here has led to difficulties in conceptualizing problems facing women in Pakistan and uncertainty within WAF about what issues to support. The earlier mentioned decision by WAF in Lahore not to support trade union women in a conflict with their employer, because it was not seen as a feminist issue' was informed by a very narrow and, as outlined earlier, untenable definition of feminism. Even with this narrow definition, this issue should have been supported because of its implications for women's economic independence and their inroads into the male-dominated formal labour force and labour movement. It seems that the reason these women were not supported has more to do with the class composition of WAF membership[31] and their failure to employ class and feminist analysis than with feminism.

Mumtaz and Shaheed suggest that because of instances such as this, WAF should focus on "women's rights rather than 'feminism'". The problem is that the former does not provide the necessary tools for generating fundamental social change. The concepts and analyses of feminism cannot be dispensed with. Feminism is a body of thought which analyses and furthers understanding of patriarchal society and subordination and exploitation in male–female relations. This is necessary in order to understand what one is struggling against and striving for, to instruct action and to provide direction to the movement. Many of the disagreements WAF has encountered can be seen as stemming from the lack of a coherent and consistent theoretical base, leaving the organization prey to the particular backgrounds and inclinations of its individual members.

In addition, closer links with feminism are necessary to avoid problem, encountered by WAF in the past, of giving in to some aspects of patriarchal culture in order to gain support. Mumtaz and Shaheed state that "[WAF's] desire to raise consciousness among the widest section of society, and elicit their tacit, if not overt, support meant that in making concessions to Pakistani culture it compromised a purely feminist line."[32] As a result, for example, smoking in public was avoided by members and there was a concern that WAF's protest against the exclusion of women from spectator sports would cost them supporters. However, while women smoking and playing spectator sports may be an affront to Pakistani patriarchal culture, and while these may not be issues which directly affect the greatest numbers of Pakistani women, there are female athletes in Pakistan and there are women who want to smoke. The question is one of whether WAF is a feminist organization or whether it is going to join the ranks of those who say women cannot behave in certain ways because they are women. It does not matter whether one's position on such issues is based on the belief that they are, indeed, wrong, or on the fact that other people think that they are wrong—the end result is the same. By not wanting to alienate anybody, there is a risk of backing away from a challenge to patriarchal culture and alienating feminists themselves.

Conclusion

During the last ten years, Pakistani women have shown that they will not submit themselves to state attempts to remove them from the public sphere and diminish their legal rights. While showing strength in this regard, certain tendencies within the women's movement discussed here have the potential to weaken this movement considerably. One example lies within the bureaucratic arm of the women's movement in Pakistan which tries to develop programmes and policies to benefit women. The danger is that it may too narrowly define the societal institutions which are acceptable targets of change and exclude others which must not be touched. Women in Pakistan have also united to seek change outside established organizations and agencies and official bureaucracies. However, their ability to go beyond the conservatism of the bureaucratic women's movement may depend very much on whether or not the movement consistently adheres to a feminist platform and abandons the attempt to work within Islam.

The transformation of the women's movement in Pakistan to a radical, secular, feministic movement faces many difficulties. One problem is that, gradually, in Pakistan, the ability to come out openly in favour of secularism in mainstream political discourse has been lost. Women must fight this trend. Obviously a secular state is no guarantee of women's rights. However, the inability to talk of the separation of Islam from the state, laws, educational systems, the media and other institutions is muting the current struggle against the *Shariat Bill*. Many politicians are looking for ways to attack the Bill without questioning the premise that it is the role of the state to ensure that all people live according to Islamic laws and that the *Shariat*, as interpreted by a select group, should become the supreme law of Pakistan. Progressive forces must counter this tendency away from discussions of secular democracy and not give into it as has happened, not just in parts of the women's movement, but among other groups as well.

The women's movement and WAF are not alone in their fight against the *Shariat Bill*—it is opposed by many who see the danger in increasing the power of the Islamic clergy within the state. The move toward re-establishing secular democratic politics in Pakistan is an endeavour which concerns a number of groups. Thus, the women's movement could derive strength from building links with other groups fighting for political and social change. Some such links have already been made, particularly by the Karachi chapter of WAF. However, there is always the problem of women's concerns being subordinated to other issues when such links are made. The extent to which groups with a common agenda come together probably depends not so much on WAF and the women's movement as it does on whether or not the left in Pakistan is willing to make feminism part of its own struggle.

Accompanying an attempt to bring a secular ideology into the women's movement would be a stronger focus on the material problems of everyday existence faced by women in Pakistan. A possible starting point for the attempt to redirect the efforts of the women's movement in this direction is increased research and study into women's life and their position in Pakistan. The state of the majority of women in Pakistan remains largely unknown, un-researched and invisible. The small amount of information that exists is often inaccurate due to improper research procedures, leading, for example, to ridiculously low official estimates of the proportion of women who are economically active in Pakistan. The absence of accurate information on Pakistani women allows people to speak for them, without knowing what they would say given the opportunity to speak for themselves. There is a need to base the agenda of the women's movement on knowledge, rather than assumptions, about what issues are of primary concern to women and what will mobilize women to join or support the movement.

In addition, the women's movement in Pakistan may find it useful to look at the feminist movement in other countries, how they have sought support and how they have responded to attacks on feminism. It is scarcely more socially acceptable to call oneself a feminist in most other countries, including those in the West. Similarly, the attempt to use culture, or some aspect of it, to attack or subvert the cause of feminism is not unique to Pakistan. In spite of these obstacles, strong feminist movements have been forged in many countries. WAF has established links with women's movements and organizations outside Pakistan. Continuing in this direction could provide the women's movement with increased strength and knowledge: both of the commonalities of women's struggles across countries, as well as the particular features of patriarchy as it has developed in Pakistan.

Finally, analysing the history of women's movements can assist in building strong feminist movements in Pakistan and elsewhere. There is a need to look at the implications, both theoretical and practical, of past activities and work towards building frameworks for understanding women's oppression and exploitation. It is through such an endeavour that one can understand the task of the feminist movement and strategies that it should employ in the future.

NOTES AND REFERENCES

1. Mumtaz, Khawar and Farida Shaheed. 1987. *Women in Pakistan: Two Steps Forward, One Step Back?*, p. 123. London: Zed Books.
2. At the time of writing it was still unclear how this bill was to be implemented. However, trouble for women can be foreseen in two clauses of the bill. The

bill states that the government will take measures to combat obscenity, a term which has, in the past, been equated with women themselves (see ibid., pp. 81–83) Also, a clause requiring citizens to order their lives according to the Shariat has the potential to curtail the rights of women as pointed out by Asma Jahangir, "On the Offensive". 1991. *Herald*, (22)5, May: 29–30. In addition, any law giving more power to the Islamic clergy is a threat to women and the few rights they have obtained in Pakistan.

3. In addition to Mumtaz and Shaheed, *Women of Pakistan*, op. cit., see Shahnaz Rouse. 1986. "Women's Movement in Pakistan: State, Class, Gender," *South Asia Bulletin*, VI(1), Spring: 30–37 and Nighat Said Khan. 1988. *Women in Pakistan: A New Era?* Lahore: ASR.
4. See Mumtaz and Shaheed, *Women of Pakistan*, op. cit., p. 148. They address the issue of how WAF is now encountering difficulty in moving from being a reactive organization to one which takes the initiative in setting its own agenda.
5. Also, the focus is on the Lahore chapter of WAF as this is the chapter discussed by Mumtaz and Shaheed, ibid.
6. Mies, Maria. 1986. *Patriarchy and Accumulation and Accumulation on a World Scale: Women in the International Division of Labour*, pp. 8–10. London: Zed Books.
7. Other women's organizations which deal exclusively, or in part, with gender issues are mentioned by Mumtaz and Shaheed, *Women of Pakistan*, op. cit., pp. 50–70, 153. Perhaps the largest organization of women which has taken on some gender issues in Pakistan is Sindhiani Tehrik. This is the women's wing of a political party, the Awami Tehrik. Unfortunately, except for the occasional mention in the press, little has been written about this group in the past.
8. Mies, *Patriarchy and Accumulation*, op. cit., p. 9, points out how these two women's movements often conflict: "The more the movement expands quantitatively, the more it is accepted by institutions of the establishment, the more money is coming forward from international funding agencies as well as from local governments, the more acutely the conflicts are felt between those who only want to 'add' the 'women's component' to the existing institutions and systems and those who struggle for a radical transformation of patriarchal society."
9. Said Khan. *Women in Pakistan*, op. cit.
10. M. Ishaque, Khalid. 1981. Foreword in Sabeeha Hafeez (ed.), *The Metropolitan Women in Pakistan: Studies*, p. ix. Karachi: Royal Book Company.
11. Naqvi, Syed Nawab Haider. 1986. Foreword in Nasra M. Shah (ed.), *Pakistani Women: Socioeconomic and Demographic Profile*, p. xxvii. Islamabad: Pakistan Institute of Development Economics.
12. Mumtaz and Shaheed. *Women of Pakistan*, op. cit., p. 137.
13. See Jahangir, Asma and Hina Jilani. 1990. *The Hudood Ordinances A Divine Sanction?* Lahore: Rhotas Books. This is evident in their accounts of cases throughout the book, but see pp. 103, 136 in particular.
14. Cuneo, Carl J. 1990. *Pay Equity: The Labour Feminist Challenge*, p. 153. Toronto: Oxford University Press. Cuneo applies the concept of passive revolution to explain the laws in Canada designed to address the male female wage gap (see Chapter 5 and Appendix 1).

Islam, Feminism and the Women's Movement in Pakistan

15. See, for example Said Khan. *Women in Pakistan*, op. cit., p. 21.
16. Ibid., p. 21. The statement refers, in particular, to the example of a working committee set up to advise on women's issues for the Sixth Five-year Plan. The recommendations were ignored by the government.
17. Naqvi, Foreword, op. cit. This is a central argument in the entire Foreword, but see especially, pp. xxviii, xxxii.
18. Rouse, "Women's Movement in Pakistan: State, Class, Gender,", op. cit., p. 36.
19. Mumtaz and Shaheed, op. cit., p. 131.
20. Ibid., pp. 131–132.
21. Duncan, Emma. *Breaking the Curfew: A Political Journey Through Pakistan*, p. 231. London. Arrow Books.
22. Mumtaz and Shaheed. op. cit., p. 156.
23. Rouse, "Women's Movement in Pakistan: State, Class, Gender", op cit, p 36.
24. The following was stated by a WAF working committee member in Islamabad during an interview in May, 1991: "Our line has been that WAF should not be wasting time with [secular versus Islamic] issues. The real issues are development and why women have to slog it out more than men. That is a different line where one is trying to veer WAF" "I don't agree with the idea that women will join you in terms of Islam. More people will join you if you talk about violence, issues of survival. Islam is not on their minds."
25. Mumtaz and Shaheed, op. cit., p. 150.
26. These women were from the lower-middle and working class in urban areas ibid, p. 132, 142n. The majority of support for rightwing Islamic parties tends to come from the new urban middle class. It would be interesting to investigate whether these two facts are related.
27. The author was told, for example, by a WAF working committee member in Islamabad, that most members in that chapter would not call themselves feminists.
28. See Kazi, Shahnaz and Bilquees Raza. 1991. "The Duality in Female Employment in Pakistan", paper presented at the Seventh Annual General Meeting, Pakistan Institute of Development Economics, Islamabad. Published in *South Asia Bulletin*,10(2).
29. Mumtaz and Shaheed, op. cit., p. 151.
30. Ibid.
31. They are largely from upper-middle or upper class backgrounds.
32. *Women of Pakistan*, op. cit., p. 131.

6

WOMEN, NATIONALISM AND WAR: "MAKE LOVE NOT WAR"[*]

Rada Ivecovic

I analyse the relationship between women and nationalism and argue that women's identity and relationship to the "Other" is different from that of men, hence even when women participate in nationalism it is in a less violent form. It is true that this may be the case for historic and no "natural" reasons whatsoever. I argue, further, that the structures of nationalism are fundamentally homosocial and antagonism toward women of one's own nation is one of the first forms of attack on the "Other", and is constitutive of "extreme nationalism". I would add today (2004) that I don't believe in "moderate nationalism".

The British suffragist movement came abruptly to an end when the contradiction of *women as members of the human race, and women as signifiers of difference and the particular, became historically significant.* This happened with World War I when suffragists became war factory workers and were released from prison in exchange for a "patriotic" attitude and for refraining from feminist-suffragist activities. Which were they first, "women" or members of the "nation"? As Jane Marcus writes, "World War I practically destroyed the women's movement in England, an extraordinary mass movement of

---

[*]First published in *Hypatia*, Vol. 8, No. 4, Fall 1993 as "Women, Nationalism and War: 'Make Love, Not War'", special cluster on Eastern European feminism ed. by Nanette Funk, pp. 113–126. I thank *Hypatia* for letting us reprint it here, and Nanette Funk for her own work and the interaction we had over all these years that meant so much to me. The present version is slightly updated. Also published in *Women Unlimited*.

women who struggled for nearly fifty years to obtain political justice and equality with regard to education, the vote, and legislation concerning marriage, divorce, child custody, and labour practices" (Marcus 1989: 129).

Women were subsequently granted the right to vote largely as a reward for their attitude during the war. War and nationalism were used as arguments to give up feminism, which said that women had to choose between feminism and the war effort, between their identity as women and as members of the nation state.

It divided feminism between those who maintained their pacifist position and those who argued for support of their men folk by working in the armaments industry or driving ambulances at the front. Pacifist feminists turned out to be in a minority.

A similar situation happened with the downfall of socialism. The feminist movement over the past fifteen years in some of the former East European countries also lost its drive because of more "urgent" political goals. Some East European feminists were overpowered by a more primary anti-communist orientation, others became involved, for much the same reason, with overt nationalist movements. Some East European feminists remain tied to "socialist" ideals that can sometimes be aggressively nationalist, as was the case in Serbia, and are not necessarily progressive. Only a small part of feminism remained, split and independent. But the transition and the conflicts gave rise, at the same time, to new feminist groups, preoccupations and urgencies and, strangely enough, it also favoured feminist public activity, publishing, peace, human rights and relief activism addressing transborder populations and not aimed at the promotion of the activists themselves. In that sense, post-socialist transition, as well as conflict—the latter, in countries of the former Yugoslavia—was also a remarkable women's political school.[1]

At the same time, a significant part of the organized feminist movement and the new feminism merged with or actually organized the new pacifist movements in those places where nationalist civil wars and wars of territorial conquest were threatening or were being fought. In both cases—Great Britain then and some former socialist countries at the beginning of the transition or as the transitional conflict was starting—the feminist movements were divided and in need of reorganization.

A great deal is at stake, not only for women but, through women, for democracy as such, especially in those East European countries where the formal human rights women acquired during socialism are threatened. The status of women in some East European "socialist" countries such as the German Democratic Republic (GDR) or Yugoslavia was *formally* in many ways comparatively better than in the West, especially as regards women's reproductive rights, collective rights, and social services that were supportive of women's work for the family. Not that the real position of women was better—no comparison is possible here, or no measurement—but there was a *general egalitarian commitment*, not particularly feminist in its intention, from which women benefited.

Yet it was women in these countries, along with men, who willed and urged the downfall of the very socialism that granted them these rights. *Women wanted both the end of socialism and the maintenance of the rights granted by socialism.* The problem was particularly visible in East Germany where women fought fiercely to keep those specific rights threatened by the return to capitalism.

In addition, in the recent series of wars in the former Yugoslavia, it is mainly women who organized the pacifist movements and local humanitarian help. Women seem to be socialized as "more pacific" and it is overwhelmingly women who run pacifist movements in countries at war. This is only partly because men are deserters from the army and thus unable to appear in public as activists, where they would be caught and sent back to the front.

Yet, in spite of the fact that women resort to arms in fewer numbers than men (indeed they are traditionally barred from power, arms and large instruments and machines), they are also, without being aware of it, complicit in war because the system as such, and its symbolic order,[2] supports the war policy and favours the dominant group, which historically has been men. It is the dominant gender, too, that defines the "interests" of war and, later, likewise of peace—indeed the negotiations are done by the warlords themselves—although those interests are considered to be gender-neutral and universal ("human").

What the socially weaker do, may well be used by the state to their disadvantage. In what follows it will be shown how the war in the former Yugoslavia was, in significant ways, an affair of "brotherhood" and not of "sisterhood".

I

To understand this situation it is necessary to analyze what is *symbolically* at stake for women and men within the war machine, because gender is one of its main organizing principles. It is characteristic of the symbolic order and of social relationships, that every power-complex uses as its model other pre-existing power complexes, projecting itself onto those models where possible. Binary models—and in particular the binary model of gender—are those symbolic power-systems through which the symbolic system works and onto which it projects itself. This projection "legitimizes" practices and domination. In particular, the extreme cases of war and nationalism take over and adopt the models of gender inequality, using them as justifying references. They exploit and manipulate gender difference to their advantage, and organize themselves along its lines. The gender order, accepted as it still is globally as "natural", is used by analogy as *the* paradigm to justify other inequalities. Hence its tremendous importance and its reappearance in any case of an institutionalized inequality or injustice.

In this process the enemy, the other nation, is made to be the Other, as is the Female within the unequal gender régime. In many cases, they can be identified for purposes of appropriation or of domination, and the Other is attributed "feminine" characteristics. The general patriarchal consensus about the lesser value of the feminine and female can then be instrumentalized. The symbolic system of nationalism in fact needs the construction of "the Other" as an indirect means for its domination; "the Other" is thus its constituent part painted in the negative and associated with values considered to be feminine.

The appropriation of gender in nationalism does not mean that there is a one-to-one correspondence between gender roles and roles in war. Not every man, perhaps not even the majority of men, identify with war, but the whole framework which permits or calls for war is organized in such a way that it favours the stronger, whether socially, politically, historically or militarily stronger. The political and symbolic systems are socially "male" only because the historically dominant gender is male and not in the sense that it is the responsibility of every individual man or of maleness as such. In fact, even when they are willing to give up their domination and make visible efforts in this direction, past history continues to provide support for the politically and gender dominant group. The will to give up historically acquired privileges alone is not enough to radically exorcise them. These privileges remain attached to the dominant group like "karma" because the past also constitutes the present.

At the level of the symbolic order, cultural or social stereotypes used in the militarist ideology, in the dominant propaganda of the war-machine, and in the new mythology are all "sexed". Every term, utterance, and concept is given a sexual "value" with a distinct preference going to the male-identified form. Thus it is men who are the "brave soldiers defending their womenfolk", the national hero is a man and women are only the mothers of sons and soldiers. It is men who "sacrifice themselves for the nation," represent the ideal national type and have the duty and privilege of resorting to arms. If it were not for courage (as a "male" characteristic) of "our boys," the nation would meet with disaster.

II

As Klaus Theweleit (1987) has argued, fighters or warriors are "brothers", sharing all sorts of rites based on strong feelings of a group identity founded on being of the same generation of "sons" of the Nation (symbolic as well as real). They are "equals" among themselves, but no other is regarded as their equal. The brotherhood is articulated, group identity constructed by excluding the "other"—the enemy (the "Outside Other")—and women (the "Inside Other"). The "brothers" only get a sense of identity through belonging to the group and by developing an image of exclusion and domination of the Others. The better the "brothers" chances for identity formation, the greater is their cruelty. The image of the woman is a split one: "our" women are the "white" ("good") ones, the enemy's are the "red" ("bad") ones. "Brotherhood" in this sense is formed by a group identity; "sisterhood" is not. Brotherhood also has a longer history through religious orders, which are also called brotherhoods even when they include or consist of women.

These "brotherhoods" operate in nationalist conflicts. There are different types of nationalisms including anti-imperialist, anti-colonialist ones and those directed against exploitation or political domination. In the anti-colonial and anti-imperial strife and resistance of some decades ago, in the period of the first postcolonialism, nationalism definitely had a positive connotation, at least for "us" in the Third World. But it is a basic assumption of the present paper that the "radical nationalisms" that have become operative at the end of the 20th century in the republics of Yugoslavia, and in other places, are both mechanisms of binary, dual oppositions and that they *invariably lead to war* in the long run. By "radical nationalism" I mean a very belligerent conquering, aggressive nationalism and/or an advanced phase of a previously contained form of nationalism.

"Radical nationalism" conquers territories, chases other nationalities away, introduces "ethnic cleansing", defines the other as such, etc. From a politically positive and affirmative movement nationalism can develop, depending on historical circumstances, into something very dangerous, as in National Socialism (Nazism). No simple definition can be given of nationalism or even of radical nationalism because these are not fixed concepts and cover changing contents, realities and processes. Between "nationalism" and "radical nationalism" there would only be a difference of quantity or intensity and, of course, differences in historic contexts, but not of principle.

III

Civil war, *guerre fratricide, Bruderkrieg, bratoubilački rat*, are wars that evoke, in their very name in some languages, a gender division and even a family structure. It is brothers who are supposed to be waging war while the sisters, according to the stereotype, are supposed to knit socks for the beloved soldier or nurse the wounded. Within revolutionary battles fought to displace some dominating group from power, women stand some chance to get a piece of the pie. Margaret R. Higonnet states:

> For women, the struggle to shift from subordination to equality is necessarily an act of insubordination and must therefore be

assimilated to regicide, the murder of the *pater populi*, rather than fratricide (Higonnet 1989: 81).

There seems to be no "space" for women within fratricidal wars. Indeed several authors, Higonnet included, interpret these wars as wars against the feminine, which they are certainly too.

In adopting this interpretation, I do not mean they are necessarily wars against women, although there are such wars in which atrocities against women are particularly brutal and conspicuous, as in the recent and contemporary wars in Bosnia-Herzegovina or Rwanda. It is rather that in civil wars, it is the incorporation of the other and the constant interaction with the other that is attacked. But it is the feminine that is regarded as representing the principle of interrelation, as well as the Other. Women are less anguished than men about inner boundaries and bodily limits, not particularly obsessed by boundaries unless under attack; this bears on women's socially "gentler" attitude to outer, political borders. They are "the place of all places" (Irigaray) and construct their social being at and with borders. These issues have to do, in part, with identity and the way a subject is constructed. Historically female and male subjectivities are differentially constructed. Women's subjectivities have had historically less support and therefore less support for autonomy. It is therefore through wayward strategies which include interiorizing borders and selfhood that women have learnt to subjectify themselves in an insubordinate and much clandestine way.

Women are traditionally accustomed and expected, both corporeally and through their socialization, to incorporate the other. Women are more accustomed to accept the "other" within themselves as evidenced in intercourse and childbearing. While women's supposedly primary love object, the mother, is the same for women and of the same sex, they are socially strongly encouraged to accept the other and to be socialised in a man's world though they are not in conformity with the dominant (masculine) figure. Traditionally, women also adapt to different cultures more easily, giving up their origins more often than men when marrying into another community: this is also learnt, and anyone could learn that. They are made to give up their family names or have no family names. In some traditions, such as the Hindu, women sometimes also give up their first names as a symbolic change of identity. Even in women's self-identity, women are socially more related to the other (a positive way of understanding it) in their strong identification with the family and their historically and socially prepared dedication to others. Boundaries for women are *made* relational rather than obstacles to relations. The division of inner and outer space is less radical for women and they move more easily in both dimensions or switch from the one to the other. Society has attributed women those obligations and capacities, necessary for its survival, which it has spared men of. But clearly, anyone could serve the purpose given when exposed to it.

Women's genealogies are also different from men's in that, in being born of woman, a man is born of the other sex while a woman is born of the same sex. Much of psychoanalysis derives from the social interpretation of the consequences of this simple fact. It is also the first and best evidence of both biological as well as social asymmetry.

At the same time, in "man's fantasies" there is a whole imaginary of how dangerous it may be for the male individual, for maleness as such and for society—to cross boundaries towards the other. That imaginary is full of myths of origination within the male power principle (for example, the myth of the *vagina dentata*; the myth of Sita being born from father's ploughing, of Athena born from Zeus directly without a mother).

These differences just discussed partially explain the fact that in the recent Balkan war(s), as in many others, women were incomparably less violent and showed on the whole more compassion and willingness to help and understand the other side. In practice, women organize whatever resistance is possible to the state-led violence and whatever humanitarian help they can.

But none of what is said here should be understood as an essentialist or biological determinism regarding the "nature" or "destiny" of women "doomed" to stay in their present social position. On the contrary, there is a permanent interaction of the "biological" and the "social" for all human beings, which makes it impossible and pointless to say whether something is "natural" or "social". I reject the very distinction itself,[3] and, without this distinction, the problem of "essentialism" or biologism cannot arise. It is a characteristic of humankind that human nature should be socialized as much as society is naturalized.[4] In this sense, woman as "the place of all places" should be understood not in the biological sense, but in the sense of a *reformed symbolic order* where women would have a say and were represented as well as represent able.

Women represent, certainly for historical and social reasons, symbolically, more then men, a space of mixture and meeting, *métissage, brassage*. It is this *métissage*, which women accept, create and represent, rather than necessarily women themselves, that is actually being attacked by those who want to purify their origins, "liberating" them from the other and denying the other. Mixture is something, which is not merely destroyed by the aggressor, but he also appropriates it as a power of creation, since it is at the origin of both life and culture. Creation both in the cultural as well as in the biological sense occurs in mixture and hence emerges the wish to appropriate it and the necessity to control women as its symbol and embodiment. It is for this reason, as a matter of logic and not by chance, that the aggressor in the Yugoslav wars destroys cities.[5] Cities are the birthplaces of culture and culture is necessarily mixture in that culture always presupposes culture and can never originate from a *tabula rasa*. Yet, the radical nationalist, paradoxically and suicidally, claims culture as a *tabula rasa*.

The Yugoslav aggressor in this senseless and eventually self-destructive war constructs a national "we" with emphatic male sexist and racist characteristics—male to the exclusion of anything/anyone else. Hence emerges the figure of the Rambo-like warrior in a ruthless, sexually powerful and racist brotherhood and the racist war songs sung not only against the enemy-nation but also against the non-European members (called "monkeys") of the UN peacekeeping forces. The city is not the birthplace of this new "hero" who, at best, comes from the grim socialist suburbs whereby he shall never be integrated in to the city's sophisticated, feminized life. Symbolically, life in a city of *early phase of urbanization* is seen by the rural person as that of an emasculated individual, because it is supposed to be an easy and comfortable life compared to the rough and "manly" life in the countryside. The new hero hates it because he envies it. He has been brought up with the traditional epic saying, "Don't be a woman," meaning "Don't be a coward".

He wants to destroy this place he doesn't understand and which never accepted him by confirming his own origin in himself in his autistic dream.[6]

For all these reasons, these wars are symbolically anti-feminine. But none of this should induce us to believe women are the only victims; the whole population is the victim, regardless of sex, regardless of nation.

Of course, war and nationalism are also practically anti-feminine in many respects. As real and not only symbolic victims (and they are most often real victims), women are "entitled", once again, to specific types of suffering, atrocities, rape, etc. Rape is, among other things, a re-appropriation by the rapist of mixture-as-power from the woman.

IV

Let us consider more closely the role of binary models in nationalism and war. As has been frequently stated, binary models of thinking hide asymmetrical structures behind an "official" symmetry. In binary thinking one of the terms of a pair is regularly thought of as feminine and "lower", and the other as masculine; in it, the feminine has been thought of as negative ever since the Pythagoreans, as reported in Aristotle's *Nicomachean Ethics*. Other examples of such pairs of concepts are not completely parallel but they are essentially sexed and they have been so appropriated by the whole history of Western thought. The models are "sexed" even when they do not mention the sexual difference explicitly, that is, good/bad, right/left, square/rectangle, etc.

In reality there is no true parallelism between the two terms of each pair; one of the terms of the duality is subordinated to the other. The subordinate term is automatically thought of as feminine and imperfect compared to the dominant term, which is seen as masculine and perfect. This configuration *precedes reflection*,[7] it is given within and with Western thought itself and we accept it unawares unless we specifically question the unconscious. This binary model of thinking has been entertained, nurtured, and further developed by our tradition of thought so as to become part of it. Such dual patterns also materialize in opposed nationalisms and wars.

Thus, in a remarkable essay, Barbara Freeman (Freeman 1989) quotes Elaine Scarry:

> War is a contest where the participants arrange themselves into two sides and engage in an activity that will eventually make it possible to designate one side the winner and one side the loser.... In consenting to enter into war, the participants enter into a structure that is a self-cancelling duality ... a formal duality, that, by the very force of its relentless insistence on doubleness, provides the means for eliminating and replacing itself by the condition of singularity. A first major attribute here is the transition, at the moment of entry into war, from the condition of multiplicity to the condition of the binary; a second attribute is the transition, at the moment of ending the war, from the condition of the binary to the condition of the unitary (Scarry 1985: 87–88).

In nationalism and nationalist wars, there is also identification with the father figure (the Father of the Nation). *In psychological terms this is a regression* (identification with the parent, the origin). This regressive identification with a "higher" or "older" office (and the consequent splitting of the father-figure into a positive and a negative figure) means, for men, taking refuge in the same sex, and for women, taking refuge in the other. In both cases, as both men and women can become nationalists, it is through this identification that a "community", not a "society", is formed. Community is created by contrast with the other community, that of the neighbour, but for women it is a double-bind relation.

It is a double-bind relation because women owe allegiance to the nation but at the same time national interests may conflict with their interests as women. Second, in identifying with the father, they identify with that which is different and they will be equally true and untrue to both the Father-symbol and to their own self-representation.

The splitting of the father figure means that "their" leader (the leader of the other ethnic group) will be the "bad father" and "ours" will be the "good one". These groups give themselves a "higher" authority much the way religion does and the identification with that authority legitimizes the violence of those who accept that office. Every individual sacrifices his or her personal identity to it as if governed by a powerful superego. The groups so constituted soon call themselves nationalities and lean towards a nation-state to give them, externally, the skeleton they lack internally. In fact, they rely on violence toward others for their identity.

A remarkable difference lies in men and women's identification with the father figure. Identifying with it means exclusion of the other(s) for men, who thereby identify with the same. It implies a paradox for women who identify with that which is different. Nationalism, for women, doesn't mean one's symbolic origin in the same or the exclusion of the other (sex), but coexistence with it, since identification with the Father-figure itself means mixture and inclusion and is represented in the ideal case as a willing and permitted "incest".[8] Men's faithfulness, on the contrary, to the father-figure (soldiers in the ideal case) is maintained in principle through the realization of "purity". It is symbolically represented as accepted and acceptable male homosexuality or homosociality, although it doesn't prevent men from having sexual intercourse with women. But, women are despised and the relationship to them is seen as being of secondary value, much as in the Socratic–Platonic tradition as read by feminists or by Foucault. It means for them a symbolic origin with(in) the Other.

Because of this different symbolic investment of women and men in nationalism, as well as for the reasons discussed above, female nationalism is thus less fierce and murderous and women will be less prone to violence in defence of the nation. Women are also *socialized* to be less violent as well. None of this, however, means that women are less cooperative with nationalism and, therefore, with that violence which we take to be essential to the main currents of radical (male) nationalism.

Nationalists also need foundation myths and these myths make claims about the "birth of the nation" and of "our" culture being the oldest and the best, "manly" and "heroic". The re-appropriation of the origin for the male nationalist is necessarily a claim both at the "national" as well as at the "sexual" symbolic levels. "Origin" means birth, and it is through a claim of a "pure" origin or "birth of the nation" that the nationalist ideal is given shape. *Women and an origin in women cannot guarantee a "pure" origin for the male nationalists since women symbolically represent mixture.* Therefore the dream of an origin in oneself or from the same[9] Women as representing evil and women as representing mixture is in no way a contradiction since mixture is considered to be evil. This myth of origins then accounts for the resulting exclusion of the other in culture and tradition.

In opting for nationalism, violence and war with its exclusion of that which is different, men have to unlearn their love for their first object, the mother, as a love of that which is different and which would divert their attention. It is here that the role of the "brotherhood" becomes apparent, and it is not in contradiction to the patriarchy to which it is itself subordinate. Its first function is thus to eliminate the "sisters", starting with *the sisters within the same nationality*. Brotherhood's first enemy is thus the one within the group, the internal other, including the symbolic woman within themselves and the *feminine principle* (Theweleit 1987). Women or the feminine are not to be trusted.

V

The basic principle of (male) nationalism as the exclusion of the other thus means the *negation of the origin in and with the other(s)* It is a claim for purity and monism, both national and sexual. The national "reason" is regularly articulated as a sexual one; "our" nation is "heroic", "straight", "moral" and "manly", the other nation is "emasculated", "cowardly", "feminine" and "dishonest". It is the sexual element that permits and structures representation—that very important figure of thinking and instrument of political domination and one of the mechanisms in the symbolic realm whereby the dominant group exercises its power. God-the-Father, the Father-of-the-Nation or the political Leader, is represented by the Son, by Man who is his true envoy and image. The figure of political representation in parliament and in public life is appropriated by that group which is in accord with, and the basis for, this norm—the man, white and powerful. All those who differ from it are misrepresented, badly represented, or non representable and they appear, if at all, as exceptions confirming the rule. At the same time this misrepresentation is not openly recognized. It is men (the norm) who in the representational system stand for both men (the "Same") and women (the "Other"). Obviously, they will not be able to represent the specificities of that which is different. There is the same basic asymmetry between the male and the female as there is between the representant and the represented. The first term is "stronger" (also, grammatically) because it appears on both sides of an equation and also at a higher, all encompassing level, as in languages such as English and French. Thus one can say that man = man *and* woman.

Women relate to representation as the *object*, as that which is represented (signified) by the representant (signifier). They are reduced to a mute position since someone speaks in their name. Politically, their situation is complex. It is certainly better to be represented by the Other than not to be represented at all (which is the real alternative) but it would be still better to present oneself. One must hope that such an asymmetric symbolic order will one day be escaped and such escape should be attempted and pursued on all fronts, obliquely and subversively, and in and through language as well, which is part of that symbolic order.

Although the sexual element may appear as instrumental to the national one, it is also basic and *structures* the idea of national purity which ultimately is sexual. Sexuality and gender difference is older than the conception of the nation, which, in Europe, can only be traced back to the 19th century. The sexual/gender difference is inscribed in language itself, whereas the national difference comes much after language and uses the examples ready at hand.

By being totally autistic, nationalism is also suicidal, because life necessarily involves having one's origin in and with the other. Since we are necessarily born of the Other—the other sex, the other person, and the other culture—the death of the Other sooner or later implies one's own death. It is mixture and not monistic solipsism that is culturally or naturally fruitful. Being "born of the Other" may also be understood in its symbolic meaning, thereby bringing into consideration *social power*, and not only in the biological sense. While cleansing the world or our surroundings of the other, we are dangerously jeopardizing our own existence and security, as well as the very possibility of our renewal. In the recent Balkan wars, as the war in Bosnia-Herzegovina raged, this was the position official Serbia and nationalists had put themselves in.

The suicidal drive in nationalism is not willed or overtly conscious; it is the result of the *insane attempt to be born retrospectively by oneself*, from oneself, not to owe anything to the other. It is actually an attempt to control birth and take it over completely. Since it cannot be done physically, it will be done symbolically.[10]

VI

The philosophical reasons for this identification of the nation with a male figure are deeper still and well known: in our symbolic order, only the masculine is universalisable, never the feminine. Universalization, like representation, is another figure of thinking that has a direct bearing on social power, since thinking is, among other things, a means of subduing the world. There is, therefore, no equivalent divine figure of a woman comparable to that of God the Father in monotheism, none that would *be both universal (and supposedly sexually neutral) and at the same time solely based on the model of the feminine sex.* The same applies to the would-be national leader-figure.

The fact that the Nation and the State are often identified with a female figure should not puzzle us. Feminine figures often *embody* and *bear* symbolically the ideal, hence "the Motherland", and in ancient religions, local goddesses. But the fact that women "embody" ideas, thereby serving to justify them, doesn't mean that what is embodied, the principle or mechanism, is a "feminine" one. One has to distinguish between the carrier of an ideal and the ideal that is carried. What is symbolically "embodied" in the female figure can still remain a male ideal, activity, or experience.

The feminine embodiment of such high ideals as "Liberty", the "Nation", "Wisdom", "Motherland", and "Purity" are often used as a pretext to eliminate concrete women, both in traditional mythologies and in contemporary politics. The supposedly female figures for such great male ideas have nothing whatsoever to do with a concrete feminine experience. In addition, it is clearly the same structure whether it is Thatcher or Major who is in office; in both cases it is a "male" lineage whereby name and power are transmitted, while the "other", the non-transmitted and un-named female lineage, guarantees the continuity of the masculine discontinuity.

Therefore, one should not yield too easily to the belief, sometimes maintained by feminists as well, that the nationality (nation) being aggressed upon "is the woman", which has been said of Croatia. According to this belief, "Croatia is being raped and thus is a woman". Woman is the incarnation of the Nation, or the Nation, precisely because women do *not* have a proper position in it, but only obliquely. Secondly, "Croatia" can be so readily identified with a woman because of the *all too ready identification of woman as victim*. Victim/aggressor is another pair of opposites that is symbolically "sexed" like any other opposition. Thirdly, the above discussion shows that rather than nationalism giving women a central position, it tries to usurp the feminine and is oppressive of women, first within the national group itself. At the symbolic level both the feminine principle as well as the feminine element in men will be suppressed. For all these reasons, the image of the aggressed nation being a "woman" and being attacked by a neighbouring (male) nation is erroneous, although rape is certainly a regular feature of war.

The masculine/feminine war is present as a war within a war, first within a nation(ality) and only secondly between two national groups, although the latter happens most visibly at the level of war atrocities. But it is complicated by the fact that women are accomplices at every level, both on the visible as well as the invisible side of the war, whether they collaborate or not. The whole system and the war-machine are all-encompassing frameworks. They are set in motion much before the belligerents resort to arms.

VII

Yoshikazu Sakamoto has described the post-cold war situation as an "orderly disorder". "A paradoxical combination of stabilization of the global framework but of disorder in the substance itself... Globally the world has become more homogeneous (military unipolarization, extension of the capitalist market and economy to practically the whole of the globe, the universal diffusion of nationalisms and the globalization of democracy). Yet new conflicts have multiplied" (Sakamoto 1992: 2).

At the time of the crash of socialism the world is unipolar, and Western-Nordic at that, a unipolarity which the national-ethnic-religious fragmentation bitterly and unconsciously resists. At the same time, if what is slowly and with difficulty being shaped in Europe and through the United Nations succeeds, an international centralized higher government-like body will be organized. Nationalism at the end of the 20th century seemed to be the most widespread of the fragmentary interests. The problem with this fragmentation is that it knows no limit. The principle of self-determination must urgently be reconsidered by the international community. But who is the subject who can do it? Where is the equilibrium between the Nation-State and the suicidal drive of the nationalisms, especially of smaller would-be nationalities who, in the assassination, murder, destruction and killing of the Other or others, are thereby suicidal, given their interdependence on the Other?

Pierre Achard talks about the linguistic use of the "expanded 'we'" when a speaker non-explicitly comprehends his/her addressee in the "we" used. In a local utterance, the speaker holds a position of power. This is the usual situation with the statist "we". Achard relates this to nationalism. He writes:

> So the notion of nation appears when there is some problem between practical politics and its citizenry. For example, when an expanded "we" considers that it deserves its own state, different from the one it is in (Achard 1992).

Not every "we" need be a national "we". We all belong to different groups and confusions concerning subject identity are not peculiar to women. *Universal values and interests are usurped by particular dominant interests.* Yet at these times of crisis a national identity emerges, felt as a "we".

Although women are, in general and abstractly, addressed by the statist and nationally expanded "we", the whole grammar, linguistic structure, and syntax make it clear that women do not belong to the model of the dominant subject-speaker. They can, at best, confirm men in that position. In the case of an expanding "we" used by a speaker in power to include not only men but also women, the two will not be included in the same manner. Women will be included rather formally, in a paradoxical way, which never fits their specificity; they will be considered the exception. But men will be included de facto since they are, of course, the model.[11] Women always imperfectly belong and belong with specific, not general, characteristics—as mothers of (unknown) soldiers, as nurses—and if they "belong" to the enemy, it is as "whores" good only to be raped (and wanting it). Given that men, under the guise of neutrality and universality, are the main agents of nationalism, women's incorporation in it is always subordinate.

This is also why "we, women" cannot be a credible political project from the standpoint of traditional politics and thinking, in which the male model has won globally, being taken as that which is universal and neutral. Within that model, women do not stand a chance. That whole system has to be changed. Within the general framework of humankind, there are other options and some of them have never been attempted. The gender difference is a historic one. One can then imagine that it too is subject to change and one can hope and act to change it.

Notes

1. This could not yet be seen at the time of the publication of this paper's first version, as the war was raging in the Yugoslav space and distance for a retrospective insight was difficult to achieve.
2. I don't use the concept of "symbolic order" so much any more nowadays, since some orientations within psychoanalysis have made it into a normative idea which they endorse. Without approving it as normative, I do however see its utility to denote a limitation which is there in the transmission of "values".
3. In the meantime, in dealing with that distinction, I have developed the concept of the *division of reason* which accounts for the distinction natural/social, nature/culture, sex/gender etc. See the other two chapters in this book.
4. The biological argument as well as the social one should never by used against someone just as past injustice or a difference should never justify a present or future injustice.
5. Bogdanović, Bogdan. 1992. Le massacre rituel des villes, in *Lumières de la vill*, November 6, pp. 95–103.
6. Iveković, Rada. 1995. *La Balcanizzazione della ragione*. Rome: Manifestolibri.
7. Today (2004) I call it the *division of reason*: it is an *inter-section* dividing thinking which is also expressed as sex.
8. Mussolini or Hitler represented the ideal and unattainable lover for women and also the "Father" without any apparent difficulty, coming from the fact of the incestual and conceptual contradiction, much like God.
9. *svayambhū*.
10. For a philosophical elaboration of this topic, see Sloterdijk (1989).
11. In the example I have given, women and men obviously cannot identify with God the Father or the Father of the Nation in quite the same way.

REFERENCES

Achard, Pierre. 1992. *Discourse and social praxis as building up nation and state.* Typescript.
Cooper, Helen M., Adrienne Munich and Susan Merrill Squier (eds). 1989. *Arms and the woman: War, gender, and literary representation.* Chapel Hill: University of North Carolina Press.
Freeman, Barbara. 1989. "Epitaphs and epigraphs: 'The end(s) of man'", in Helen M. Cooper, Adrienne Munich and Susan Merrill Squier (eds), *Arms and the woman: War, gender, and literary representation.* Chapel Hill: University of North Carolina Press.
Higonnet, Margaret R. (1989), "Civil wars and sexual territories," in Helen M. Cooper, Adrienne Munich and Susan Merrill Squier (eds), *Arms and the woman: War, gender, and literary representation.* Chapel Hill: University of North Carolina Press.
Marcus, Jane. 1989. "Corpus/corps/corpse: Writing the body in/at war", in Helen M. Cooper, Adrienne Munich and Susan Merrill Squier (eds), *Arms and the woman: War, gender, and literary representation.* Chapel Hill: University of North Carolina Press.
Sakamoto, Yoshikazu. 1992. Un entretien avec Yoshikazu Sakamoto. *Le Monde*, December 2.
Scarry, Elaine. 1985. *The body in pain. The making and unmaking of the world.* New York: Oxford University Press.
Sloterdijk, Peter. 1989. *Eurotaoismus. Zur kritik der politischen Kinetik.* Frankfurt am Main: Suhrkamp.
Theweleit, Klaus. 1987. *Male Fantasies.* Translated by Stephen Conway in collaboration with Erica Carter and Chris Tunner. Minneapolis: University of Minnesota Press.

Section II

Movements

INTRODUCTION

Kalpana Kannabiran

The occupied territory presents a very inhospitable terrain for feminist mobilization. And yet, across the world women have built movements for peace, rebuilt communities blown apart by weapons of war, and nurtured those that have been scarred by the violence of conflict in unimaginable ways, returning them to "normalcy" under the most difficult conditions. What are the concerns that arise in the course of this "return" to peace?

Questions of women and peace must be located, at the outset, within larger arenas of culture as ideology and practice, which shape the ways in which communities act on women prior to, during and after conflict. In a sense, culture makes women's lives intelligible within patriarchal moorings, seeking to entrench them further in patriarchy times of disturbance. The more one looks at women's engagement with conflict therefore, the more necessary it becomes to look at ideas/ideologies of culture and belonging that undergird these responses. One part of the question of culture—an important part of it—is that of religion as belief and community of belonging. The impossibility of silence on the troubled relationship between women and war is brought home, for instance, by the question that has become the cornerstone of patriarchal legends in different regions in the world, most certainly in South Asia: "Haven't the greatest battles been fought over women?" The power of hegemonic-patriarchal versions of mythology, in a religio-political context that witnesses frequent violent polarization between different religious groups can scarcely be understated. Mythology and legend run into the history of the present re-inventing the agency and/or the victimization of women in occupied territories, replaying themes of abduction, sexual assault, forced pregnancy, chastity/wifely virtue, and selfless motherhood, the war cry dismembering women's bodies, extending the battlefield into homes and communities.

Minow draws an interesting parallel between intimate violence and inter-group violence, pointing to the similarities, continuities and disjunctions in experience and law with respect to these two kinds of violence.[1] This is particularly relevant in situations where inter-group violence on women, especially in times of conflict, often involves "intimate" violence—sexual assault, forced marriage, forced pregnancy/sterilization. The use of the word "intimate" (my usage, not Minow's) in this context is without doubt deeply problematic. Yet, it is in the context of this very problematic usage that one needs to look at intimate violence (within the family) in conflict and post-conflict situations. Take the case from India for instance. Gudiya's experience in the past couple of years—the return of her "disappeared" soldier-husband from a Pakistani prison, the public [national] debate on whether she should return to him or continue to live with the man she married out of choice subsequently, whose child she was carrying; the decision of the community to return her to her first husband and return her child, when born, to her second husband who must now divorce her; the birth of that child; her unsuccessful attempts to bear a child for her "original" husband; her illness and death in an army hospital; all in the space of a couple of years encapsulate women's predicament within families and communities in times of conflict. And this draws for us, in very poignant ways, the connections between intimate and inter-group violence against women.

The history of Partition, especially of the Punjab—especially women's experiences of abduction, recovery and rejection—echo the eerie timelessness of women's experiences of glorious battles and their sacrifice at the altar of family honour in times of war. Abduction is not a story of one side of a border alone, and it is often countered by deceit, appropriation and assault on women from the other side. The experiences of women across borders are starkly similar, and women tell stories of loss even in times of victory, although stories of loss and violation in times of defeat, occupation or subjugation are numbing in their raw endless pain and victimization, the experiences of women in Gujarat in 2002 being yet another signpost in a long history of violation. The public humiliation of women, especially in times of escalated conflict, is an experience that women's movements have had to confront time and again. The violence of conflict is always etched on women's bodies, as the recent experience of women in Manipur demonstrates.

While the recovery of women in the aftermath of Partition and their rejection by their families has been written about, Minow's observation that situations of conflict also lead to an escalation of domestic violence bears reiteration. The precariousness of existence of those engaged in combat is often offset by increasing conflict and violence in the home—virtually the only space where combatants are certain of their authority and control. This could of course be extended to argue that armed conflict, militarization and militancy rely on the use of weapons of war, which are essentially also symbols of masculinity and domination. For women in combat, the test is inevitably about how well they are able to master masculinist discourses and strategies, and how well they are able to mask their "femininity". For those, who nurture men in combat, part of that nurturance is complete acquiescence, and submergence under the larger goals of combat, personal liberty in the home being but a small casualty—the chaste compliant wife and the selfless devoted mother being the ideal supports of men out at war.

Efforts by women to rebuild their lives in this situation, therefore, attains a new significance because these efforts are in a sense pitted against heightened patriarchal cultural sensibilities and try in very poignant ways to subvert the power of entrenched patriarchy—a far more painful project in the context of conflict and its aftermath than in the context of "normal times."

Work on conflict in the past two decades has looked at the specific implications of conflict for women. Feminist writing has attempted to understand the politics of mothers' fronts; the specific mobilizations by women to promote peace and resist war; the ways in which family and community lock women into inescapable custody, through non-consensual marriage, the denial of choice in widowhood and remarriage practices; the experiences of combatant women within militant movements and resistance struggles; the relationship between the violent masculinity of the armed forces and women at contested boundaries or on the borders of nations, to cite a few concerns in the subcontinent.

The critical element in feminist politics that is the need for women to build alliances across borders, boundaries and identities, even while acknowledging the fact of diversity, comes to life in the letter written by Pakistani feminists to the women of Bangladesh apologizing for the violence perpetrated by the Pakistani army during the Bangladeshi war of Independence. Mothers' fronts across the sub-continent have consistently questioned the gains of war and juxtaposed them to the loss of kin, of homes, of land and livelihoods.

While the "maternalization" of post-conflict mobilizations might echo in troubling ways the valorization and reification of motherhood within patriarchy (especially on the sub-continent), instances from Sri Lanka and Northeast India demonstrate both the conjunctions with patriarchal constructs and the spin offs that interrogate and transform the original construct itself.

Patriarchy speaks with a forked tongue to women. Where the subjugation of women simultaneously involves their reification as mothers and the colonization of their bodies, womanist mobilizations (as distinct from "feminist" if one can call them that) appropriate the potential of the forked tongue—sometimes using the pedestal of the "reified mother" to reclaim bodies of disappeared sons, sometimes throwing back the shame and humiliation of violation back at the perpetrator in ways that rock the complacency of the habitual masculine appropriation of female sexuality. Moving the naked female body into the street and forcing public gaze on it, captures the collective predicament in occupied territories. The assault on one woman is experienced as the vulnerability of all women whose bodies bear the scars of that violence.

This brings us to the relationship between identity, belonging and citizenship in times of conflict. Women engage with the realities of conflict from specific locations—Bengali, Chakma, Hindu, Muslim, Naga, Tamil, Sinhala, Buddhist, Mohajir, or one of several others on the sub-continent. In articulating their position with respect to specific episodes/contexts of violence, therefore, they rely on the notion of belonging which refers primarily to patterns of trust and confidence, constantly grappling with the shifting relation between forces of community and society. The longing for a stable national, indigenous and cultural territory is situated within the material context of strife, displacement and instability with the state playing a critical role in the shaping of this context. The politics of assertion therefore directly addresses state power and state culpability in aggravating conditions in areas of conflict and the notion of belonging gets inextricably linked to this politics of assertion/ resistance. Clearly then, belonging is constantly in the making through a process of becoming that draws on the contingencies of politics from one phase of struggle to another. The fact of belonging, therefore, is located sometimes in the past, at other times in the "re-claimed" past, and sometimes very clearly in the history of the present.

Finally, the problem of exclusion. Despite the fact that women have mobilized against heavy odds to retrieve stability and rebuild communal life, official peace initiatives in periods of suspended conflict rarely invite women to negotiate peace. On the other side, movements of resistance scarcely move beyond rudimentary paternalism in their understanding of the women's question, both within their own movements and in relation to civilian communities that bear the burden of their resistance without respite. And yet, women continue to pull communities together, build bridges and make the forked tongue speak for them.

The essays in this section address these and related concerns drawing on the experience of Sri Lanka, India (Andhra and the North Eastern region) and Bangladesh, and attempt to understand the texture of women's engagements with peace process in situations of conflict in South Asia.

NOTE

1. Minow, Martha. 2000. "Between Intimates and between Nations: Can Law stop the violence?", *Case Western Reserve Law Review*, 50 (4) Summer: 851.

7

WOMEN IN SRI LANKAN PEACE POLITICS

Saro Thiruppathy and Nirekha De Silva

INTRODUCTION

This chapter focuses on women's involvement and influence in Peace Politics in Sri Lanka. The scope of the chapter is limited to women's involvement in Peace Politics in relation to the civil war in Sri Lanka between the Government and the Liberation Tigers of Tamil Eelam (LTTE). This chapter concentrates on the contribution of Sri Lankan women in the decision-making processes in political dialogues, conflict situations and peace efforts in Sri Lanka. It analyses the role of women in peace making, by discussing Sri Lankan Women's Movements for Peace, selected personalities of women peace activists, women's civil society organizations campaigning for peace through advocacy, lobbying, networking and through research and intellectual contribution by women towards the peace process in Sri Lanka. The chapter also discusses the role of women in militarization. The role and the position of women in the LTTE and in the Army are presented as part of the analysis. Also discussed are the contributions of women towards peace through legal mechanisms and instruments.

Peace politics is the process that influences the content and implementation of the goals, polices, etc., of a state or organization in order to facilitate a united and harmonious relationship between state and society. The political norms, values and beliefs of the state or organization involved is acquired and internalized through the process of political socialization.[1]

Women's Role in Peace Making

Women's Movements for Peace

"The contemporary Sri Lankan Women's Movement stand-out for its inspirational clarity and insights and will assuredly become an important resource for academics and activists seeking to track and learn about strategies of mobilizing women on peace and democracy."[2] The use of the local tradition of *devale kannalaawa*, that is, beseeching the gods in hysterical public bouts of weeping and cursing at shrines, is used in Women's movements and motherhood politics in Sri Lanka.[3]

Mothers and Daughters of Lanka is the re-grouping of the Women's Action Committee, which ceased to exist in 1987. It was disbanded due to the dilemma experienced in responding to the International Peace Keeping Forces' (IPKF) presence, Sinhala nationalist outrage and militant Tamil nationalism. Movement of Mothers and Daughters of Lanka was formed to take up the challenge of militant nationalism and state authoritarianism.

The Sinhala Mothers Front of the South was founded by two (male) members of Parliament belonging to the left *Naval Sama Samaja Party* (NSSP), who were inspired by the *Mothers of the Plaza de Mayo* (The Argentine Mothers Front).[4] Within two years of establishment, the membership of the Sinhala Mothers Front grew to 25,000.

The Sinhala Mothers Front, *co-opted* by the Sri Lanka Freedom Party (SLFP) became an instrument of its oppositional politics against the United National Party (UNP) Government of President Ranasinghe Premadasa. It organized a protest against the State-sponsored policy of abductions and disappearances in the Government's fight against the *Marxist Janatha Vimukthi Peramuna* (JVP) in 1987. The Mother's Front Movement had a significant impact in bringing the agenda of human rights to the public forum.[5] The Movement collapsed after the SLFP party came to power in 1994.

The Sinhala Mothers Front failed because of the lack of *cosmopolitanness*.[6] It acted only against state sponsored violence and did not call upon either the JVP or the LTTE to stop violence or to disarm. The Movement also had neither inter-ethnic nor inter-religious solidarity.

The Jaffna Mothers Front in the North was mobilized to protest against the atrocities of the Indian Peace Keeping Force (IPKF) and state security forces. The Jaffna Mothers Front also had to be disbanded due to the LTTE's disapproval on references to non-state violence and anti-democratic practices of the militant groups in the North and the East. A failure of the Mothers Front Movement was the lack of inter-religious and inter-ethnic solidarity between them. This failure indexed the weakness in building a national pro-peace platform.

"While the women have been able to appropriate their motherhood as a political force to bring about significant change in the political power balance, they have not been able to sustain this activism or use it as a means of achieving genuine empowerment. Nor have women's aspirations for peace and their activism within the peace movement been translated into a force that can determine the content or direction of peace process."[7]

Women Peace Activists

The women political leaders in South Asia are mostly the daughters and widows of male leaders, with kinship privileges over gender and co-opted by a male dominated political and institutional culture.[8] Some of the Women activists and leaders also have risen to power as a result of kinship privileges. President Chandrika Bandaranaike Kumaratunge and the late Prime Minister Sirimavo Bandaranaike can be given as examples.

Some of the women activists and leaders involved in Sri Lankan Peace Politics include the following.

President Chandrika Bandaranaike Kumaratunge came to power on a pro-peace platform and was backed by a broad coalition of civil society groups, but failed to establish an inclusive peace process and alienated the supporters and the opposition.[9] One of the factors that contributed towards the failure of Her Excellency Kumaratunge's efforts in the peace process is her failure to involve women parliamentarians from her own party or other non-party women professionals.[10]

Dr Radhika Coomaraswamy is the Chairperson of the Human Rights Commission of Sri Lanka and Director of the

International Centre for Ethnic Studies (ICES). As Director of the Centre, she oversees projects and programmes on multiculturalism, federalism and constitutional reform as well as education policy and judicial approaches to pluralism. She served as the UN Special Rapporteur on Violence Against Women from 1994. Dr Coomaraswamy has published widely on women's issues and ethnic issues. Dr Coomaraswamy has been appointed to many Boards and Committees and is a working committee member of the Civil Rights Movement, a member of the University Council of Colombo and a member of the National Committee on Women. At the international level, she is a member of the Board of Minority Rights Group and The International Human Rights Policy Group. Dr Coomaraswamy has won many awards, which include: The International Law Award of the American Bar Association, The Human Rights Award of the International Human Rights Law Group, The Bruno Kreisky Award of 2000 and The Leo Ettinger Human Rights Prize of the University of Oslo.

Ranjini Thiranagama: Analysing two events held in Colombo[11] to commemorate the 10th death anniversary of the feminist Peace Activist Ranjini Thiranagama, de Mel argues that "Ranjini's name and face had traveled from the North to the East and the South to enter the consciousness of women transcending divisions of class, ethnicity and religion, demonstrated the possibility of forging intra-national and intra-regional coalitions."[12]

Kumudini Samuel, has played a key role in the women's movement and the antiwar movement in Sri Lanka. In 2002, she organized a campaign involving international feminists to press for the inclusion of women in the peace process aimed at ending Sri Lanka's two-decades-old civil war. Her campaign led to the appointment of a Sub-Committee on Gender Issues to advise Peace negotiators and she is one of the five women nominated by the government to serve on this body.

Monica Alfred, Co-founder and Programme Coordinator of *AHIMSA*, the Center for Conflict Resolution and Peace, promotes stability throughout Sri Lanka by working to repair trust between the two groups. She directs workshops to unite Sinhalese and Tamil religious leaders, youth, teachers and staff members of government and non-governmental organizations (NGOs), educating them about conflict resolution, nonviolence, ethnic diversity, and peace education. Working to repair relations in the next generation, Ms Alfred also directs numerous youth programmes and gives lectures on national integration and reconciliation.

Visaka Dharmadasa is the Founder and Chairperson of Parents of Servicemen Missing in Action and the Association of War-Affected Women. She is also the Secretary of the Kandy Association for War-Affected Families. Working to end the civil war that has gripped Sri Lanka for the last 20 years, she educates soldiers, youth, and community leaders about international standards of conduct in war and promotes the economic and social development of women across conflict lines. She has designed and facilitated Track II dialogue processes, bringing together influential civil society leaders from both sides of the conflict. Ms Dharmadasa was asked by the LTTE leaders to carry messages to the government when talks were floundering and Tamil representatives refused to speak directly with foreign embassy staff members and Norwegian negotiators. In January 2004, Ms Dharmadasa authored an analysis on the unraveling of the current peace efforts, which she presented to Yasushi Akashi, Japanese special envoy for the Sri Lankan peace process.

Neela Marikkar is also President of Sri Lanka First. This powerful group of leaders from the country's business community struggles to end the 20-year conflict by advocating for peace and regional stability through a negotiated settlement between the Government of Sri Lanka and the LTTE. Ms Marikkar is also the Managing Director of Grant McCann–Erickson, a member of the international network McCann Erickson Worldwide, USA, and a consultant to the UN Development Programme's initiative "Invest in Peace", which promotes foreign investment for post-conflict reconstruction in Sri Lanka.

Justice Shiranee Tilakawardane, is a Supreme Court judge in Sri Lanka and a member of the International Panel of Jurists of the International Bureau for Child Rights (UN-affiliated). Justice Tilakawardane has led many workshops and done extensive training on gender sensitivity, equality issues, child witness sensitivity, and child abuse for groups ranging from

Government officers, Police Force and clergy to attorneys at law in Sri Lanka. She is a member of the advisory board of the South Asian Regional Program on Equity (SARI–Q) to reduce trafficking and violence against women in South Asia and an advisory committee member and international panelist for human rights and equality to the International Courts of Judges (also UN-affiliated). Justice Tilakawardane was the first woman judge appointed to the Court of Appeal, President of the Court of Appeal, High Court Judge, Admiralty Court Judge, State Counsel in the Attorney General's Department and Prosecutor in the Air Force Court Marshals. She has received numerous awards including the Sakshi of India Women's International Award for contributions to human rights and equality rights, the Shakti Award in recognition of contributions to equality rights and law from the Canadian International Development Agency on International Day, 2000 and a Human Rights Award in 2001 from the University of Sri Lanka.

Women's Civil Society Organizations

The Sri Lanka Women's NGO Forum (SLWNGOF) consists of over fifty women's organizations working on gender issues. SLWNGOF was founded in 1993 as a way to disseminate information and coordinate activities around the Fourth World Conference on Women in Beijing (1995). Since then, the Forum has focused on lobbying and advocacy and national, regional and international levels to ensure the implementation of the Beijing Platform for Action.

The Association of War-Affected Women, based in Kandy, is working to end the civil war that has gripped Sri Lanka for the last 20 years. The Association educates soldiers, youth and community leaders about international standards of conduct in war and promotes the economic and social development of women across conflict lines.

Kantha Handa (Voice of Women), campaigns for the economic, political, social and legal rights of women in Sri Lanka. It publishes a trilingual journal, organizes trainings, conducts research, and has a Women's House for women displaced by the conflict.

The International Centre for Ethnic Studies (ICES), was founded in 1982 to engage in culturally sensitive research in

Sri Lanka and outside. ICES implements projects on capacity building of women in conflict areas in Sri Lanka, the "Women's Constitutional Convention: Towards Engendering Constitutional Debate in Sri Lanka", one of the many projects initiated by the ICES in the recent past, violence against women in Sri Lanka, women and governance in South Asia, gendering peace movements in the context of armed conflict and displacement in South Asia and the programme on gender, citizenship and governance.

The Centre for Women's Research (CENWOR), conducts a variety of action-oriented activities, information dissemination, trainings and advocacy pertaining to women's rights, women's entry into non-traditional occupations and the creation of a general awareness of gender issues.

Intellectual Contribution of Women towards the Peace Process in Sri Lanka

Many Sri Lankan women have made intellectual contributions through research work and publications. A bibliography[13] of books published by Sri Lankan women, or on women involved in peace politics is hereto attached.

MILITARIZATION OF WOMEN

Traditionally, feminism and militarism have been configured as dichotomous—men and militaries and women and peace.[14] Chenoy argues that class, ethnicity, race and the position in the conflict become determining factors of women's response to militarization. Yet, Chenoy agrees on the masculine culture of militaries and the cooption of women by way of adopting masculinized ways.[15] Masculinized pride and expertise, discipline, centralization, secrecy, hierarchy and a belief in violence are integral to a militaralist ideology.

Women in the LTTE

The Women's Wing of the LTTE was formed in August 1983.[16] At the initial stages the LTTE women cadres were mainly involved in the task of political propaganda. Since mid-1984, women cadres had been given the military training and established as an organized guerrilla unit. Currently, women cadres are divided into the different platoons vis-à-vis Medicine, Education, Health, Social Science, Justice, Commando and Teaching. Roles and responsibilities of the cadres are determined by the Platoon Leaders. Peter Schalk estimates that there are 3000 women fighters ready and willing at the disposal of the LTTE command.[17]

LTTE women cadres include children, youth and middle-aged women. LTTE asks each Tamil family to contribute one member to the organization.[18] There also have been allegations of forced conscription. Yet, according to Alison's findings, most LTTE women recruits seem to be voluntary.[19] Alison has pointed out some motivations for women to join the LTTE as: 1) Nationalist sentiment, 2) To overcome suffering and oppression, 3) Educational disruption, 4) Sexual violence against women and 5) Ideas of women's emancipation.[20] The primary reason for active recruitment of women is not based on ideological commitment to equality and women's rights but is a pragmatic response to the need for more fighters created by the loss of men through death, as refugees and as emigrants.[21]

The armed cadres of the LTTE women's wing were also involved in the task of politicization and mobilization of Tamil Eelam women, campaigning against national oppression and social discrimination and emphasizing the need for women's emancipation. Towards this objective of emancipation of women, a radical women's journal called "*Sunthanthira Paraivagal*" was launched in December 1984.

The LTTE's women's wing has been expanding its political structures in the Jaffna peninsula, which was under the administrative control of the LTTE, since early 1985. They coordinate and work with women organizations, trade unions, industrial training centres, health and welfare associations, educational institutes and campaign towards enlisting women for the national struggle. Despite the fact that women are playing a significant role in combat and in political propaganda, they are not a part of the elite decision-making process.[22]

With the transformation of women's activism from the domestic sphere to the political sphere, by women joining the LTTE, the social identity as well as the role of women has changed.

South Asian women's ideal identity as *"Sita Devi"* has been transformed into "guerrilla fighters" who are willing to sacrifice their lives in pursuit of a political cause. Discriminatory social practices such as dowry, intra-caste marriages and the seclusion of unmarried women et al., which existed in the traditional Tamil society, have diminished as a result of the changes in social values and the traditional role of women.

Yet, Coomaraswamy argues that inducting women into a fighting force is not a step toward empowerment and equality, as the militarization of civil society destroys the important human rights values of due process, non-violent resolution of disputes and the celebration of humane values of compassion and tolerance.[23] Also, completely eradicating positive feminine qualities such as networking among people, nurturance, social bonding, gentleness, compassion, tolerance, etc., in the LTTE and, instead, giving prominence to masculine qualities and values, such as aggression, hierarchy, authority and empowerment, cannot be treated as a victory for women but as a triumph for the masculine world view.[24] In responding to Neloufer de Mel's query, whether LTTE women are agents or victims, Coomaraswamy responds that "the answer must lie in the appreciation that Tiger women are not given the freedom to determine their own destiny; they are helping to act out the perceived destiny of someone else."[25]

Women in the Army

The Women's Corps of the Sri Lankan Army was formed in 1980 as an unarmed, noncombatant support unit. This unit was set up with the assistance of the British Women's Reserve Army Corps, who contributed in training the first generation of officer cadets was. The structure of the Sri Lanka Army Women's Corps was identical to the structure of the British Women's Reserve Army Corps.

Eligibility criteria for the Women's Corps included being a Sri Lankan citizen (woman) between the ages of 18 and 20 and who has passed the lowest level of the General Common Entrance examinations. (Officer candidates must have passed the GCE Advanced Level examinations also.)[26]

Enlistment entailed a five-year service commitment (the same as for men) and recruits are not allowed to marry during this period. Women cadets are given a 16-week training course at the Army Training Centre at Diyatalawa. Although drill and physical training given during the course is similar to the men's programme, weapons and battle craft training is quite different.[27] In late 1987, the first class of women graduates from the *Viyanini Army Training* Centre were certified to serve as army instructors.

Women recruits are paid according to the same scale as the men, but are limited to service in nursing, communications, and clerical work.

Military Women in the Post-Conflict Situation

Although men and women are encouraged to act out similar roles as fellow soldiers in an Army or in a Guerrilla Movement during a war situation, in post-conflict society, the role women have to play is significantly different from that of men. As a result, the priorities of a post-conflict society are quite different from the priorities of a conflict society and women's contributions during the conflict rarely receive recognition when the war is over. The differential socialization patterns during a war situation and a post-conflict situation has significant consequences for former combat women. During the transitional process, the women ex-combatants, who have broken rules of traditional behaviour and gender roles, risk being marginalized. In many cases, female ex-soldiers prefer to conceal their military past rather than face social disapproval.[28]

CONTRIBUTION OF WOMEN TOWARDS PEACE THROUGH MECHANISMS AND INSTRUMENTS

Recommendations Presented at the Peace Negotiations in Oslo by Sri Lankan Women's Organizations to the LTTE and the Government

On 7 June 2002, Sri Lankan women's organizations presented a set of recommendations to the representatives of the LTTE and the Government at the Oslo peace negotiations. In addition to calling for full implementation of Security Council Resolution 1325, women recommended that both the Tamil Tigers and the

Government pay attention to the following substantive issues: Violence and Sexual Violence against Women, Refugees and Internally Displaced Women, Protection of the Rights of Women During Resettlement, Property Rights and Repossession of Homes, Land and Title, Women in Custody, War Widows, Families of Detainees, Families of the Disappeared, Families of Soldiers, Combatants and those Missing in Action, Women Combatants and Women in the Armed Forces, Provision of Food, Housing, Clean Water, Healthcare, Education, and Basic Services, Trauma and Counseling, Economic and Social Rights of Women, Trafficking of Women and Forced Prostitution.

Women's Charter

The Government's intention to fulfill its obligations towards women's rights is articulated in the Women's Charter (1993) document, and therefore considered integral to the ratification process of the Convention on the Elimination of All Forms of Discrimination Against Women (CEDAW). Currently, the Women's Rights Bill, of which the Women's Charter forms a part, has received Cabinet approval and is on its way to Parliament. Part 1, Section 2 of the Women's Charter refers to the Government's obligation to guarantee the rights of women in political and civil processes, equitable political representation and the right to participate in the formulation of state policy. Hence, by inference, it can be deduced that the state has acknowledged a duty to include women's active participation in peace negotiations and resultant policy formulation.

Gender Sub-Committee

At the peace negotiations in 2002, it was decided to form a Sub-Committee on Gender Issues to advise the main negotiation team on the effective inclusion of gender issues in the peace process. The Sub-Committee consists of five women appointed by the Government and five women appointed by the LTTE. The Government chose its nominees on the basis of a list of women leaders compiled by national women's organizations. The LTTE chose its members from its own cadres from the North and the East. In January 2003, at the fourth session of peace negotiations, the parties asked Norway to appoint a facilitator and senior advisor for the Committee and to contribute financial support.

The first meeting of the Sub-Committee on Gender Issues was held on 5 and 6 March 2003. The purpose of the Sub-Committee was to ensure the full inclusion of gender issues and analysis in all phases of the peace process. At the first meeting, the Sub-Committee decided to focus on the following issues: Sustaining the Peace Process, Resettlement, Personal Security and Safety, Infrastructure and Services, Livelihood and Employment, Political Representation and Decision-making and Reconciliation. However with the suspension of the peace negotiations, the Sub-Committee has not been active.

Women's Manifesto

Though there is no legislation directly addressing the right of women to participate in political and peace negotiations in the country, provisions in the Women's Charter address the right of women to participate equally with men in the political and public life of the country. While the mechanism of the Sub-Committee on Gender Issues has been in place since 2003, it has been dormant since its initial meetings, due to the stalling of the peace process itself.

The Women's Manifesto 2005/6 published by the Women's Political Forum in Sri Lanka stresses the importance of women's equal participation and full involvement in the prevention and resolution of conflict and in peace-building. The Women's Manifesto also emphasizes the need to take action in raising public consciousness on issues of women affected by conflict and that gender sensitive women should be brought into policy making and implementing mechanisms. Some of the recommendations made by them include:

a) Institutions created to carry the peace process forward must be sensitive to gender issues and take steps to ensure effective participation by women at policy making level. They should also network with women's organizations island-wide to develop and implement appropriate programmes.

b) Gender issues must be given priority during the peace and constitutions-making process through the Sub-Committee on Gender Issues.

c) Rehabilitation and resettlement programmes must take special circumstances of female heads of households and widows into account and address their needs including the allocation of lands to them.
d) Welfare schemes, as well as employment and skills training programmes must be implemented for women affected by the conflict.
e) Women and girls affected by conflict must have better access to education and employment and be afforded protection from all forms of harassment.
f) Trauma counseling must be made available for women and girls from conflict-affected areas.

Conclusion

Women in Sri Lankan peace politics have hailed from both the North and South of the island over a 20-year period and have been active in many different areas of advocacy and awareness raising. However, it has been just a few women such as Her Excellency President Chandrika Bandaranaike Kumaratunge who have been in a position to take decisions and make changes at policy level. As such, while advocacy on peace politics continues through a variety of women's organizations and at individual level as well, the role of women in direct peace negotiations is not yet a reality. In Sri Lanka, the representation by women in Parliament also needs to increase dramatically and women need to be seen both at national and international levels, actively participating and bringing the voice of women to the negotiating table of the Sri Lankan peace process.

Notes and References

1. Jary, D and J. Jary. 1995. *Collins Dictionary of Sociology*, p. 500. Glasgow: HarperCollins.
2. Quoted from Manchanda, R. (ed.). 2001. *Women, War and Peace in South Asia: Beyond Victimhood to Agency*, pp. 148-9, based on de Mel's work. New Delhi: Sage Publications.
3. De Alwis. 1998. Maternalist Politics in Sri Lanka: A Historical Anthropology of its Conditions of Possibility, Ph. D. Dissertation, University of Chicago and de Mel, N. 2001. *Women and the Nation's Narrative: Gender and Nationalism in the Twentieth Century*, 2nd edition. Colombo: SSA

4. The Argentine Mothers Front had forged a unique women's way of doing politics, of taking the private act of mourning into public space and politicizing it into a formidable tool of moral protest against state injustice.
5. De Mel. 2001. p. 236.
6. Ibid., p. 247
7. Kumudini Sammual quoted in Manchanda. 2001. p. 1472.
8. Manchanda. 2001. p. 1472.
9. Kumuduni Sammual's argument in "Gender Difference in Conflict Resolution—The Case of Sri Lanka" presented in Manchanda. 2001. p. 1472.
10. Sammul, K. 2003. quoted in Manchanda. p. 1472.
11. In one event, the Indian feminist Kamala Bhasin delivered a Key Note Address on Ranjini's contribution to South Asian Women's Movement, foregrounding a South Asian sisterhood. The other was a picket that tapped into different collective identity as women activists, commemorating Ranjani's death, appealed with a renewed urgency to citizens within the nation for peace made urgent following an incident of aerial strafing by the security forces and LTTE reprisal killings.
12. De Mel. 2001. p. 234.
13. The National Peace Council has the copyright to the bibliography. It is presented with the consent of the NPC.
14. Manchanda, R. 2003. p. 1470.
15. Chenoy's work in *Militarism and Women in South Asia*. 2002, analyzed by Manchanda. 2003. p. 1470.
16. "LTTE Women Guerrillas: A New Revolution". February 1990. *Voice of Tigers Bulletin*
17. Peter Schalk quoted in Coomaraswamy R. 1996. p. 8.
18. Margaret Tarwic. 1999. "Reasons for Violence: A Preliminary Ethnographic Account of the LTTE", in Siri Gamage and I.B. Watson (eds), *Conflict and Community in Contemporary Sri Lanka: "Pearl of the East" or the "Island of Tears"?*, p. 143. India: Sage Publications.
19. Mirinda Alison. 2003. "Uncovering the Girls in "the boys": Female Combatants". *Nivedini–Journal of Gender Studies*, 10(May–June): 43.
20. Ibid., pp. 44–54.
21. Ibid., p. 44. Has cited Hoole et al.. 1990: 326; De Silva. 1994: 28 and Samarasinghe, 1996: 213.
22. Coomaraswamy, R. 1996. *Tiger Women and the Question of Women's Emancipation* in *Pravada*, 9(4): 8.
23. Ibid., p. 8.
24. Ibid., p. 9.
25. Ibid.
26. AllRefer.com: http: //reference.allrefer.com/country-guide-study/sri-lanka/sri-lanka170.html
27. AllRefer.com: http: //reference.allrefer.com/country-guide-study/sri-lanka/sri-lanka170.html
28. Barth, Elise. 2003. *Peace as Disappointment: The Reintegration of Female Soldiers in Post-Conflict Societies: A Comparative Study from Africa*. Oslo: Peace Research Institute.

8

MOTHERHOOD AS A SPACE OF PROTEST: WOMEN'S POLITICAL PARTICIPATION IN CONTEMPORARY SRI LANKA*

Malathi de Alwis

During the years 1987 to 1991, Sri Lanka witnessed an uprising by nationalist Sinhala youth, the Janatha Vimukthi Peramuna (JVP) and reprisals by the state that gripped the country in a stranglehold of terror. While the militants randomly terrorized or assassinated anyone who criticized them or supposedly collaborated with the state, the state similarly, but on a much larger scale, murdered or "disappeared" anyone they suspected to be a "subversive", which included thousands of young men, some young women and several left-wing activists, playwrights, lawyers and journalists who were either monitoring or protesting the violation of human rights by the state. Bodies, rotting on beaches, smoldering in grotesque heaps by the roadsides and floating down rivers, were a daily sight during the height of state repression from 1988 to 1990. It was in such a context that the Mothers' Front, a grassroots women's organization with an estimated membership of over 25,000 women was formed in July 1990 to protest the "disappearance" of approximately 60,000 young and middle-aged men. Their only demand was for "a climate where we can raise our sons to manhood, have our husbands with us and lead normal women's lives".[1] The seemingly unquestionable authenticity of their grief and espousal of "traditional" family values provided the Mothers' Front with an

---

* Previously published in Patricia Jeffery and Amrita Basu (eds). 2001. *Resisting the Sacred and the Secular: Women's Activism and Politicized Religion in South Asia*. New Delhi: Kali For Women.

important space for protest, unavailable to other organizations critical of state practices.[2]

The Mothers' Front phrased their protest in a vocabulary that was most available to them through their primary positioning within a patriarchally structured society—that of motherhood—which I define here as encompassing women's biological reproduction as well as their interpellation as moral guardians, care-givers and nurturers. While I am fully in agreement with the argument that maternalist women's peace groups project essentialist views of women, that re-enforce the notion of biology as destiny and legitimize a sex-role system that, in assigning responsibility for nurture and survival to women alone, encourages masculinized violence and destruction, I think we need to consider carefully the reasons why "motherist movements" adopt the strategies they do, and what effects they have.[3] In light of such a project, I would like to consider here, the contingent usefulness of maternalized protest at a particular moment in Sri Lankan history. However, such an attempt at a positive reading cannot ignore the complex interplay of power within this space that also re-inscribed gender and class hierarchies and re-enforced majoritarian ethnic identities while those of minorities were erased.

Though the Mothers' Front's agenda remained very limited, its few, brief, and spectacular appearances on the Sri Lankan political stage nevertheless placed a government on the defensive, awoke a nation from a terrorized stupor and indelibly gendered the discourses of human rights and dissent. It also created a space in which a much larger, non-racist and more radical movement of protest could be launched to overthrow an extremely repressive and corrupt government that had been in power for 17 years, at the general elections of August 1994.

Due to limitation of space, my chapter will only concentrate on exploring how the Mother's Front created a space for themselves within a predominantly patriarchal political landscape by articulating their protest through an available, familiar and emotive discourse of motherhood. While this space was mediated by a powerful political party that was also predominantly male, Sinhala and middle class, I would like to suggest that the repertoire of protest employed by these women, albeit under the sign of the mother and mainly limited to tears and curses, were the most crucial components in an assault on a government that had until then held an entire nation to ransom on the pretext of safeguarding the lives of its citizens. It is in this sense that I assert the contingent value of the Mothers' Front's repertoire of protest.

> Tears ... are common to all. Yet, there is nothing more powerful on earth that can wring tears from others than a mother's tears.[4]

The first branch of the Mothers' Front was inaugurated on 15 July 1990 in the southern district of Matara, a region severely affected by "disappearances".[5] The meeting was held under the auspices of *Mangala Samaraweera and Mahinda Rajapakse*, members of Parliament representing the main opposition party—the Sri Lanka Freedom Party (SLFP) from *Matara* and *Hambantota* respectively. The meeting was attended by 1,500 women from the Matara district who elected office bearers from among themselves to coordinate the work of the group. They decided to work out of Mr Samaraweera's home in Matara as the climate of violence warranted some protection for the women[6] and as the majority of them were severely traumatized: "At that time we were like children constantly needing to be told what to do. Sometimes I would come away from one of our meetings not remembering a single matter that was discussed" noted one office bearer.[7] Within six months, branches of the Mothers' Front were set up in ten other districts (often under the patronage of an SLFP Member of Parliament (MP) of that area) and the Front's membership increased to 25,000 by 1992. The majority of these women were from rural and semirural areas belonging to the lower and lower middle classes, acquainted with much poverty and hardship.

Initially, the Front's focus was mainly regional and it made little headway, except in compiling systematic and extensive documentation about the "disappeared" from each district. Visiting police stations, army camps and local government offices with these lists and petitioning various state institutions and officials for information produced few results. The women often viewed their reception at such institutions of power with a certain resignation and cynicism, tolerating politicians who promised the earth when canvassing votes but refused to give them the time of day once in power and accepting that the everyday provision of state services was often contingent upon one's wealth and status. Yet, what fuelled their continued pursuance of such activities and an increasing anger at being thwarted was an over-riding confidence that their "disappeared" was alive and should be sought urgently before his trail grew cold. No amount of persuasion would sway them from this ceaseless search except the actual display of the body. As one mother eloquently pointed out to me, "I gave birth to that boy. Surely won't I sense it if he dies?" The first seeds of protest were sown in such moments of stubborn refusal to give up hope, to concede failure. The "absence of bodies", noted Jennifer Schirmer, creates a "presence of protest".[8] By early 1991 the Mothers' Front was to "show its muscles" by targeting its protest on the epicentre of power—the capital city of Colombo—and capturing the attention of the entire country.[9]

On 19 February 1991, the Mother's Front organized a massive rally in a suburb of Colombo. Clad in white and holding photographs and pieces of clothing of their "disappeared", thousands of these "chronic mourners", mobilizing under the sign of the mother demanded that a nation not forget them or their "disappeared".[10] The rally also commemorated the death of well-known actor, newscaster and journalist Richard de Zoysa who was abducted, tortured, murdered and dumped upon the beach by a paramilitary squad the year before. Richard de Zoysa's mother Dr *Manorani Saravanamuttu*, who had publicly accused senior police officers in being involved in her son's abduction (and had then to flee the country for her own safety), also returned to the island at this time and was invited to serve as the President of the National Committee of the Mothers' Front. The Front portrayed itself as a grassroots movement of mothers who had dedicated their lives to seeking their "disappeared" with the support of the SLFP (because of the threat posed by the government). The mothers' seemingly conservative and apolitical rhetoric, as well as certain unorthodox avenues of protest that were subsequently employed by them, made a counter-attack by the state especially difficult and complicated. Unable to contain the Mothers' Front through the usual practices of authoritarian control, the state was constantly placed on the defensive—countering the Front on their terms rather than its own. Such a counterpoint took the form of counter-rhetoric, counter-allies and counter-ritual.

Counter-Rhetoric

As in the case of the Madres of Argentina or the Mutual Support Group for the Reappearance of our Sons, Fathers, Husbands and Brothers (GAM) of Guatemala, the rhetoric of protest used by the Mothers' Front too can be read as confronting a repressive state by revealing the contradictions between the state's own rhetoric and practices. By appealing for a return to the "natural" order of family and motherhood, these women were openly embracing patriarchal stereotypes that primarily defined them through familial/domestic subject positions such as wife and mother. However, by accepting this responsibility to nurture and preserve life, which is also valorized by the state,[11] they revealed the ultimate transgression of the state as well, for it was denying women the opportunities for mothering, through a refusal to acknowledge life by resorting to clandestine tactics of "disappearance".[12] The Sri Lankan state's major rhetorical counter to such implicit accusations was very interesting. On the day the Mothers' Front organized their first rally in Colombo, President Premadasa acknowledged that he sympathized "with the mothers whose children have been led astray by designing elements. Many now in custody are being rehabilitated".[13] In a similar vein, Ranjan Wijeratne, Minister of State for Defence pontificated: "Mothers are not expected to stage demonstrations. Mothers should have looked after their children. They failed to do that. They did not know what their children were doing. They did not do that and now they are crying".[14] In both statements, there is an overt suggestion that these protesting women have not been "good" and "capable" mothers but the President's statement goes one step further and suggests that because of this, the state has taken on the responsibility of motherhood by rehabilitating these children so the mothers should have no reason to protest but rather, should be grateful to him and to the state for taking on their rightful responsibility. By also focusing on "rehabilitation", the President carefully circumvented accusations of the state's complicity in "disappearances" and arbitrary killings.

Several government ministers also used various rhetorical ploys to slander the Mother's Front, their most vociferous critic being Ranjan Wijeratne, the Minister of State for Defence.[15] He denounced the movement as being "subversive," "anti-government", "against the security forces who saved democracy", threatened to "get at the necks of those using the Mothers" Front' and stepped up police surveillance of its leaders.[16] The SLFP was also consistently accused of trying to use the Mothers' Front to further their power by both the government-owned media and various government ministers.[17] The central thrust of the rhetorical responses of the state attempted to undermine the primary subject position of these women by suggesting that they had not been "good" mothers while also attempting to question their credibility by insinuating that they were mere puppets of a political party which was using them for its own ends.

COUNTER-RALLIES

The state attempted to disrupt the first Mothers' Front rally by banning demonstrations and creating an atmosphere of distrust and panic with suggestions of possible bomb explosions and an Liberation Tigers of Tamil Eelam (LTTE) infiltration of Colombo. However, when the Mothers' Front organized their second rally in Colombo a month later, the state implemented yet another counteractive under the aegis of the First Lady, Hema Premadasa. While the Mothers' Front organized a rally to commemorate International Women's Day on 8 March 1991, in one part of the city of Colombo, the government organized a massive counter women's rally in another part of the city by bussing-in women from various *Seva Vanitha*[18] units affiliated to government departments—especially the armed forces. While the Mother's Front mourned the "disappearances" of their male relatives due to state repression, the state-organized women's rally mourned the death of their male relatives who had been killed by the JVP in the south and Tamil militants in the north and east of Sri Lanka. The state-owned *Daily News* carried an entire page of photographs from the state-organized rally while no mention was made of the Mothers' Front rally.[19]

In July 1992, the United National Party (UNP) government even inaugurated a UNP Mothers' Front in the Gampaha

District, the stronghold of the Bandaranaike clan and thus synonymous with the SLFP. At its first meeting, the only female Cabinet Minister in the government, Health and Women's Affairs Minister Renuka Herath, categorically claimed that "it were the children of those mothers who slung photographs and marched, who killed the children of you innocent mothers".[20] She promised to provide financial support for the members of this Front and to erect memorials to their children's bravery; two and a half years later these women were still waiting to see these promises fulfilled.

RELIGIOUS RITUALS AS RESISTANCE

The practices of the Mothers' Front that most unnerved the government, especially the President who was known to be an extremely superstitious man, was the skilful use of religious ritual as resistance. As Marx has so perceptively pointed out, "religious distress is at the same time the expression of real distress and the protest against real distress".[21]

Most families of the "disappeared" were intimate with such manifestations of religious distress which ran the gamut: from beseeching gods and goddesses, saints and holy spirits, with special novenas (Catholic masses), penances, offerings, donations, and the chanting of religious verses over a period of months, taking vows, making pilgrimages and performing *bodhi pujas* (offerings to the Bo tree), as well as resorting to sorcery and the placement of charms and curses on those deemed responsible. The SLFP first realized the powerful potential of such "publicized" religious practices when members of the Mothers' Front participated in the SLFP-organized 180 mile long *Pada Yatra* (march) to protest various government policies and human rights violations, in March/April 1992. The absolute abandon and passion which the mothers displayed as they broke coconuts and beseeched the deities to return their sons and husbands, and heaped curses on those who had taken them away, at the *Devinuwara* and *Kataragama devales* (temples) even surprised the SLFP organisers of the *Yatra* and provided tremendous photo opportunities for the image-hungry media men.[22] The President apparently took this collective and ritualized display of ill feeling personally: on the advice of his

Malayalee Swami, he immediately participated in a counter ritual in which he was bathed by seven virgins! While Sirimavo Bandarnaike (the Leader of the SLFP) publicly linked the two events at the second National Convention of the Mothers' Front on 23 June 1992, her daughter Chandrika Kumaratunga suggested that the mothers' curses during the *Pada Yatra* had effected the sudden and much publicized disclosures by former Deputy Inspector General of Police, Premadasa Udugampola. Premadasa Udugampola was the mastermind behind the paramilitary hit-squads, that terrorized the southern and central provinces of Sri Lanka at the height of the JVP uprising in 1989-91.

The ritual of religious resistance that received the most publicity and generated much comment was the *Deva Kannalawwa* (the beseeching of the gods), which took place in the afternoon of 23 June 1992. The Mothers' Front specifically picked this day for their second National Convention because it was President Premadasa's birthday and coincided with the commencement of his extravagant brainchild—the *Gam Udawa* (village reawakening) celebrations. Not surprisingly, therefore, many of the wrathful speeches made at the Convention focused on his autocratic style of governance (he had just foiled an impeachment motion against him). Afterwards, the SLFP provided lunch to the mothers and bussed them to the *Kaliamman Kovil* (Hindu temple) at Modera. On arrival however, the mothers were greeted by the locked gates of the *kovil* and a battalion of policemen standing guard. Not to be deterred, SLFP MP Alavi Moulana, instructed the first group of mothers to break their coconuts outside the *kovil* gates. Almost simultaneous with this and the loud chanting of "*sadhu, sadhu*" that rent the air, the gates were hastily opened by a somewhat chagrined senior police officer though access to the inner sanctum was still denied. The small kovil premises soon became packed with weeping and wailing mothers, many of whom boldly named President Premadasa and cursed him and his government. Asilin, one of the mothers was chanting over and over again: "Premadasa, see this coconut all smashed into bits, may your head too be splintered into a hundred bits, so heinous are the crimes you have perpetrated on my child". Another mother wept saying: "Premadasa, I bore this child in my womb for ten months, may you and your family be cursed not for 10 days or 10 weeks or 10 months or 10 years or 10 decades but for 10 eons".

The passion, the anger, the pathos, the power of these weeping, cursing, imploring mothers riveted an entire nation. Not only did these mothers make front page news the next day and for much of that week, but their display of grief at the *Kaliamman Kovil* was a constant topic of discussion for several months, and spurred some alternative as well as mainstream Sinhala dailies and Sunday editions to being a series of articles, which focused on the individual stories of the families of the "disappeared". And editorial warning issued when the Front was first begun now seemed prescient:

> When mothers emerge as a political force it means that our political institutions and society as a whole have reached a critical moment—the danger to our way of life has surely come closer home.[23]

COUNTER-RITUALS

To ward off the mothers' curses President Premadasa sought refuge in an elaborate counter ritual—the *Kiriammawarunge Dane* (The Feeding of Milk Mothers) an archaic ritual that is now connected with the Goddess Pattini.[24] On the day of his birthday/commencement of *Gam Udawa* and the Mothers' Front's *Deva Kannalawwa* at Modera, on 23 June 1992, he offered alms to 68 (grand) mothers and, at the conclusion of *Gam Udawa* and another *Deva Kannalawwa*, organized on a much smaller scale at Kalutara (south of Colombo) by the Mothers' Front, on 3rd 1992, he offered alms to 10,000 (grand) mothers while the North Central Provincial Council Minister for Health and Women's Affairs, Rani Adikari, chanted the *Pattini Kannalawwa* to bring blessings on the President, the armed forces and the country.[25] Though the commonly held belief is that *Pattini* is predominantly a guardian against infectious diseases, she is also the "good mother" and ideal wife whose chief aim is to maintain "a just and rationally grounded society" and can thus be read as a counterpoint to the goddess that the Mothers' Front appealed to—the "bad mother" and evil demoness Kali who deals with sorcery and personal and familial conflicts.[26]

It was not only President Premadasa who was disturbed by such rituals but even the urbane Minister of Industries, Science and Technology, Ranil Wickremasinghe warned: "If your children have disappeared, it is alright to beseech the gods. After all, if there is no one else to give you succour it is fitting to look to one's gods. But if one conducts such *Deva Kannalawwas* with thoughts of hate and revenge, it could turn into a *huniyam* (black magic) and backfire on you".[27] Ironically, despite such dire warnings and counter-rituals, President Premadasa was blown to smithereens by a suicide bomber before a year was out. A few days after his death, a beaming Asilin came to see me with a comb of plantains (considered to be an auspicious gift): "He died just like the way I cursed him" she said triumphantly.

Tears and Curses

The complicated interplay between the Mothers' Front and the state operated upon a common terrain that took for granted the authenticity and efficacy of a mother's tears and curses. Though the state could retaliate that these women were not "good" mothers or that they were the pawns of a political party, it could not deny the mother's right to weep or to curse, for after all that was what was expected of women. Rather, when these women wept or cursed *en masse* and in public, it became an embarrassment for the state which then attempted to organize its own Fronts of weeping women or to counteract the Mothers' Front's curses through the deployment of even larger masses of mothers to participate in counter rituals. In a context of violence and terror, it was the tears and curses of the mothers that finally stirred a nation and shamed a government.

However, it is also important to bear in mind that tears and curses differed in signification. While a mother's tears were a familiar, emotive trope in literature, songs, films etc., as well as public practices of grieving such as funerals, her curses were a familiar, yet less discussed practice, that was mostly restricted to the private, religious domain. While the SLFP had cleverly manipulated the emotive power of tears at the Mothers' Front rallies that they organized, it was the spontaneity of the women themselves, during the *Pada Yatra*, that suggested an alternative/parallel avenue of protest that was not merely emotive but powerful—in its staging, as well as in the ferocity of its call for revenge. The presumption inherent in a curse is that it could bring about change through the intercession of a deity which also complicates efforts (for a believer such as the President) to stall such changes for they now transcend the human aspect. The use of curses as public protest and religious ritual as resistance not only had no precedent in Sri Lanka, but it could also circumvent emergency laws enforced by the state that were applicable to standard forms of political protest such as demonstrations and rallies.[28] To have banned people's right to religious worship on the other hand, was something even an autocratic government, which repeatedly defined itself as one that had the best interests of the populace in mind, would not have dared. It is not that the government did not toy with this idea. After all, the gates of the *Kaliamman Kovil* remained locked when the Mothers' Front first arrived and the alternative media was quick to highlight such attempts as a blatant and public violation of human rights.[29]

For the members of the Mothers' Front however, weeping and cursing was nothing new. The only difference now was that the gaze of an entire nation was upon them and the focus of their wrath/protest had shifted from the local to the national. From such a perspective one could also point out then, that despite their participation in a mass movement, their agency continued to be limited to tears and curses. It was quite common for politicians at the Mother's Front rallies to exhort the mothers that it was "time to stop weeping and move beyond", while at the same time, congratulating them on how successful their curses had been by crediting them with bringing upon the sudden disclosures by ex-DIG Udugampola, the unnerving of President Premadasa and even the death of Ranjan Wijeratne, Minister of State for Defense. This particular circumscribing of the mothers can be chiefly attributed to the fact that these women had merely exchanged one structure of power that was riven with gender and class inequalities, for another. Socialized within a society that defines women primarily through familial subject positions such as wives and mothers, these women may have nevertheless managed to both mobilize and transcend these categories if they had chosen to organize themselves as the Mothers' Fronts in the north and east had done (see further). Funded by a group of men, who also happened to be representatives of a powerful political party, these women of the Mothers' Fronts in the north and the east were never pushed to break out of their gender and class stereotypes or to form links with other women's groups.

SRI LANKA FREEDOM PARTY AND MALE ORCHESTRATION

On an everyday level and in organizing rallies and rituals, the financial backing and infrastructural support of the Sri Lanka Freedom Party (SLFP) were crucial. The Mothers' Front women elected their own office bearers and ran their regional offices relatively autonomously, but remained under the control of their respective SLFP MPs, who provided much of their funding and office space. The SLFP coordinators of the Front (such as Mangala Samaraweera) set the agenda for rallies planned in Colombo, handled the advertizing, sent out invitations and hired buses to transport women from various regions of the country. As a professional dress designer, Mr Samaraweera was central in designing the Mothers' Front logo—the Sinhala letter "M" containing a mother cradling a baby. He also openly acknowledged that he was instrumental in identifying the Front with the colour yellow as it was not identified with any Sri Lankan political party and because it echoed the yellow ribbons that symbolized hopes for the return of the American hostages who had been held in Iran. His office drafted petitions for the Front—demanding the appointment of an independent commission to inquire into "disappearances", calling for the state to issue death certificates and to compensate the families of the "disappeared"—and organized the lobbying of key government departments to bring these demands into effect.

However, it was the events that were held in Colombo that made visible the SLFP/male dominance of the Mothers' Front in the most blatant fashion. This account of the 19 February rally in Nugegoda (a suburb of Colombo) is especially telling:

> Most of the people on the stage in the shade, are men, with perhaps two or three women visible.[30] Most of the mothers, dressed in white, are seated at the foot of the stage in the sun. As the meeting starts, the press, cameras, videos spill onto the stage ... sometimes even blocking the microphone and the speaker ... the disrespect for the speakers is more apparent when a "mother" is speaking ... About twenty women's testimonies were interspersed among the politicians'

speeches, which often took over fifteen minutes, to the five minutes the women seemed to use.[31]

Though representatives of other opposition parties had been invited to speak, they were a mere "smattering" compared to the SLFP MP's jostling of the stage' who in their speeches "were hell bent on making it a party political rally".[32] Even the two leading women in the SLFP, the party leader Sirimavo Bandaranaike and her widowed daughter, Chandrika Kumaratunga were obviously not committed to the Mothers' Front; their late arrivals and early exits from the meeting annoyed many mothers who had hoped that these "powerful women" would be more "approachable".

Unfortunately, no attempt was made to rectify the errors of the previous year at the second National Convention which was held indoors and drew a more modest crowd on 23 June 1992. Once again, the stage was predominated by males mainly representing the SLFP. Of the 20 speakers, only eight were women, of whom four represented the SLFP. This gender imbalance created a marked spatial hierarchy that was completely contradictory to the goal of a national convention where one would have thought that at least once a year, these mothers would get an opportunity to come to Colombo—the seat of power—and speak, and the politicians and concerned citizens would listen. On the contrary, what occurred was that the politicians on the stage spoke and the thousands of women seated below listened and wept and wailed almost on cue. However, there were a few instances where women exceeded their roles as listeners; when women's wailing drowned out the voice of a speaker, or a woman was so moved by a speaker that she insisted on sharing her own tragic story or another demanded that she be allowed to come up on stage and hand a petition to Chandrika Kumaratunga while she was giving her speech. Yet, the majority of women felt that at least this part of the meeting had been a useless exercise. As one woman noted rather cynically, "at least this year they gave us a free lunch packet."

These women's disillusionment with the SLFP-organized meetings and rallies not only stemmed from a frustration at being marginalized but also from a certain impatience with the use of such orthodox forms of political protest where "one politician after another either tried to absolve himself of blame for having participated in similar kinds of repression in the past or who attempted to blame the state for all ills" (views of some Mother's Front members from the Matara District). While the SLFP went to great lengths to build an anti-government coalition by incorporating the participation of various political parties, progressive religious dignitaries and specific interest groups such as those representing the Organization of Parents and Families of Disappeared, the Organization for the Disappeared Soldiers in the Northeast etc., the majority of the mothers viewed such attempts as mere political ploys. The only worthwhile participation they were involved in, they felt, was when they were able to collectively beseech the deities on behalf of their "disappeared" and call for the punishment of the perpetrators of such crimes. For someone like Asilin, who may never see her son again, the knowledge that she may have had a hand in the death of the President was indeed a powerful weapon in the hands of the weak.

CLASS DOMINATION

The only woman who rose to national prominence as a spokesperson for this movement, along with Mangala Samaraweera and Mahinda Rajapakse, was Dr Manorani Saravanamuttu. There were several reasons for this and they all hinged on her class position and social status. Dr Saravanamuttu, a scion of a prominent Tamil family in Colombo had married into an equally prominent Sinhala family—the de Zoysas. Her single progeny from this marriage—Richard—was a popular public personality as an actor, broadcaster and journalist. Divorced from her husband for many years, she supported herself through her extensive medical practice as a general practitioner. Her ancestry, professional status and stately and dignified bearing afforded her much respect among all ethnic groups in middle class Sri Lankan society. She was transformed into a public personality when she courageously pressed charges against senior police officers for murdering her son, and an entire nation's sympathy was focused on her when many moving photographs of her grief-stricken face watching her son's burning pyre were published in local newspapers. When she had to flee the country because of threats to her life, she was also embraced by an international community concerned with issues of human rights.

Dr Saravanamuttu's main link with the rest of the women in the Mothers' Front was the searing pain of loss and grief that she shared with them. Yet, here too, she counted herself more fortunate than them: "I am the luckiest woman in Sri Lanka— I got my son's body back".[33] Dr Saravanamuttu was conscious from the outset about the chasm of inequality that divided her from the other mothers; they could not afford to flee the country when their lives were threatened, they were not fluent in English or literate enough to file *habeas corpus* reports ... the list was endless. But what the mothers appreciated about Dr Saravanamuttu was that she made it clear that she genuinely cared about them and constantly tried to form bridges of friendship and support. Her speeches, often uttered in faltering Sinhalese or simple English, always directly addressed the concerns of the mothers present—cautioning them to remain as watchdogs of all political parties including the SLFP, reminding them that they were not alone in their grief, but that Tamil women in the north and east too suffered like them as did women in far away Latin America and sharing with them the news that women across the globe had pledged their support to the Mothers' Front. When she realized that the mothers had been sidelined at the 19 February rally, Dr Saravanamuttu quietly left her seat on the stage and mingled with the women below. Her individual mission to fight her son's murderers in court was also articulated as a battle waged for all mothers: "[m]ost of them don't have the means to obtain justice. But I have the means and the social position I'm doing this for every mother in Sri Lanka who has lost a son".[34] Unfortunately, Dr Saravanamuttu's overtures were not sufficient to shatter an entrenched class and patronage structure. When the mothers sought the help of their MPs, they were following a familiar route of patronage that exists between politicians and their constituencies; the people vote for the MP and expect him/her to look after them. Even if this system may not often work in practice, it is always a last resort in the face of despair. As Mangala Samaraweera noted, in his father's day, people would line up outside his office requesting jobs, while in his day, people lined up outside his house asking him to find their sons and husbands.[35]

Erasing Tamil Women's Agency

It was also extremely unfortunate that the SLFP, in their efforts to build an oppositional coalition against the government through the Mothers' Front rallies in Colombo, did not make a sustained effort to form links with minority ethnic parties or organizations except for a token representation from the Eelam Peoples' Revolutionary Front (EPRLF). The most glaring absence of all was that no member of the original Mothers' Front, which was begun in the north of Sri Lanka in 1984 and later spread to the eastern part of the island, was invited to speak, or even mentioned as providing inspiration for the Mothers' Front in the south, at any of the southern Mothers' Front meetings. In fact, when I questioned Mangala Samaraweera on the Fronts' antecedents, he promptly mentioned the Madres of Plaza de Mayo in Argentina, whose strategy of marching with photographs of their "disappeared" he had introduced among the Sri Lankan women as well. I found it quite astonishing that he did not think it worth mentioning that there had existed a group with the same name in his own country. Thus, in a seeming move to internationalize the southern Mothers' Front, its organizers were completely erasing the agency of Tamil women not just from their memory, but from the memory of an entire population in the south of Sri Lanka. In fact, it was another Sinhalese gentleman, Gamini Navaratne, the former Editor of an important English weekly in Jaffna—the *Saturday Review*, and one of the few Sinhalese civilians who chose to remain in the north during the height of the Civil War in the 1980s, who attempted to set the record straight, albeit in a somewhat skewed fashion.[36] In his article, Mr Navaratne disputed the claims made by the organizers of the southern Mothers' Front that it was "the first of its ten in 1984 reporting on the first march organized by the northern Mothers" Front to protest the arrest of over 500 Tamil youths by the Sri Lankan state.' Unfortunately, he trivializes the agency of Tamil women by portraying himself as the instigator and ultimate heir of this protest campaign.

The northern Mothers' Front, like its southern counterpart, was mainly active only for about two years.[37] However, unlike the newer Front, it was controlled by and consisted of women from all classes who

> mobilized mass rallies, and picketed public officials demanding the removal of military occupation and protesting against arrests. Not only the spirit, but also the enormous numbers that they were able to mobilize, spoke loudly of the high point of which such mass organizations, especially of women [could] rise.[38]

The northern Mothers' Front also inspired Tamil women in the east to begin their own branch. In 1986, the eastern Mothers' Front took to the streets with rice pounders to prevent a massacre of members of the Tamil Eelam Liberation Organization (TELO) by the LTTE.[39] In 1987, one of its members, Annai Pupathi, fasted to death to protest the presence of the Indian Peace Keeping Forces (IPKF). She was subsequently immortalized by the LTTE (it was common knowledge that the LTTE had forced her to keep her fast) who now offer a scholarship in her memory. It was finally the increasing hegemony of the LTTE and their suppression of all independent, democratic organizations that did not "toe the line", which pushed the Mothers' Front in the north and east into political conformism and lost its wide appeal and militancy. "It became another Young Women's Christian Association (YWCA)"; its central structure which was mainly made up of middle-class women finally confined its activities to works of charity.[40] Many members also migrated abroad or to Colombo.

Several of those in Colombo continue to work with southern feminist organizations with whom they had always shared close ties as members of the eastern and northern Mothers' Fronts. These women were thus an available resource that the organizers of the southern Mothers' Front chose to ignore with the exception of one instance—Ms S. Sujeewardhanam from Batticoloa was invited to be part of the presidium at the first National Convention of the Mothers' Front on 19 February 1991, along with Dr Manorani Saravanamuttu (Colombo) and Ms D G Seelawathi (Matara). In contrast to the huge open air public rally which was held later on that day and attended by over 15,000 people (which made it one of the biggest public gatherings in this country in recent years), the first National Convention of the Mothers' Front was much more focused on procuring international support and was attended by over 100 foreign invitees representing embassies, NGOs and the press. It was thus in the organizers' interest to create a good image which proclaimed that the Mothers' Front was not anti-government but pro-peace, and more importantly, that it was being run by women from different ethnic groups and classes. Much concern was also expressed about the plight of the mothers in the north and east of the country and the need to form branches in those regions as well.[41] The organisers had dispensed with such rhetoric, however, by the time of the second National Convention. Only two out of the 20 speakers mentioned the suffering of Tamil mothers and, with the exclusion of Dr Saravanamuttu, no Tamils were given an opportunity to address the gathering. The absence of Tamil or other minority participation in the Mothers' Front meetings reduced the possibilities of launching a more integrated, national protest campaign that could have also gained much from the experiences of Tamil women in the north and east of the Island.

Conclusion

The members of the Mothers' Front were not motivated by ideology, but rather by circumstance to participate in a protest campaign against the state. Despite repeated assertions that they were not political or anti-government, the Front generally identifies representatives of the state as perpetrators of "disappearances" and the President—the supreme repository of state power was the key target of their curses. Indeed, the fact that the main opposition party—the SLFP was coordinating this organization removed all doubts that the Front would be anything but apolitical or uncritical of the government. However, the political participation of so many women articulating a specific subjectivity, that is motherhood, had been unheard of until the Mothers' Fronts in the north and east took to the streets in 1984 and 1986 and the southern Mothers' Front went one step further and demonstrated their despair and anger through public, collective, ritualized curses. Despite the limitations inherent in the identification with the familial and the nurturing, and the mobilization of feminized repertoires of protest such as tears and curses, these women did manage to create a space for protest in a context of terror and violence. In fact, the contingent power of their protest stemmed from their invocation of "traditional" sensibilities and the engendering of emotional responses by presenting themselves before a government and a nation as grief-stricken, chronic mourners for their "disappeared", whose only resort now was to beseech the deities for justice. Ironically, in a time where the protesting voices of several left wing, feminist and human rights activists had been silenced with death, it was the mothers' sorrowful and seemingly apolitical rhetoric and practices that nevertheless alerted a nation to the hypocrisy of the state.

The Front's politicization of motherhood by frequently linking it to a discourse of rights and dissent was continued to its full realization through the campaign strategies of SLFP politician and Prime Ministerial candidate Chandrika Bandaranaike Kumaratunga, at the 1994 general elections.[42] Herself a grieving widow and mother, she cleverly articulated the mothers' suffering as both a personal and national experience; she too "sorrowed and wept" with them but also made it clear that she was capable of translating her grief into action, of building a new land where "other mothers will not suffer what we suffer".[43] Ironically, Ms Kumaratunga's embodiment of these grassroots women's suffering also usurped their space of protest; the materiality of their lives was sacrificed for an election slogan. What has become of these thousands of women? Have their lives changed significantly with a more progressive government in power? The new government has appointed three Commissions of Inquiry to investigate the "disappearances" and killings that occurred during 1988–1991.[44] We cannot yet predict what concrete measures will transpire from these hearings. Maybe these women will receive individual hearings, another chance to demand that the perpetrators of violence be brought to justice. May be their "disappeared" will be restored to them. Perhaps they will receive financial compensation, although that would be extremely meager in comparison to all that they have lost, sometimes even their sanity.

It also remains to be seen how their involvement, however liminal, in a protest campaign has changed their lives. While the majority of women who were part of this movement had been relegated to the "home" and the margins of an increasingly militarized society throughout much of their life, the Mothers' Front did provide them with some opportunities to air their grievances and anger in public for, and to create, strong networks among themselves. Several groups of these women have now formed links with feminist groups and other non-governmental organizations (NGOs) who are providing them with trauma counseling and help with establishing self-employment projects. Yet, the numbers are minuscule compared to the thousands of women and their families across the country who continue to grieve and bear the livid scars of a nation-state that has blood on its hands.

NOTES AND REFERENCES

1. *Island*, 1991. February 9.
2. The Mothers' Front has been inspired by and shares much with similar organizations in Latin America, but I want to highlight here the importance of historical and material specificities rather than make comparisons between different movements.
3. Enloe, Cynthia. 1989. *Bananas, Beaches and Bases: Making Feminist Sense of International Politics*. Berkeley: Univ. of California Press. Hartsock, Nancy. Prologue to a Feminist Critique of War and Politics, in Judith Stiehm (ed.), *Women's Views of the Political World of Men*. New York: Transnational Publishers. Lloyd, Genevieve. 1982. Selfhood, War and Masculinity, in Carole Pateman and Elizabeth Gross (eds), *Feminist Challenges*, pp. 63–76. Boston: Northeastern University Press.
4. *Lankadeepa*. 1992. June 28.
5. On 20 May 1990, the Organization of Parents and Family Members of the Disappeared (OPFMD) was formed to do similar work among the families of "disappeared" trade union workers and left-wing activists. This group was closely aligned with Vasudeva Nanayakkara, opposition MP and polit-bureau member of the left-wing NSSP (*Nava Sama Samaja Pakshaya*). They rarely received as much publicity as the Mothers' Front but they supported the Front and joined their rallies while members of the Front often participated in their rallies (see fn. 10 for example).
6. Mr Samaraweera reports that a branch office set up independently in Weligama (in the Southern Province) was attacked by thugs.

7. The event of "disappearance" not only inscribed the minds of the families with anguish but also turned their bodies into ciphers of agony. Most families of the "disappeared" seemed to suffer from trauma-related neuroses; children who stopped speaking, old and young women who complained of memory loss, fainting spells, seizures, weight loss, severe chest pains etc., and fathers who died of sudden heart attacks.
8. Schrimer, Jennifer G. 1989. "Those Who Die for Life Cannot be Called Dead: Women and Human Rights Protest in Latin America", *Feminist Review*, 32 (Summer): 3–29.
9. *Island*. 1991. January 27.
10. Schrimer, Jennifer G. 1989. "Those Who Die for Life Cannot be Called Dead: Women and Human Rights Protest in Latin America", *Feminist Review*, 32 (Summer): 25.
11. Malathi de Alwis. 1994. "Towards a Feminist Historiography: Reading Gender in the Text of Nation", in Radhika Coomaraswamy and Nira Wickremasinghe (eds), *Introduction to Social Theory*, pp. 86–107. Delhi: Konark Press.
12. Schrimer, Jennifer G. 1989. "Those Who Die for Life Cannot be Called Dead: Women and Human Rights Protest in Latin America", *Feminist Review*, 32 (Summer): 28.
13. *Daily News*. 1991. February19 .
14 Ibid., February 15.
15. Whe Wijeratne was killed in a bomb blast in late March 1991, many Front members and SLFP organizers directly connected his death with the efficacy of their collective protest.
16. *Daily News*. 1991. February 23 and March 14. *Island*. 1991. February 20 and *Sunday Time*, 1991. March 29.
17. *Daily News*. 1991. February 19, March 23, 1991; *Sunday Observer*, 1991. February 24.
18. All wives of government officials and all female officials must join this national social service organization which replicates the hierarchical structures of government in that the President's wife is the leader, the Cabinet Minister's wives are below her.
19. *Daily News*. 1991. March 9.
20. *Divaina* . 1992. July 27.
21. Quoted in Comaroff, Jean. 1985. *Body of Power, Sprit of Resistance*, p. 252. Chicago: University of Chicago Press.
22. *Divaina*. 1992. April 4.
23. *Island*. 1991. February 20.
24. For a brief description and analysis of this ritual see Gombrich 1971, and for a discussion of its origins see Obeyesekere 1984 especially pp. 293–296.
25. *Daily News*. 1992. June 7. However, this is not the first time the President has publicly participated in this ritual (e.g., *Lankadeepa* 1/113/92 and *Island* 3/22/92). Nevertheless, the repetition of this ritual within such a short period and on such a grand scale suggests it was not mere coincidence. The ritual is usually performed with just 7 (grand) mothers and the chief (grand) mother rather than a politician leads the chanting. See also *Silumina*, 28 June 1992.

26. Gombrich, Richard and Gananath Obeyesekere. 1988. *Buddhism Transformed: Religious Change in Sri Lanka*, pp. 158–160. Princeton: Princeton Univ. Press.
27. *Divaina*. 1992. July 13.
28. Besides their efforts to ban demonstrations in February 1991, the state also attempted to ban and later curtailed a protest march of the Mothers's Front organized in Kalutara on 3 July 1992 (to co-incide with the end of the *Gam Udawa*) by forbidding the Front to carry their banner and insisting that the women walked in single file. As a news report pointed out, there were as many policemen as were mothers! (*Divaina* 7/4/92). On World Human Rights Day—10 December 1992, a sit-down protest organized by the Organization of Parents and Family Members of the Disappeared (OPFMD) and joined by some Mothers' Front organizers like Mahinda Rajapakse, was tear gassed and baton charged by the Riot Squad leaving several of its leaders injured (*Island* 12/11/92).
29. *Aththa*. 1992. June 24. *Divaina*. 1992. July 6.
30. Mahinda Rajapakse did make an effort to rectify this gender imbalance halfway through the meeting, but since the stage was already very crowded, few women took up his offer (Confidential Report, INFORM, no pagination).
31. Confidential Report, INFORM: no pagination.
32. ———. no pagination.
33. *Amnesty Action*, Nov/Dec 1990.
34. Ibid.
35. *Lankadeepa*. 1992. June 28.
36. *Island*. 1991. March 3.
37. I gratefully acknowledge the help of R. Cheran, Sarvam Kailasapathy and Chitra Manuguru in writing the following section.
38. Hoole Ranjan, Daya Somasunderam, K. Sritharan and Rajani Thiranagama. 1990. *The Broken Palmyra: The Tamil Crisis in Sri Lanka— An Inside Account*, p. 324. Claremont, CA: Sri Lanka Studies Institute.
39. Hensman. Rohini. 1992. Feminism and Ethnic Nationalism in Sri Lanka, *Journal of Gender Studies*, 1(4): 503.
40. Hoole Ranjan, Daya Somasunderam, K. Sritharan and Rajani Thiranagama. 1990. *The Broken Palmyra: The Tamil Crisis in Sri Lanka—An Inside Account*, p. 325. Claremont, CA: Sri Lanka Studies Institute.
41. Confidential Report, INFORM: no pagination
42. Schrimer, Jennifer G. 1989. "Those Who Die for Life Cannot be Called Dead: Women and Human Rights Protest in Latin America", *Feminist Review*, (32) Summer: 26.
43. Excerpted from Ms Kumaratunga's final advertisement before the elections that was published in both Sinhala and English newspapers.
44. While the previous government did appoint a commission to investigate "disappearances" due to intense pressure exerted upon them by the Mothers' Front as well as international human rights organizations, it empowered this commission to only look into such events that occurred from the commissions' date of appointment—11 January 1991—rather than during the height of the repression in the south—January 1988. The commissions

appointed under the new regime, while rectifying this error, continue to ignore the atrocities that were perpetrated in the north and east by the previous regime by not being empowered to investigate "disappearances" of Tamil youth under the guise of the Prevention of Terrorism Act from as far back as 1979 (cf. *Pravada*, Vol. 3(10), Jan/Feb 1995).

9
NEGOTIATING PEACE: FEMINIST REFLECTIONS[*]

Kalpana Kannabiran, Volga and Vasantha Kannabiran

> Our lives begin to end the day we become silent about things that matter.
> —Martin Luther King Jr.

BACKGROUND

The peace process initiated by the Maoist rebels (who were in conflict with the state) that began in Andhra Pradesh (AP) in 2004 was the result of several factors that relate to the democratization of socio-political fabric over the past decade. It was an immediate result of the people's mandate, given to the Congress and its allies, to bring peace to the state. It must not be forgotten that one of the key commitments made by the Congress during its election campaign was that it would invite the Maoists and other Naxalite groups to the negotiating table and create the conditions for the restoration of democracy and the rule of law in a state where the previous Telugu Desam regime had completely abdicated on both these counts. Even prior to the election phase, citizens' groups, notably the Concerned Citizens' Committee had over a period of five years painstakingly pieced together a framework within which peace could be negotiated, in

---

[*] Adapted from three essays in the *Economic and Political Weekly* and from Kalpana Kannabiran and Vasanth Kannabiran. 2002. *De-Eroticizing Assault: Essays on Modesty, Honour and Power*. Calcutta: Stree. Parts of this paper was published in *Economic and Political Weekly*.

case the possibility arose. A new government meant the creation of the possibility.

It was not easy reposing confidence in the Congress, given its own notorious history during Emergency in the state, yet, the people decided to set the past aside and give it another chance. It is also true of course that not giving the Congress a chance meant risking the catastrophic consequences of continuing the Telegu Desam Party (TDP) and its allies in power. Post-Gujarat riots and the TDP's deplorable human rights record in the state, voting the Congress in and forcing accountability on it seemed a better possibility. The victory for the Congress was only possible because of the support by different parties (including the naxalites) and ordinary citizens concerned about the crisis in democracy. Initiating the peace process therefore was not an act of benevolence by the Congress government, but the first step towards fulfilling a commitment on the basis of which it had been given the mandate of the people—a mandate that had its conditions. We also know that non-compliance with conditionalities, especially where it concerns the people, inevitably results in being ousted from power.

In a state that has the longest history of radical political movements, especially left movements, we have also had the longest history of the criminalization of political dissent in post-independence India. Areas where political activism is highest therefore, are in the eyes of the state "naxalite infested" areas. Arms, extremist propaganda and extortion are equal and co-existing evils. Political literature, specifically communist literature is censored (sedition sections were used well into the 1970s) and the right to free speech curtailed even while C grade cinema spreads its poison through a flourishing industry. And yet, although this effort at criminalization of radical politics through law, in popular perception, has been backed by the might of the state, it has failed to achieve its objective. As a result, "rule of law" has been interpreted by the state to mean "law and order", a euphemism for arbitrary and unlimited police powers.

Despite the incessant negative propaganda by successive governments and direct engagements with the press by the police, the popular perception of the Naxalites is far from negative.

The people have questions on specific actions by naxalite groups; they have criticisms of specific actions (killing/abduction of informers, *sarpanches* and local officials, extortions etc.); they have doubts about the larger meaning of bearing arms since they are the ones who bear the brunt of the coercion that results from the bearing of arms in most contexts. But despite these questions and doubts, what was clear at the commencement of the peace process in October 2004 was that the people did not see naxalites as criminals.

Although the government initiated the peace process, even while the Home Minister was closeted with the peacemakers working out a time bound blueprint, the Chief Minister was reported to have made a series of adverse statements to the press, in his routine public engagements, on the very questions that were being negotiated. On the other side, the head of the police force went aggressively to press, taking issue with the naxalites' demand for fair wages and working conditions for police constables. These were not accidental but in fact a sign of things to come.

A month after the conclusion of the first round of talks, the encounters resumed. Naxalites were being hunted down with unfailing regularity even as discussions were on for the possible timing of the second round of talks. The Prime Minister reiterated the commitment of his government to go ahead with the talks and move towards a peaceful solution in the state.[1] The Home Minister continued to be in touch with representatives of different groups, seeking their advice and reiterating the commitment of the government to peace. The encounters continued unabated. All those concerned about the peace process hoped the naxalites would not pull out, till it reached a point where even that hope became unreasonable. The naxalites pulled out of the peace process in January.

Even as we came to terms with the gravity of the situation, the state was gripped with the news in the first week of February that the Nallamalla forests had been surrounded by a 5,000 strong force of Greyhounds who were closing in on the Naxalites and all the leaders were on the verge of being killed in an "encounter". It needed intervention from the highest level to stall what would have been the worst instance of arbitrary state action by any standards.

Issues in the Peace Process

It is now time to address several questions pertaining to the entire process spanning eight months. The first is the role of the media. If the media is to fulfil its watchdog role, what should have been at the forefront of reporting on the issue is the concern for peace. In this process of ethical politics, neither individualism nor romanticism has any place. All parties involved in the process are equal participants and must be represented as such. And in a peace process, there are no adversaries because there is a common interest that binds all the parties, a collective interest. When the Maoist leaders were in Hyderabad, the media was suddenly gripped with the romanticism of the forests and the revolution, so that there was an over-exposure of the teams that came for the talks—the leaders, the women, what they wore, what they ate, driven by the very individualism that this persuasion of politics is meant to eschew. Alongside this was the tendency to play up the adversarial mode of politics, in a situation that called for the foregrounding of ethical politics. Instead of focusing on the different parties as participants in the peace process, reports focused on participants as political opponents, statements of one party being pitted against statements of another. This was clearly a distortion of the process that was underway, and contributed in no small measure to undermining it.

The second issue has to do with the bearing of arms. The critical issue in the talks with the naxalites was on whether they could bear arms in public. There are as many views on this as there are groups involved in the process. But what is the reality? The ruling party has legitimate access and entitlement to arms, even military might; in a state where faction politics has come to stay, a leader is one who carries arms and has a private army that is fully equipped with the latest weapons;[2] criminal gangs carry arms; cinema actors and members of their fan clubs carry arms;[3] naxalites carry arms. Of all these categories, it is only the naxalites who declare openly that they will carry arms as part of their political ideology. The others not only carry arms but use them at will while pretending to respect the constitutional framework, a pretence that is somewhat like the emperor's new clothes, one which the general public, while aware of, will not expose. Further, it is the bearing of arms that precipitates political crises and distinguishes the ordinary practice of politics from the politics of conflict. How in this situation can the demand be made by the state or the police that the naxalites lay down arms?

But clearly this is not the end of the argument. For the people, all arms are instruments of coercion, and there is no detracting from that. They are weapons of assault that even when used "in the interests of the people" are by definition used arbitrarily, and thorofore unjustly. That the gun gives a sense of power which ordinary participation in politics does not, is true. It is the power of coercion and disproportionate authority. This is a debate that must go on with radical groups in the interests of democracy. The test of course is in the construction of martyrdom. The martyrs are those that die by the gun. In our times political persuasion is largely irrelevant in this canonization. For instance, if the attempt on Naidu's life in Alipiri had been successful, he would have been immortalized as a martyr, his deplorable human rights record notwithstanding. His escape was a stroke of luck for democracy, because it made it possible for the people to consign him to political ignominy and irrelevance through the vote.[4] This, for us, juxtaposes the democratic alternative with the bearing of arms for people's causes.

The third question has to do with land reforms, another commitment made by the ruling party, as well as a demand by the naxalite groups in the peace process. For the Congress, land reforms is a programme that must be effected by giving *pattas* to those already cultivating the land, without in any way changing existing relations leave alone transforming them, while for the naxalites, land reforms are specifically with reference to redistribution of land and equitable distribution of resources. There is a fundamental contradiction in ideology and a divergence of interests, with the state finding itself in the uneasy position of having to safeguard the interests of the landed dominant classes (of which it is a part) and the people looking to the naxalites and civil society groups for the fulfillment of their aspirations.

The fourth question has to do with neutrality in political matters. The reluctance to take sides and be seen as partisan can insidiously eat into the core of otherwise vibrant processes.

Most often postures of neutrality serve to shield the status quo and keep it in place, which is why debates on political processes, including peace processes, must present extreme positions and evaluate them against the yardstick of human rights and democratic governance. When political dissenters are under siege by the state, there can be no "neutral" assessment of state action in relation to them. All parties involved in the peace process must be willing and able to take a firm and unequivocal position against state action and in defence of dissenters. There is in this context no question of whether the state is justified' in its action, especially if that action violates the core terms of the peace process, viz, ceasefire. There can also be no neutrality or equivocation ("was there provocation?") with respect to uncontrolled and autonomous policing that refuses to subserve political processes, persisting in treating politics as crime. For instance, when the Greyhounds surrounded the naxalites and were closing in on them, there was no possibility of a "balanced" view. For the police it was only "the biggest catch" they would ever find; the peace process for them only had nuisance value. For the people of the state and their representatives in the peace process on the other hand, it was an unpardonable error and breach of faith.

This leads us to the final point in this section. The undoing of a laboriously crafted process of democratization with callousness and irresponsibility by a newly elected government is cause for serious concern. In less than a year, there has been a negation of the people's mandate in the state. With four more years to go, questions relating to the forcing of accountability, transparency and the rule of law on the newly elected government seek urgent reflection and resolution.

FEMINISM IN NAXALITE POLITICS

Within this framework it is important to understand the position of women in Naxalite politics. Over a week before the commencement of the peace talks in October 2004, Ratnamala, former President of AP Civil Liberties Committee and a founding member of Stree Shakti Sanghatana in the early 1980s published an article in Telugu in *Vaartha* on 9 October in which she raised the problem of the lack of visibility for gender concerns within the party agenda. The only demand on the revolutionary agenda, she said, was total prohibition which women achieved through a historic struggle, and went on to ask, "Is the women's question limited only to prohibition?" Critiquing revolutionary perspectives, she said, they define our society as neo-colonial and semi-feudal only, whereas they ought to speak of it as being defined in terms of patriarchy, caste, class, and religion. Discussing the indicators of women's status in Indian society today, she placed twelve issues that she felt needed the parties' attention for mobilization: equal wages; mobile crèches and crèches in neighbourhoods; rehabilitation of sex workers; working women's hostels and student hostels in the districts; shelters for women at the district level; prohibition; implementation of the Supreme Court Judgment on Sexual Harassment at the workplace; media portrayal of women; identity cards and Employees' State Insurance (ESI) for domestic workers; prohibition of amniocentesis.

Around the same time, Jayaprabha, a feminist poet published a satire in *Andhra Jyothy*, "Does War[5] Mean Only Men's War?" (4 October 2004). Both these pieces in fact reflected the feminist critique of revolutionary left movements in AP over the past two decades and more.

The issues raised in these pieces seem to have generated a demand for further dialogue from women comrades in the party. With the first phase of the Peace Talks coming to an end, the party following Ratnamala's initiative, sent out invitations to women's groups, activists and writers for a dialogue on women's issues. Although it was short notice, many women turned up at the venue well prepared with a barrage of questions and doubts. Groups like Chaitanya Mahila Samakhya, Progressive Organization for Women, Stree Shakti, All India Praja Pratighatana and other individuals, writers, activists and journalists attended the meeting on 19 October 2004.

On arrival we were welcomed by three unarmed women guerillas of the People's Guerilla Liberation Army (PGLF) in their early twenties. The two banners on the stage declared "no revolution without women" and "there can be no women's liberation without the liberation of the working class".[6] Everyone was given literature, including a red book, which stated the Communist Party of India's (CPI) (Maoist) position on the women's question. It is worthwhile at this point to mention the key areas of concern in the little red book. The first chapter speaks of the social system and the origin of patriarchy, stating interestingly that while socialist feminists locate patriarchy in the superstructure, the party believes that patriarchy is at the base and must be destroyed to achieve an equitable social order. The second chapter speaks of the economic system, of which the first section deals with housework, and the rest with women's role in social production, the role of family and marriage in women's oppression. The third chapter looks at culture and the perpetuation of discrimination against women through education, media, religion and religious fundamentalism, caste, and goes on to speak of the role of law, motherhood, the position of single women, the issue of sexual orientation etc. The fourth chapter speaks of politics, beginning with an analysis of violence against women, and then goes on to delineate the various trends in feminist politics today. While the document itself merits a detailed discussion and dialogue with the party leadership and cadre, just the diversity of issues that it attempts to grapple with and the prioritization of issues speaks volumes about the influence of feminist discourse in Andhra Pradesh.

THE NAXALITE–FEMINIST DIALOGUE

As feminists who have engaged critically with revolutionary politics and writing in the state on the one hand, and have been actively involved in human rights advocacy on the other, we went to the meeting with a written statement voicing our concerns on the relationship between revolutionary praxis and women's lives/feminism.

Open Letter to Revolutionary Parties[7]

The discussions today with women's groups come at the end of 25 years of incessant efforts at democratization by women, within parties and groups outside, concerned about the position of women within political structures. This marks a watershed in the demand by women to be recognized as citizens and the demand for treatment as agents in the creation of new and radical political structures. We sincerely welcome your effort to understand women's political concerns particularly relating to equal citizenship.

While governance is something that is immediately relevant in the public realm of the state and civil society, it also proliferates to the other niches of civil society and politics, the same basic principles governing all realms. And representation is critical to effective governance. While it is generally true that leadership is drawn in movements and the state from the middle classes, the movement towards a radicalization of the polity inevitably involves the gradual and increasing delegation of power and authority to those classes, whose interests must be represented in order to eliminate oppression. For us as women, this immediately raises our central concern. Why is there no significant representation of women in the upper echelons of your political structure and leadership? If the number of women in leadership reflects a corresponding disproportion in membership, our question is, what is it about the questions you are raising or the manner that these questions are being articulated that does not draw women in significant numbers. If there is a parity of membership among women and men, why is it that women are unable to rise to the position of intellectual and political leaders of the movement?

We have been raising the concerns stated here for two decades now, as is evident from our writing and work over this entire period. Even when the Concerned Citizens' Committee was set up four years ago, we asked why it was that there was only one woman on the Committee at that time who dropped out very soon, when in fact there were so many in the state who had an active interest in various aspects of this issue. When the talks were fixed and all sides chose their representatives, none thought of inviting women to be part of deliberations, which by your own admission, affected thousands of women who lived in remote areas and were victims of the conflict. Yet after the peace process commenced, we were asked by one of the mediators what women's groups were doing in the peace process.

We would also like to state that as women we have an active interest in processes of democratization, and secularization of civil society. We believe that women's survival rests on the complete abatement of conflict and the elimination of all forms of conservatism and orthodoxy. Gujarat 2002 is a stark reminder of the grave assaults that women must bear in situations of conflict and moral policing. And this has more to do with patriarchal ideologies than with any specific religious ideology. All ideological mechanisms predicated on an understanding of the subordinate status of women during periods of crisis exhibit a range of unanticipated and uncontrollable assaults on women. And these assaults and threats of assaults are viewed even by visionaries and leaders as part of larger cultural questions that cannot have immediate remedies, rather than as the simple derogation of the life and security of person of women, which must be handed over to the due process of law. We hope, therefore, that in engaging in this dialogue, we are beginning to work towards a transparent, democratic public space that will fulfil the promise of true equality for women.

The questions we have raised in the past have often been dismissed as diversionary and bourgeois. What are these questions?

Why are women confined to marginal roles in struggles? Even where they wield arms, responsibilities for caring and providing reproductive labour is still that of women. While we have information that there has been some change with men also sharing in the cooking and fetching of food, the sexual division of labour has not significantly altered. And this is visible in the fact that women are completely absent from any accounts of intellectual creativity or agency in the struggle, and consequently in the leadership, as is evident from the composition of the front face of the parties.

What is the exact nature of the part played by women in the struggle, and how has this participation been theorized by the party? Women's questions are generally dismissed as devoid of ideology and political perspective. Yet, it is our belief that a political perspective that is not nuanced by an understanding of gender as a structural and ideological fact is seriously flawed. By not taking questions raised by women seriously and by not dealing with those questions both at the ideological and programmatic levels, by dismissing women's questions as trivial and "personal", there is an active disempowerment of women as a class within the movement. While parties are willing to examine power relationships between classes, castes and the state, the more fundamental and ubiquitous power relationship between men and women never enters the account. This serves to mask the power that men wield over women and guarantee impunity especially to perpetrators of violence against women both within the party and outside. The control of sexuality, which is the cornerstone of patriarchy, operates not only in feudal neo-colonialist societies, but also in semi-feudal patriarchal revolutionary attitudes. The inherent belief that female sexuality must be controlled to maintain social order is responsible for the multi-layered oppression of women, which revolutions have been totally unable to eradicate. This results in forced marriages, the belief in the inevitability of marriage for women, abduction of minor girls for marriage and sexual harassment of women. Sexual harassment includes accusations of sexual and moral-ethical misconduct when women refuse to conform, or when they ask questions related to democratic governance within parties. At a more pernicious level, this internal ideology of male domination gets projected onto grassroots work, with similar solutions being implemented outside. Witness accounts of the marriages of rapists to victims as the solution to rape.

We strongly recommend that the terms "*veeramatha*" and "*veerapatni*" be expunged from revolutionary vocabulary, as they are extremely sexist terms. The glorification of motherhood masks the active denial of entitlements and equal citizenship in practice while idealizing sacrifice, service and unquestioning surrender to sons. This glorification of motherhood is a mirror image of the simultaneous worship of the mother goddess and the debasement of women in reality. This mystification of reproductive labour serves to keep women in chains.

Finally, the collapsing of all issues of women's rights into liquor and prohibition reflects a blindness to the much larger, much more pervasive violence against women. In order to address the issue, we must begin to understand it. This effort is particularly important because the climate is now conducive for revolutionary parties to mobilize and work with mass organizations. We hope that this will mark the beginning of the process to write women into public discourse in more meaningful and far reaching—truly revolutionary—ways.

The Revolutionary Position

The party leadership, Ramakrishna, Sudhakar and Ganesh from CPI (Maoist) and Amar and Riyaz from CPI (Janashakti), personally met each participant and sought detailed introductions, before going on to state their respective party positions on the women's question. The position as delineated both in the individual statements and as a response to the discussion that followed may be simply stated as follows:

Although there has been a significant increase in the number of women coming into the movement, and also a significant increase in women's leadership at the *mandal* and district level, the situation still left much to be desired. The spokesperson for the Maoist group, Ramakrishna was candid in his observation that the internal structure of the party was bound to reflect a patriarchal orientation, as the cadre is drawn from different sections of society who bring their knowledge and consciousness from those backgrounds. However, since the process of change is continuous and dynamic, transformation cannot be seen as a one-time measure. Since it is easier to gain political authority than it is to eliminate patriarchy, the revolutionary route will make more deep-rooted change easier. While there was a feeling that women writers and activists, who had written on this issue, had done so without factual information and probably irresponsibly, there was simultaneously an undisguised concern about the persistence of patriarchy within the party. The question was an ideological one. The problems women face are ideological, yet there are "practical problems" in women's situation arising from "natural factors" (*prakrutiparamaiyna ibbandulu*) that constrained women's complete, efficient and equal participation in party leadership. A possible reason, suggested was the failure of women's movements to provide support to women within the party in terms that enabled them to destroy patriarchy within the parties. Even in mass mobilization, Janashakti, for instance, was able to address questions related to labour without difficulty, but found itself unable to address patriarchal oppression effectively. Further, during times of extreme state repression, several issues get pushed back to deal with immediate contingencies.

The concerted opposition to patriarchy is part of a larger democratic process. Given the encrustation of patriarchy within party structures and personal lives within the party, women a decade ago organized themselves separately and apart from the men, primarily as supports rather than as independent agents. The year 1995 witnessed the beginning of more open discussion on the fact that the family ideology governed gender relations within party and on the need to bring personal issues out into the open. The Peoples' War Group in that year undertook a "*diddubaatu karyakramam*"[8] (rectification programme) to bring about awareness on issues of patriarchy and to eliminate it. The demand for this programme came from women comrades. Although as a result of this campaign, the number of women coming into the party today is higher than the number of men, women are not yet able to transcend the limitations of family ideology. The solution to the problem does not lie in the formalizing of representation through reservations, as there is a difference in capabilities between women and men, with women's understanding and development being limited by their exclusion from the public domain prior to their entry into the movement, creating an "efficiency problem". So the effort of the party would be to focus on the creation of leadership that will alter the character of the base within the party. "It is only when all other sites of oppression are eliminated that the family can be wiped out, and that would be the road to women's liberation." But, "it is easier to eliminate imperialism, and feudalism than to eliminate patriarchy."

The Feminist Response

The discussion then grew very animated with each group firing questions at the leadership.

One point that was underlined was the fact that it was because of a faith in the movement and a shared vision of a just social order that women were present at the meeting. The faith in revolutionary politics went hand in hand with the right to question and critique every flaw in the party's programme or perspective. The glaring lack of women at leadership levels and their lack of visibility needed to be addressed. The death of women leaders in encounters cannot account fully for the absence of women's leadership. Then there were questions about the silence of women in the party that put them out of reach. There were also questions about how far feminist writing and criticism have influenced the party's thinking. Women present pointed to the need to look at the institution of the family, what happened to women and children in the areas of conflict, particularly children born to cadre after they had joined the party. The need for diversity, the centrality of land and the exploitation of dalit women in the "*devadasi* system" could be effectively addressed, women activists felt, by asking the government to allocate endowment lands to dalit women who were trapped in this system. The use of extremely demeaning images and language about women that either spoke of "barrenness" or glorified motherhood by people, as distinguished as the peoples' poet Gaddar, did tremendous disservice to women's struggles for dignity and recognition.

Many women who had left the party were working with poor women and felt that it would strengthen democratic processes generally if the party built alliances and working relationships with people and groups engaged in similar work. Women felt that they had plenty to contribute practically and intellectually and that this potential should be drawn upon by revolutionary parties. But for this the party had to be willing to engage with criticism on its treatment of various aspects of the women's question. It was also pointed out that the women's movement could only provide an impetus, support and intellectual tools to dismantle patriarchal biases within the party, but it cannot actually break the patriarchy within the party. Since the parties had repeatedly asserted in the course of the peace process that they would function within the constitutional framework, representation, in terms of physical numbers, at every level were an intrinsic part of democratic structures. And in a situation where there is a concentration of power and authority in a certain class, in this case men, bringing about equal representation would mean that women could only assume leadership to the extent that men are willing to relinquish the authority that is already with them. The failure to do this would only mean an unequal struggle and the further concentration of power in the hands of men. If the parties were actually mobilizing the masses on women's issues as well, and if the resistance included a resistance to patriarchy, then the rule of equal participation in governance must first be applied and achieved within the party before being applied outside, as it is only the actual application of the rule that would result in an understanding and a commitment to it. Finally, the question of class, caste and patriarchy, as interlinked systems of oppression, was yet to figure in revolutionary discourse, especially in revolutionary writing. This debate has a history in Andhra Pradesh, which will be useful to look at briefly.

REVISITING HISTORY

Step back by half a century and you will hear identical echoes from the leaders of the Telangana Peasant Struggle with regard to their women comrades. It is as if the women's question is on a treadmill rather than on a revolutionary track.

The debate on the woman question in radical Left politics is an ongoing one. Radical Left movements have been critical to the birth of feminist groups in Andhra Pradesh over the past decade and have shaped feminist thinking in several very interesting ways. The history of the Progressive Organization for Women is too well known to be reiterated. The Feminist Study Circle was yet another group that consisted predominantly of people from the radical Left. These groups came up at a time when neither revolutionary movements nor struggles had any clearly defined programme that took account of women's issues. Three decades after the women in the Telangana Armed Struggle had raised questions relating to the gendered division of labour and equality for women within the Communist Party, women in radical Left groups were still echoing the concerns of the earlier generation of women.

In the late 1970s, no communist party had so much as attempted an analysis of women's oppression. Women's wings of these parties served primarily to provide official status to wives of the leadership, but did not work in any concerted manner to either mobilize large numbers of women or to address the critical concerns of these women. Women who participated in these movements and became members of these parties, were people who had thought through issues of class and class struggles, but had not reflected on their predicament as women.[8] Questions of feminist praxis and socialist feminism had already found fertile ground in the women's groups that has come up in the late 1970s in the country, Stree Shakti Sanghatana being one of the most active groups in Andhra Pradesh.

The relationship between feminists and communists, however, has always been a troubled one. Fundamental questions related to women's oppression, the division of labour and the theorizing of patriarchy evoked a strong negative reaction from the leadership of these groups, particularly in the late 1970s and early 1980s. To begin with, the leadership attempted to sidetrack the new questions with traditional, well-worn answers. The revolution would resolve the woman question as it would resolve all other issues. Until then, these questions are best unasked, as they would only serve to divert attention from the real, important issues that confronted the movement. The leadership came down very heavily on all those who felt the need, the seriousness and the inevitability of having to reckon with these issues. These people were isolated, ridiculed and expelled from organizations.[10]

Although the raising of these questions was linked to an imperialist plot, of which bourgeois feminists were part, the history of this dissent within the Unity Centre of Communist Revolutionaries of India (Marxist- Leninist)UCCRI (ML) is interesting. The precipitation of issues had little to do with the West. Matters came to a head when the dissenting group (the feminists within the party) moved a resolution, condoling the death of Chalam, well known and prolific Telugu writer who wrote about sexuality, oppression, and women's liberation in very radical terms. His powerful articulation of issues of sexuality, motherhood and social control on women caused considerable unease to the male leadership of the time, bound on the one hand by the ideological limits of doctrinaire Communism, which saw issues related to women as essentially personal, not political, and if articulated at inappropriate moments, even diversionary. On the other hand, their own entrenched feudal patriarchal values served to strengthen the ideology.

Quite apart from the substantive differences in ideology that were emerging to which gender was central, other critical issues regarding the lack of internal democracy and autocratic leadership also formed an important part of the same critique. This is particularly significant to our present purpose because what we find time and again is the fact that a gendered articulation is never confined to "women's issues" alone even if it starts at the point. Members of the Jana Sahiti cultural group that was part of the UCCRI (ML), went through the entire process, which also foregrounds a different history of the debate in Andhra Pradesh, where the so-called Western feminism did not provide the major reference point. While debates, discussion and writing within the radical Left, of which the Revolutionary Writers' Association was part, were alive and throbbing with newly emerging questions, the power of the traditional leadership was too strong and the official stand on issues too heavy for the small, creative groups to counter effectively. The trajectory of the protagonists of feminism leaving radical Left parties was common to the several groups active during the past two decades.

The Progressive Organization for Women (POW) did manage through its practice to attain a fair degree of autonomy, and the women who left the POW actually rose to positions of leadership within the party as well. Yet, as late as 1999/2000, women who had stayed with the party and believed that they had fashioned a democratic space both through presence and work, found themselves quitting because of the lack of internal democracy.[11]

Yet, this does not imply that radical Left parties have been completely untouched by gender. *Adaviputrika* (Daughter of the Forest), published in 1995, recounts the life and struggles of a woman, tracing her transformation from an illiterate, exploited woman to a literate, militant, guerrilla leader. Critically examining family values in a poor working-class family and the unequal gender division of labour within the family, the novel contrasts this with the more democratic, accommodating and educative environment of the squad.[12]

Clearly, radical Left politics by the mid-1990s had begun to address gender questions centrally in the constituencies they worked in. As Vindhya points out, however, there is no official account of the problems this might create between party cadre and the local people. Fraught with complexities and conflicting often contending interests, did party interventions in tribal and other rural areas on questions that were centrally about patriarchy, alter in any way the relationship between the party and the constituency? Further, questions of internal democracy raised within one group interestingly find resonances elsewhere as well. Sandhya's questions, for instance, are echoed in Vennela's critical review of *Adaviputrika*, where she observes that the "lack of clarity in revolutionary organizations regarding the sexual division of labour is responsible for perpetuating women's subordinate position, especially in urban hide-outs."[13]

Margaret Randall, in a sense, provides a useful point of departure with accounts of her work in the Cuban and Nicaraguan revolutions. The questions she raises about the rolling back of hard won gains after a consolidation of political power over ten years are critical. There were gains on issues of the gendered division of labour within the Nicaraguan movement in political and military roles, the struggle for equal rights during, instead of after, the struggle and the wresting of key positions by women within the newly formed Nicaraguan revolutionary government:

> Suddenly these were all just men.... Political leaders who had waged a guerrilla war with cunning and courage, often with innovative and exceptional skill, and who went on to tackle the running of their country with varying degrees of competency. Most are authoritarian in manner; several are womanizers in the crudest sense of the term. Only one, perhaps two, have the slightest interest in or respect for a feminist agenda. [It is doubtful] if any of them understands a feminist agenda as something beyond the proverbial "equal rights for women".[14]

Again the space of the political constantly shrinks till finally it sits on the essential interpersonal relationships (especially sexual) between two people. Resolutions, therefore, are continuous and necessary in progressively diminishing circles: the party in its constituencies; the party and its internal constitution; two members of the party engaged in a relationship that is both political–ideological and sexual. And gender is critical to each of these resolutions, each of them radically political. As the final piece in the collage of the radical left, the letter written by a woman to her parents about her experiences with her partner and the rest of the members of the division she is with, is telling.

> [We] are separating.... The reason for our separation: his accusation that I am a prostitute. Now, whatever I say is a lie. Whatever I do is pretence. The most honorable things he has said to me are these. If I were to recount all his accusations and the incidents to prove them, this would not remain a letter any more. It would be pornography. I am perhaps the first woman in the party to face this degree of humiliation and torture. I say first because it does not seem like this

will stop with me. He is not alone. There is a section like him that is bent on using their authority and position to oppress women in the party and stamp them down. Coming to me, the party can go to hell, but I wanted to stay and fight. But it is of no use. These are all vengeful extremists. This is the concentration camp.

...

What was at that time limited to an accusation of "mental prostitution", then became an effort to convince everyone about my pregnancy. Now [he] wants to convene a division plenum and get me punished by the members for my crime.

It is perhaps not correct to lose faith in the party because of the goings on in one division or the actions of one person. Countless times we have seen issues like this come up.... Each time we have seen that peoples' consciousness develops according to their nature, their social background, and class, but the party itself has not succeeded in creating a better culture.... Now, whether I get out of UG a prostitute or a chaste woman makes little difference.[15]

The inseparability of sexuality from politics and the centrality of sexuality to a larger "culture of politics" are critically foregrounded in this letter. Further, this interlocking of sexuality and politics reflects the entrapment of the age-old dichotomy of immorality and chastity, a dichotomy that serves to circumscribe women's participation in politics across the board. And chastity continues to remain the index determining a woman's value even in a politics that is admittedly the most radical in the country, and perhaps the only one to actually engage, even rhetorically, with feminism.

A further point of interest in this letter is its simultaneous invocation of different registers. While the letter, immediately after disclosure, was seen by the father as an infringement by the state on a "private" filial relationship, the letter is in fact a political communication couched in personal terms. The moment of disclosure is the moment before the woman is to face a public trial on charges of sexual misdemeanour initiated by her partner who is also a party leader. The disclosure is to her father, a leader who wields greater authority than her partner in the party hierarchy. And the disclosure is about the erosion of democratic norms within the party, sexual terrorism (to use Kramarae's term)[16] epitomizing this erosion. Significantly, while the father's pain may have been personal, his embarrassment was political, and the private nature of the communication is invoked to deflect public attention from the public and political implications of the content of that devastating letter.

On a different register (personal, in a manner of speaking), the author reminds her mother of a conversation they had about her choice of partner:

> Amma, the other day, when you were troubled about the life I had chosen for myself, I reiterated Volga's observation that people must keep experimenting with life, saying I wanted to experiment with my life. Remember? Little did I think my experiment would fail so miserably. This is a learning experience. My life and my experiment with life lie ahead of me. The future gives me immense courage and hope.[17]

This different register then is the map of another world—one that is more hospitable to women and one that exists concurrently with the mainstream world (which is an essentially hostile environment for women), an alternate "woman's world" that is feminist. The world itself, "is created when women act in ways other than those sanctioned by the mainstream...[where] women do not have to resist and cope with the mainstream world and can construct themselves and their relationships in ways different from those normalized by the mainstream."[18]

The letter by the woman guerrilla also, interestingly, maps out the fields of masculinity and femininity in politics. Masculinity is mapped between two poles, as it were. On the one side, revenge, suspicion, sexual aggression and the general exercise of authority by men over women as a part of more pervasive patriarchal, ideological formations. On the other side, the paths of disclosure, as we have seen, are gendered. The invocation to reason, rationality, "the common good", morality and the consequent regret at the "inherent" disability of a woman to respond to sexual terrorism on its own terms are the other sides of masculinity, a part of the same ideological formation.

At the centre of the field of masculinity, however, is the archetypal revolutionary, whom Sheila Rowbotham caricatures brilliantly:

> The individual militant appears as a lonely character without ties, bereft of domestic emotions, who is hard, erect, self-contained,

controlled, without the time or ability to express loving passion, who cannot pause to nurture, and for whom friendship is a diversion... Members of this elect will tend to see the people around them as bad, lazy, consumed with the desire for material accumulations and sundry diversionary passions.... And always the weight of the burden of responsibility, the treachery and insensitivity of everyone else is bearing down on them.[19]

Against this, the woman guerrilla says of her revolutionary partner,

I don't know whether it is self-confidence or arrogance. Whatever it is, he has too much of it. To him, friendships, relationships are all subservient to party norms and discipline. He respects and loves people only within those limits. Yet he cannot bear it if some one does not show him respect.[20]

Femininity is then structured around this dominant masculinity. The creation of a different register, another world, different words mark feminine sites. These sites are also marked by disability—the disabling power of gender and the will/compulsion to silence. All these are part of the cultural artefacts of patriarchy, of which this letter is a moving testimony.

When I am told that even if not emotionally, I sought sexual variety, I am too disgusted to even reply. At times like this I feel our beliefs, our values and our culture are of no use at all. If it weren't for those, *I would have lived out those accusations and taught him a lesson* instead of retreating into silence... I now know how much humiliation and betrayal a woman can bear.[21]

At the centre of the field of femininity is the virtuous woman/wife-immoral woman/prostitute dichotomy, which scarcely needs elaboration. Suffice it to say that in this instance chastity is marked by unflagging love/devotion:

No matter how much [he] hates me, even now I am unable to sever my relationship with him totally. I can't help hoping that he will return to me after days/years. Even while bearing the brunt of this treatment, I tried to win him over with love and goodness. I compromised totally.[22]

And part of the burden of chastity is built on the need to constantly remind oneself of one's chastity, since accusations of immorality in patriarchal schema take on the character of the real. And interestingly, this appeal for exoneration is made not to the mother, but to the father, the moral authority, in this instance, both in the home and the political arena.

> Bapu, I don't need to say this to you, but I am telling you the truth. I have not had that kind of intention in my mind, let alone my behaviour. I have not looked at even one man from the angle. I have not been attracted towards anyone in this division.[23]

Both sexuality and domestic violence are juxtaposed in political discourse against the unqualifiedly non-deviant emotion/location, that of the Mother: as bearer of pain, of loss, the epitome of self-denial, endurance and love. Interestingly, "mother's love" is not a bourgeois emotion even within the revolutionary paradigm. Politico-cultural narratives like the work of Gaddar or Varavara Rao, for instance, weave themselves around the mother's grief at the loss of her sons (daughters too) and her infinite capacity to nurture and bring forth offspring for the revolution. And yet, interviews with several mothers who lost their children in the conflict reveal the feeling of futility and despondency coupled with a tinge of regret at the paths the offspring had chosen. There were only a few women who prided themselves on the martyrdom of their sons and daughters.[24]

In this situation of escalated and aggressive confrontation, all parties in the confrontation are deploying strategies of organizing and policy based on the politics of masculinity with impunity, a deployment that seriously restricts women's engagement with politics across the board. The manner in which the gendering of revolutionary politics defines and circumscribes women's political activity can be mapped on the different sites of struggle: ideological or practical. The persistent, reductionist beliefs that the revolution will resolve the women's question, that the class struggle will automatically result in the overthrow of patriarchy, and the definition of the subject as an ungendered "worker" have resulted in an absence of a vision for women's emancipation in revolutionary struggles in the state. This absence of vision has then consistently served to erase the question of women's emancipation from revolutionary agendas. This erasure and silencing have been sustained and systematic in censoring women's voices and concerns. The accusation that "bourgeois feminism" (which in this view is all feminism) is dismissive of the revolution as a vehicle of social transformation has been a key instrument of censorship.

The argument that the foundational structures of patriarchy as it intersects with other identities must be dismantled in order for the revolution *to bring about* social transformation is not yet understood or accepted. We remain frozen at a point of tokenism, trapped in stereotypical, romantic evocations of motherhood and womanhood within orthodox/revolutionary Marxist frameworks. In the context of the Cuban revolution, Randall observes that "the uncritical acceptance of the nuclear family, with the heterosexual couple and their children as the norm, where the sexual division of labour meant a devaluation of women's work, especially within the home and also within the party, and the stereotyping of women as caretakers and objects of male desire made the space of the revolution identical to the space that the revolution was fighting." As Randall observes,

> There is no question that a revolutionary movement, in or out of power, unable to address the needs of women, people of color, or any other group, will have a very hard time dealing with those needs in the society it envisions or constructs. If a revolution is unable or unwilling to address the needs of all people, it is doomed to failure. The idea of a revolution within the revolution, as proclaimed in the Cuban experience, will inevitably keep the first in the shadow of the second. It's the difference between understanding feminism as an isolated piece or as integral to struggle, as one of the motors of social change.
>
> The failure to grasp the potential of feminism as a motor of social change and the fear of moving beyond the security of time-worn stereotypes are responsible for one of the key instruments of silencing, the branding of women activists as wild, unbalanced and fanatical.

It is important to note here that in this entire discussion on sexuality and gender, the assumption is one of heterosexuality. Debates around sexual orientation have been dismissed in the past variously as immoral, Western, and so on and completely silenced. When the issue of sexual orientation did come up at a National Conference of Women's Movements in Tirupati in 1994, women's groups that were part of Marxist-Leninist (ML) parties diverted the debate and vehemently opposed resolutions supporting multiple sexual orientations. The resolution was translated to the largely non-literate rural ML constituency that was present at the conference as, "what they are saying is that women should marry women. Do you think that is correct?" This also raises the issue of the need for women to demonstrate their virtue and provide vocal and visible support to the heterosexual monogamous ideal projected by the party as principled revolutionary practice. While affirming the tremendous theoretical contribution of the Left, especially in Andhra Pradesh, and its sculpting of genres of popular culture and creative writing, there is unfortunately a silence on/distortion of the feminist problematic, most evident in its conflation with sexuality.

Conclusion

And still, there is a distinct sense of a shift and an admission of failure to democratize male–female relations within and without. The delineation of the party position in the October 2004 dialogue was far from linear and unequivocal. There were disjuncture and gaps that reflected a struggle with ideas and received knowledge systems, as also a grappling with new, unfamiliar ideological frameworks that seemed to have the answers and yet were cause for discomfort, if not hostility. The fixing of "women's natural constraints" and its natural opposition to men's ease in public domains, the generalizing of "knowledge" and "understanding" to mean knowledge from a male standpoint and the assumption of an unconstrained male experience as normal, exposes an ignorance of the long standing feminist critique of this separation.

There is also the more difficult question of the relationship between masculinity and the bearing of arms, which did not figure in the debate, but remains a critical feminist question, particularly relevant in this context because the impasse in the peace process was caused by the Maoists' assertion that the weapons they carried were extensions of their bodies, the analogy between the farmer's plough and the revolutionary's gun being particularly problematic. This inability to think through issues of gender in any far reaching way is reflected in the prioritization of the agenda for struggle as well, the critique of which has still not ruptured their traditional formula of women's liberation after the liberation of the working class. There is no engagement with the contradiction between admitting the resilience of patriarchy and pushing the most difficult struggle to the bitter end. And finally, even while recognizing the problem of inequality within, the firm denial of the need for mandatory sharing of leadership with women, positing instead a long term struggle with cultural questions in philosophical rather than material terms tends to blur the distinction between these parties and parliamentary parties on the issue of women's representation in governance. But let us hope that this is only the beginning of a long awaited dialogue that will yield results sooner rather than later.

Notes and References

1. He had a half hour one-to one meeting with K.G. Kannabiran in November and followed this up with a letter to him to the same effect in the second week of December, 2004.
2. Witness the Paritala Ravi phenomenon. Paritala Ravi, a TDP leader was shot on 24 January in broad daylight in Anantapur, even though he was under protection by armed guards who were part of his private army. A faction leader in Rayalaseema, Paritala was known for his ruthless participation in a cult of violence in the name of politics.
3. Witness the absurdity of the Balakrishna case. Balakrishna, the youngest son of Telugu Desam founder and former Chief Minister of AP, NT Rama Rao is a film actor. About a year ago, he was involved in a shootout at his residence where an astrologer and a film producer were grievously hurt, and Balakrishna was the only other person present. While it is widely believed that he pulled the trigger, a prestigious corporate hospital shielded him from arrest by providing him shelter on medical grounds and the victims who recovered claimed they had been shot by unidentified persons. Balakrishna was acquitted last week.
4. As a result, today, the single straw Chandrababu Naidu grasps to regain power is the death of Paritala Ravi who ruled by the gun.
5. The reference is to People's War, which in Andhra is often referred to as "War".
6. The second banner, it appeared to us, was an unconscious inversion of the original Lenin quote "there can be no liberation for the working class unless women are completely liberated".
7. This letter was given [in Telugu] to the leaders of the two parties at the commencement of the dialogue on 19th October 2004 by the authors.

8. "Diddubaatu" is also the title of noted early 20th century Telugu writer-social reformer, Gurajada Appa Rao's short story about a woman who reforms her husband.
9. Volga. 1995. "Feminist Study Circle", in Kalpana Kannabiran, Volga and Vasanth Kannabiran (eds), *Sarihaddulu Leni Sandhyalu: Feminist Rajakiyalu, Karyacharana, Konni Prasnalu*. Secunderabad: Asmita. Our translation.
10. Ibid.
11. Personal conversations with Sandhya and Vimala, leaders of the POW, who have since left the party.
12. For a more detailed account of the questions this novel raises see U. Vindhya. 1999. "Comrades-in-Arms: Sexuality and Identity in the Contemporary Revolutionary Movement in Andhra and the Legacy of Chalam", in Mary E. John and Janaki Nair (eds), *A Question of Silence: The Sexual Economies of Modern India*, pp. 167–191. New Delhi: Kali for Women.
13. Ibid., p. 175.
14. Margaret Randall, 1992. *Gathering Rage*, p. 30. New York: Monthly Review Press.
15. This letter, in the possession of a CPI–ML (Peoples' War Group) courier was intercepted by the police and published in the Telugu daily *Andhra Jyothi* on 10 April 1996, a year after the same party published *Adaviputrika*. While the interception of the letter and the motives behind publishing it raise another set of questions about state repression and the citizen's right to privacy, the issues the letter raises, in a sense, erase, once and for all, the line between the private and the public. Our translation.
16. Cheris Kramarae, in Karen A. Foss, Sonja K. Foss and Cindy L. Griffin (eds), *Feminist Rhetorical Theories*, p. 47. New Delhi: Sage Publications.
17. See n.16.
18. Kramarae, in Foss, Foss and Griffin (eds.), *Feminist Rhetorical Theories*, p. 47.
19. Sheila Rowbotham. 1991. "The Women's Movement and Organising for Socialism", in Sheila Rowbotham, Lynne Segal and Hilary Wainwright (eds), *Beyond the Fragments: Feminism and the Making of Socialism*, pp. 68–69. London: Merlin Press.
20. See n. 16.
21. Ibid.
22. Ibid. In a tragic sense he too surrendered totally to the prerogatives of the revolution. Kranti Ranadev was killed by the police in an encounter in Orissa on 9 August 2001.
23. Ibid.
24. *Smarana*, a video documentary of interviews with mothers of naxalites killed in encounters.

10

THE SPACE BETWEEN: WOMEN'S NEGOTIATIONS WITH DEMOCRACY*

Paula Banerjee

Proponents of democracy believe that it offers the best hope for justice in any given society. Yet, there is very little discussion on how that state of justice can be achieved. Democracy is a concept that gained popularity in the late 19th and the early 20th century. As an ideology, its rise was closely linked to the rise of the nation-state in Western Europe. In a democracy, sovereignty supposedly rests with "the people". In a nation-state it is nationalism that constitutes a legitimate definition of who belongs to the category of people. In a pluralistic society such as in India, it often leads to a reinforcement of traditional cleavages based on religion, language, ethnicity, caste and gender and transforms them into newer inequalities. This is because central to the processes of democratic (and in this case post-colonial) nation-state formation is the question of identity. The state machinery seeks to create a homogenized identity of the nation and its citizenry that accepts the central role of the existing elite. This is done through privileging majoritarian, male and monolithic cultural values that deny the space for difference. As has been pointed by Etienne Balibar (1990) and Nira Yuval-Davis (1991), the denial is legitimized through liberal and social democratic discourses of state formation that camouflages the political will that consciously decides who belong and who does not belong to a particular space.

*Previous version was published in C. Joshua Thomas and Gurudas Das (eds). 2002. *Dimensions of Development in Nagaland*, pp. 187–197. New Delhi: Regency Publications.

Feminist scholarship and women's struggles alike have drawn attention to the incomplete nature of certain political projects such as democracy. For Carol Pateman (1988) "the social contract presupposed the sexual contract, and civil freedom presupposed patriarchal right." Women were long excluded from the collective "we" of the body politic in Western Europe, even after democracy had been achieved. For example, in France the "Declaration of the Rights of Man and Citizen," negated the rights of women and all those women who could have legitimately voted when the Notre Dame was built were liable to be punished by death if they so much as demanded suffrage. Not until the 20th century did western democracies include women in their citizenry. The second wave of feminism in the second half of the 20th century portrayed that, even if women acquired civil and political rights in the West, social and sexual rights still eluded them and that had serious ramifications for democratic processes.

In Africa and Asia, the project of national independence gave certain political space to women. According to feminist writers, such as Jayawardena (1986), in the post-colonial developing world, for a time, feminism and nationalism were compatible and allied, sharing similar objectives. During the period of decolonization, political rights, including the right to vote, were given to men and women alike. Yet, during the process of state formation male–female differences were reinforced. The new states formulated rights and obligations in ways "that strengthened the masculinity of the public sphere and the femininity of the private sphere" (Moghadam). According to Moghadam (2000), "in so doing, their policies and discourses ironically recall the early Western model of exclusivity and male privilege." This chapter will discuss the gendered nature of the Indian state-building processes from the time of the Constituent Assembly debates and how, in some instances, women have been able to subvert such marginalizations.

Before beginning a discussion on the gendered nature of state formation, it is essential to clarify what we mean by gender. Lorber (1994) defines gender as

> an institution that establishes patterns of expectations for individuals, orders the social processes of everyday life, is built into major social organizations of society, such as economy, ideology, the family, and politics, and is also an entity in and of itself.

For our purpose, gender refers to a structural relationship of inequality between women and men based on perceived sex difference, which is manifested in society, politics, economy, ideology and in culture. Even in the West, modern state formation was a gendered process. The British Nationality and the Status of Aliens Act of 1914 portrayed that rights of nationality could be transferred only through the male line. Women were considered as subjects or aliens primarily through their association with men. Thus, the case of Fasbender vs. Attorney-General in 1922 showed that a female British subject could contract a marriage in good faith during war and lose her British nationality.[1] Thus, women were neither full subjects nor foreigners. Even when they were subjects they could lose their nationality through marriage to an alien.

The post-colonial states of South Asia inherited many of its legal practices from Britain. The first Indian Passport Act was formulated in 1920. This Act did not define who an Indian citizen is. But it made it mandatory for any foreigner entering India to carry a passport. In it the male pronoun "he" described the foreigner.[2] In subsequent Acts dealing with immigration and emigration, the same practice was continued. The Foreigners Act of 1946 stated that wives of foreigners were also to be considered as foreigners. The Act prohibited Foreigners to change their names while in India. Exception was made if a marriage occurred between the foreigner and a woman ("native" or foreign) who was then permitted to take her husband's name, which presumed that a women's legal status depended on that of her husband's status.[3] Thus, women as independent legal identity did not emerge in the colonial period even though women got the right to vote. Even in the Constituent Assembly debates, it was presumed by many members that the "masculine, as it is well known, embraces the feminine".[4] This made the passage of the Abducted Person's Recovery Act possible.

The Abducted Persons (Recovery and Restoration) Act, 1949 was an Act provided in pursuance of an agreement with Pakistan for the recovery and restoration of abducted persons. It defined an abducted person as "a male child under the age of sixteen years or a female of whatever age who is, or immediately before the 1st day of March, 1947, was, a Muslim and who, on or after that day and before the 1st day of January, 1949, has become separated from his or her family and is found to be living with or under the control of any other individual or family."[5] There are some outstanding features of this Act. During partition, some 50,000 Muslim women in India and 33,000 non-Muslim women in Pakistan were abducted, abandoned or separated from their families.[6] The two states of India and Pakistan embarked on a massive Central Recovery Project during which some 30,000 women were recovered by their respective states. Some incidents relating to these abducted women exemplify the politics of gender during partition. Even when the two countries could decide on little else, they decided that the abducted women must be restored to their families. Problems arose over the process and progress of recovery. An Abducted Person's Bill was brought in the Indian Parliament. The bill gave unlimited power to police officers regarding abducted persons. If a police officer detained any women under this bill, they could not be questioned in any court of law. Although numerous amendments were proposed in the House, the bill passed unchanged on 19 December 1949.[7]

According to Rameshwari Nehru, adviser to Ministry of Rehabilitation, Government of India (GOI), many abducted women showed extreme unwillingness to leave their "captors".[8] Ritu Menon and Kamla Bhasin in their recent book on partition observe that women were:

> abducted as Hindus, converted and married as Muslims, recovered as Hindus but required to relinquish their children because they were born of Muslim fathers, and disowned as "unpure" and ineligible for marriage within their erstwhile family and community, their identities were in a continuous state of construction and reconstruction, making of them…"permanent refugees".[9]

These women were forcibly repatriated though refused rehabilitation by their families. How did India and Pakistan achieve such commonality of interest regarding abducted women?

Many explanations are given for this forcible repatriation of women. Menon and Bhasin point out how national honour was bound to women's bodies. According to Jan Jindy Pettman, "repatriation was made a nationalist project because women's bodies became markers of male honour." As usual women's bodies became "part of other people's agendas".[10] Both countries made claims of moral superiority over the *other* based on their ability to protect/control female bodies. This control was essential for the self-definition of the male identity that was in a state of crisis.

Abducted women were not considered as legal entities with political and constitutional rights. All choices were denied to them and while the state patronized them verbally by portraying their "need" for protection, it also infantilized them by giving decision-making power to their guardians, who were defined by the male pronoun "he". By insisting that the abducted women could not represent themselves and had to be represented, the state marginalized them from the decision-making process and made them non-participants. For the abducted, it was their sexuality that threatened their security and the honour of the nation. Thus, their vulnerability was focused on their body. This made all women susceptible to such threats and so they had to be protected/controlled. By denying agency to the abducted women, the state made it conceivable to deny agency to all women. Even after 53 years, state politics in South Asia regarding women remain essentially similar to the partition days.

The male-centrism of the Indian project of state formation continued with the Citizenship Act of 1955. As its title suggests, the Act dealt with modes of acquisition, renunciation, termination and deprivation of citizenship. Although the Act was meant to give rise to the category of the universal citizen, in actuality it did not. It continued the gender dichotomy evolved by the colonial state. The section on citizenship by registration stated that "women who are, or have been, married to citizens of India", were to be given citizenship if they applied for it. No such stipulations were made for men marrying women who were Indian citizens. Thus, citizenship by registration was largely transferred through the male line. In the section, on the termination of citizenship it was stated that where a male person "ceases to be a citizen of India under sub-section (1), every minor child of that person shall thereupon cease to be a citizen of India."[11] This portrayed once again that citizenship was transferable largely through the male line giving women a second class citizenship. Although, in later Acts, women could transfer citizenship rights to their spouses and to their children, it did not alter the maleness of the Indian state as conceived in the formative years. Adequate testimony to this male-centrism of the Indian state is provided by the debates over the Shah Bano case and, in present day, by state attitude towards the riots in Gujarat.[12] Thus, the male character of the state ensured that women would have hardly any space in formal politics. But what about space in the informal sector? One way of understanding this informal space that women acquire within the public sector is to study women's role in peace-building processes in Nagaland and Manipur. Such interventions made by women in these states of Northeast India have not only redefined gender stereotypes but have transformed definitions of democracy, nationalism and peace. Also the diversity of women's interventions for peace in the Northeast gives new meaning to Joan Scott's contention that "politics constructs gender and gender politics".[13]

THE CASE OF NAGALAND

To understand women's role in peace-building in Nagaland, one has to keep in mind that Nagaland has witnessed protracted conflict over the last 59 years. It has also to be remembered that, during state versus community conflict, men withdraw from civic life for compulsions of war and self-defense. In such a situation, the public sphere retreats into the private and women form the civil societies. They assume roles that are completely new to them and confront and negotiate with the massive power of the state machinery in their everyday lives.

It has to be remembered that in most of Northeast India, including, Nagaland, women are marginalized in institutional politics. The Naga women have one of the worst sex ratios, even by Northeast Indian standards, but the second best literacy rate. The sex ratio is 890 and the literacy rate is about 55.72 per cent. The sex ratio for women in rural areas is 912 and in urban areas 789.[14] This shows greater out-migration of men from villages and the ongoing conflict is the main cause for that. Naga women are extremely independent and there are more women cultivators in Nagaland than men. Yet, in electoral politics, the record of Naga women is hardly any better than the women from the other regions of the Northeast. Although Nagaland had some extraordinary women parliamentarians, such as Rano Shaiza, the present day record is much worse. There are no women in either the Assembly or in the Parliament.

Electoral politics in Nagaland is thus completely dominated by men. They dominate the seats of power. Sometimes, women are given token representations but very often they become invisible.

According to one observer, this exclusion of women from electoral politics is a "deliberate exclusion" imposed on them by the men.[15] Thus, electoral politics has in no way empowered women in Nagaland, rather it has led to their further marginalization. However, there are other areas in the public sphere where women have made spaces for negotiations. It is in the politics for peace that they are able to negotiate some spaces of action. The peace movement in Nagaland is sometimes led by women, but almost always overwhelmingly supported by them. Women dominate the peace movements in sheer numbers.

Women in the peace movements negotiate with both the army and the insurgents and yet are able to carve out an independent space for their actions. The best known among these organizations for peace is the Naga Mother's Association (NMA). The head office of the NMA is in the largely Angami (a Naga ethnic group) city of Kohima. It came into existence on 14 February 1984, with a preamble that stated, "Naga mothers of Nagaland shall express the need of conscientizing citizens toward more responsible living and human development through the voluntary organization of the Naga Mother's Association."[16] Membership of NMA is open to any adult Naga women, irrespective of whether she is married or single.[17] Members can join through the women's organizations of their own tribes. The organization encourages human development through education and it endeavours to eradicate social evils and economic exploitations and work towards peace and progress.

The NMA has rendered valuable service for the cause of peace. It mediated between the Government of Nagaland and the Naga Students Federation over age limit for jobs and came to an equitable settlement. An achievement of NMA is the formation of the Peace Team in October 1994 to confront the deteriorating political situation. Their theme was "Shed No More Blood". The NMA spoke against killings not only by the army but also by the militants. In a pamphlet released on 25 May 1995, the representatives of NMA wrote that "the way in which our society is being run whether by the overground government or the underground government, have (sic) become simply intolerable". The NMA celebrates 12 May each year as Mother's Day and renews its appeal for peace.

Apart from peace initiatives, the NMA has worked for social regeneration. In Nagaland there is rampant abuse of alcohol and drug. The NMA provides facilities for de-addiction. They collaborate with the Kripa foundation of Mumbai for rehabilitation of drug-doers. The NMA has also started anonymous HIV testing. They are probably the first women's organization in the Northeast to test pregnant women for HIV virus. The NMA is providing pioneering service for care of patients afflicted with AIDS. An important issue preoccupying the doctors of NMA is the increase in HIV positive cases among pregnant women. An NMA spokesperson is of the opinion that conflict in Nagaland is a result of chronic underdevelopment. Therefore, the NMA believes that, without addressing developmental issues, there cannot be any peace in Nagaland.[18]

NMA's greatest achievement is that most Naga women's organizations are its collaborators. The members of NMA also collaborate with the Naga Women's Union of Manipur. The rallies organized by NMA are always well attended by other Naga women's organizations. The NMA work very closely with the Naga *Hohos*, the apex body of all the Naga tribes. That the NMA has assumed enormous influence in Naga politics is borne out by the fact that they are the only women's group in South Asia that has participated in a cease-fire negotiation. In 1997, they mediated between the GOI and the Nationalist Socialist Council of Nagaland—(Issac-Muivah) NSCN (I-M) faction and facilitated a cease-fire.

The NMA, however, is not the only women's group. There are a number of others of which an important organization is the *Watsu Mongdung*. This is not to say that the NMA and the other groups are of equal status, they definitely are not. The NMA is much larger than any other women's organization in Nagaland. But the other groups have some importance among certain ethnic groups just as *Watsu Mongdung* has among the *Ao* women. An extraordinary case catapulted the *Watsu Mongdung* into fame. The incident took place on 27 December 1994 in *Mokokchung* town. Ten members of the Assam Rifles entered the town and carried out indiscriminate rape and arson. Innumerable women were raped. The Naga Human Rights Commission entrusted *Watsu Mongdung* to investigate and identify the victims. The *Watsu Mongdung* formed a special committee and investigated the matter. They identified eight victims and reconstructed the incident after a thorough discussion with them. None of the other social organizations wanted to take this up. So, members of the *Watsu Mongdung* decided to litigate on behalf of the rape victims. The case is still pending. Although the *Watsu Mongdung* is largely an *Ao* organization they have participated in protest marches organized by the *Lothas* and such other tribes.[19] However, they are one of the few women's organizations that do not collaborate with the NMA. This may be because of traditional *Ao* and *Angami* antagonisms.

The *Watsu Mongdung* carries out relief work during calamities—man-made or otherwise. They have led protests against every kind of oppression and violence. Once, during a combing operation in Mokokchung, when the army wanted to separate the men and women, they refused to be separated since they feared that the army would kill the men. Ultimately, the army had to interrogate both men and women together and then released most of them.[20]

The *Watsu Mongdung* is not the only group that provides such services. There are other women's groups such as the *Tangkhul Shanao Long* (TSL) which operate both in Nagaland and Manipur. The TSL worked in Ukhrul district. It has its branches in all the *Tangkhul* Naga villages. In July 1997, after an ambush by the NSCN–IM, the Assam Rifles went on a rampage in Ukhrul town beating up the men including schoolteachers. People were so traumatized that life came to a standstill in Ukhrul town. The TSL not only spoke to the army and convinced them to release over forty civilians but also tried to instill confidence among the people of the town and its adjoining villages. They helped the people of the area to return to normal life by requesting the shopkeepers to open their shops. They appealed to the stranded people to go back home which brought back some semblance of normalcy in the town.

In recent years, groups, such as the NMA, the *Watsu Mongdung* or the TSL, have gained recognition as serious actors in the peace process. Their organized campaigns and rallies have facilitated the cease-fire. They continue working with other Naga organizations to reduce the violence and brutalization of the Naga society. They actively participate in discussions on peace and human rights. Through their negotiations for peace they have created a niche for themselves in the public sphere.

The numerous Naga women's peace groups successfully maintained their independent stand. They have convinced all the parties in the politics of peace that they are not to be dictated by any specific faction. Most of these women retain their belief in their *Cause* of self-determination and liberation. But their actions show that they are on the side of peace. They want to achieve their goals through political actions and not through brutalization of society. Women's peace groups in Nagaland have achieved enormous success. They have become an important and necessary component of the Naga *Hohos*. Yet, even the state machinery is not averse to using them for purposes of peace. There are a number of reasons for the success achieved by the Naga women. The Naga women have been able to situate their political manoeuvrings within their traditional roles. Peace to them is not just a political phenomenon; it is also economic and social in nature. They believe that without development there cannot be peace and here they differ from the majoritarian attitude towards peace. They call for a just peace that will result in equity and they equate it with progress.

THE CASE OF MANIPUR

In Manipur valley, women's activism is symbolized by the activities of *Meira Paibis*, or the torchbearers. Although Manipuri women are not entirely new to activism, yet in institutional politics they have little space. Manipuri women trace their descendence from legendary women such as *Laisna*, the wife of *Nongda Lairen Pakhangba*, who came to the throne in Kangla of 33 AD. She presided over the *Patcha*, or the women's court, that dealt with women related crimes. Women also eulogize the military deeds of *Linthoingambi* of *Ningthou Khomba*, who was known to have saved her palace from attacks by the enemy. During the last century, there were two women-led uprisings in Manipur known as the *Nupi Lal*, these were against the British. The Manipuri monarchy gave so much importance to the voice of women that political executions were stopped if enough women raised their voices in favour of the victims. Today, there is a women's bazaar in Manipur known as *Nupi Keithel* where women meet, sell their ware and discuss problems of the day, including politics. This bazaar has served as a launching pad for collective revolt by women. Yet, in electoral politics, women have not made any mark. For example, in the 1996 Parliamentary elections, female voters who were 6,47,422 in number, outnumbered male voters who were 6,38,438 in number, yet the number of women candidates were only two among a total of 28.[21] In inner Manipur Parliamentary seat, Annie Mangsatabam was only the second woman candidate to fight elections after Maharani Iswari Devi in 1952. None of the candidates mentioned any particular women's issue in their manifesto. Neither of the two women candidates won the elections.

The *Meira Paibis*, or the torchbearers, who are also the most prominent women's groups in the valley trace their origin from mythical and historical women's activism in Manipur. According to *Yumnam Rupachandra* of the *North-East Sun* the *Meira Paibis* have become an institution in their own rights today. They started as *nasha bandis*, or combat groups, for the ever-increasing consumption of alcohol by the men. Slowly, they captured the imagination of the Peoples Liberation Army (PLA). The PLA imposed a ban on bootlegging and booze in January 1990. Two months later, succumbing to this pressure, the United Legislative Front government declared Manipur a dry state. This was a victory for the *Meira Paibis*. The social cleansing drive, it is said, evoked popular support. According to some critics, *Meitei* militants actively support these women's groups. But recent events portray that *Meira Paibis* enjoy the support of most of the civil society in Manipur. In the last two years, the *Meira Paibis* have expanded their area of action. Now they campaign against atrocities by the security forces. They also keep nightlong watches to foil raids. They dialogue with security forces and convince them from picking up innocent bystanders for questioning as part of counter insurgency operations. Since July 2004, they began an unprecedented movement against the Armed Forces Special Powers Act (AFSPA) that has captured the imagination of all civil society groups working on peace. They are in the forefront of protests against violence and it is being extremely difficult for the state to ignore their demands.

It all started years before the brutal killing of Thangjam Manorama by the Assam Rifles. But it was brought to popular attention on the dawn of 11 July 2004, when the massacred body of Manorama was found. But, three years before this event, another

33 year old woman Irom Sharmila had started a fast unto death against the AFSPA. She is still being forced fed through her nose at Jawaharlal Nehru Hospital in Imphal. However, it was Manorama's death that served as a clarion call. The same day that her body was found, the *Meira Paibis* marched to the Chief Minister's residence and demanded punishment for the killers and removal of AFSPA from Manipur. The Chief Minister agreed to the former demand but refused to concede to the latter. Many civil society organizations joined the *Meira Paibis* and a huge protest movement started in Manipur against the AFSPA.

On 15 July, the *Meira Paibis* shocked the nation out of its stupor by protesting naked in front of the Kangla Fort, the Assam Rifles headquarters, holding up banners that said "Indian Army Rape Us". This was a novel way of shaming the authorities, the Indian state and a patriarchal society where women's bodies were considered as nothing better than pawns in the armed conflict between the community and the state. According to observers "initially women groups took the lead," and organized a movement that later became a more generalized protest.[22] The Assam Rifles called Manorama a member of PLA and a "baby faced murderer", thereby trying to exonerate their totally illegal action of killing an arrested person in army custody. The protestors alleged that Manorama was raped before being brutally murdered. *Meira Paibis* gave leadership to a protest that kept growing. About 32 organizations joined the protest and formed the *Apunba Lup*, an apex body of 32 civil society organizations formed to organize massive public resistance to the AFSPA. The movement continues even today with the *Meira Paibis* still stridently protesting against AFSPA. Many of the leaders of the 15 July movement were arrested under the National Security Act and the government floundered completely in trying to control the movement. The *Meira Paibis* were successful in initiating a movement against which the state had hardly any arsenal. The Assam Rifles tried to go to the hills and the Naga areas and forced marched people with banners that said the Assam Rifles were their saviours. All this polarized society to some extent but, in no way, could discredit the initiative of the *Meira Paibis*.

That brings us to a number of Naga women activists in Manipur whose activities fall within this genre of peace movement.

The Naga Women's Union in Manipur has fifteen constituent units and one of the more exceptional ones is Moyon Sanuw Ruwrkheh (MSR). The *Moyon* tribe inhabits the Chandel district that is in the southeastern part of Manipur. The *Moyon* women's organization was formed in 1950 to improve the social status of *Moyon* women. From April 1994, the Moyon women's organization included a number of political demands in their annual resolutions. They called for equal right of women to inherit property. They also began an agitation for women to participate in decision-making bodies. These resolutions were brought up for discussions in the Moyon Naga Council and the President of the MSR was given the right to vote. She was the first woman to vote in the elections of the council. In 1997, for the first time, a *Moyon* woman became the speaker of the Assembly of the Naga *Moyon* Council. No other Naga tribe in Manipur has given its women the right to vote in their Legislative Councils.[23]

The Moyon women are extraordinary in another way as well. These women tried to initiate dialogue with *Kuki* women living in proximity. Initially, they had some success, but later, the *Kuki* women activists told them that their men were unwilling to let such a dialogue continue. Notwithstanding the pressures from the men, the *Kuki* women and the representatives of the MSR organized a formal dialogue between the women activists of the two groups. But on the day of the dialogue, they were informed through an emissary that it would not take place, as the *Kukis* were unwilling to continue it. The Moyon women are of the opinion that although the *Kuki* women were willing to dialogue on peace, their men felt threatened by such a dialogue. Thus, they stopped their women from attending such dialogues. Even after this setback, the MSR has continued its activities towards peace. They established networks with other Naga groups and are trying to organize a women's dialogue between the *IsaacMuvah* and the *Khaplang* factions of the NSCN. They crossed international borders to speak to the leaders of the *Khaplang* faction. In the process, the Border Security Force (BSF) arrested them. But, as a result of interventions by the Chief Ministers of Nagaland and Manipur, all charges were dropped. Apart from these sensational endeavours, the representatives of MSR organize peace campaigns through awareness raising programmes, seminars and workshops on peace and harmonious co-existence in different localities. They collaborate with other human rights organizations on fact-finding investigations.[24]

Apart from peace activities, the Naga Women's Union in Manipur also undertakes developmental activities. It campaigns for women candidates in Lok Sabha elections. It has begun campaigning for the inclusion of women in Naga village councils. None of the Naga village councils includes women as office bearers. This is a source of great disappointment to the Naga women. Hence, campaign on this issue is a priority for the Naga Women's Union. It also works towards income generation programmes for the women. Its other priority area is to work towards equal wages for women. There is a disparity in wages between male and female workers in Naga society, which the Union seeks to correct.[25] However, its greatest achievement has been over property rights. Traditionally, Naga women do not inherit immovable parental property, such as land. But due to the campaigning of these women, the Naga tribes in Manipur are slowly trying to correct this discrimination against women. This is possible because the Naga *Hohos* (tribal councils) view this issue favourably and they have also included it in their agenda.

WOMEN AND THE POLITICS FOR PEACE IN NORTHEAST INDIA

Kumari Jayawardena in her path-breaking commentary on feminism and nationalism stated:

> Women's movements do not occur in a vacuum but correspond to and, to some extent, are determined by the wider social movements of which they form a part. The general consciousness of society about itself, its future, its structure and role of men and women entails limitations for the women's movement; its goals and its methods of struggle are generally determined by those limits.[26]

This is true insofar as the Northeast is concerned. But there is also another reality. Women's initiatives are not just determined by, but also determine, wider social movements. From this short analysis it becomes apparent that women's groups, such as *Meira*

Paibis and NMA who have a broader definition of peace are more successful than those who think that peace is only an end to armed conflict. These groups believe that peace can be achieved through dialogue and political negotiations. They believe that only military solutions cannot bring peace. They work towards a betterment of their own society and, in this way, they equate peace with justice and development.

The *Meira Paibis* in Manipur and Naga women's peace groups have successfully maintained their independent stand in the politics of peace. They have convinced all the parties that they are not to be dictated by any specific faction. Most of these women retain their belief in their *Cause*. But their actions show that they are on the side of peace. They want to achieve their goals through political actions and not through brutalization of society. Women's peace groups in Nagaland and Manipur have achieved enormous success. They have become an important and necessary component of the Naga *Hohos* and the civil society bodies in Manipur. The *Meira Paibis* led a huge civil society movement in its protest against AFSPA. Even the state machinery is not averse to using them for purposes of peace. This shows the inclusive nature of the successful manoeuvrings of women in peace politics in parts of Northeast India.

There are a number of reasons for the success achieved by the *Meira Paibis* and the Naga women. These women have been able to situate their political manoeuvrings within their traditional roles. Peace to them is not just a political phenomenon; it is also economic and social. They believe that without development there cannot be peace and here they differ from the majoritarian attitude towards peace. They call for a just peace that will result in equity and they equate it with progress. These women also successfully mix social work with their political actions. Whenever they face political opposition, they shift their focus and work on issues of health, de-addiction and rights of women. Their involvement in developmental activities has increased their effectiveness and their acceptance in Naga and Meitei societies. These women have portrayed that under the guise of social work, women can negotiate spaces in the public sphere.

The experiences in the Northeast portray that if women are successful in defining peace and making it a women's job, then they are not severely challenged. I, however, make no essentialist plea here. Peace making is often recognized by the male dominated society as women's own work. The majoritarian leadership fails to recognize the political nature of the work of peace making. The experiences of Nagaland and Manipur show that, through peace making, women are able to negotiate spaces in the public sphere. This recognition then helps them in their other negotiations such as the reworking of property rights. Women's negotiations for peace have the potential to change the situation for women even in traditional societies. Women not only influence the politics of peace but their own lives are affected by participating in the politics of peace in myriad ways. They are able to legitimize their leadership roles and question unequal distribution of resources. This leads to a democratization of society in as much as democracy can be equated with social justice. Therefore, women not only redefine peace but their own situation is also redefined by the politics of peace.

Notes and References

1. Lord Atkinson quoted in Lord McNair and A.D. Watts. 1966. *The Legal Effects of War*, p. 66. Cambridge: Cambridge University Press.
2. The Passport Act, 1920, Act No. 32 of 1920 in 1955. *The Indian Code*, Government of India, Ministry of Law, p. 1. New Delhi: The Manager of Publication.
3. The Foreigners Act 1946, Act no. 31 of 1946 in 1955. *The Indian Code*, Government of India, Ministry of Law, p. 10. New Delhi: The Manager of Publication.
4. Mr. Naziruddin Ahmad. 1948. *Constituent Assembly Debates*, Vol. 7. 22nd November.
5. The Abducted Persons (Recovery and Restoration) Act, 1949 in 1955. *The Indian Code*, Government of India, Ministry of Law, pp. 1–4. New Delhi: The Manager of Publication.
6. For a scholarly account of gender in the politics of partition refer to Menon, Ritu and Kamla Bhasin. 1998. *Borders and Boundaries: Women in India's Partition*. New Delhi and Urvashi Bhutalia. 1998. *The Other Side of Silence: Voices from the Partition of India*. New Delhi.
7. Paula Banerjee. 1998. "Refugee Repatriation: A Politics of Gender," *Refugee Watch No*, January. pp. 8–9.
8. Rameshwari Nehru Papers, Nehru Memorial Museum and Library (NMML), Delhi.
9. Menon, Ritu and Kamla Bhasin. 1993. "Abducted women, the State and questions of Honour," p. 13 in *Gender Relations Project Paper*. Canberra.

10. Pettman, Jan Jindy. 1996. "Boundary Politics: Women, Nationalism and Danger", p. 194, in Mary Maynard and June Purvis (eds), *New Frontiers in Women's Studies: Knowledge, Identity and Nationalis*. London.
11. S.C. Consul, Citizenship Act, 1955, in 1962. The Law of Foreigners, Citizenship and Passport, pp. 179–185. Allahabad.
12. For the gendered nature of the government's attitude to the Shah Bano case see Gopal Jayal, Niraja. 1999. *Democracy and the State: Welfare, Secularism and Development in Contemporary India*, pp. 101–150. Delhi.
13. Scott, Joan quoted in Sarah A. Radcliffe and Sallie Westwood (eds), *"Viva": Women and Popular Protest in Latin America*, p. 217. New York and London: Routledge.
14. Luhadia, SR. 1991. *Census of India 1991*, Series 18, Supplement 6, Paper 1.
15. Aparna Mahanta. 1998. "Working of Parliamentary Process and Empowerment of Women in Northeast India," in Phukon and Yasin (eds), *Working of Parliamentary Democracy & Electoral Politics in North East India*, p. 174.
16. *Constitution of the Naga Mother's Association*, Reprinted in Kohima, 1992.
17. Statement made by Neidonuo Angami, President NMA, in Second Civil Society Dialogue on Peace, organized by Calcutta Research Group, Shantiniketan, 14 July 2002.
18. Interview with Ms Kheseli, Secretary NMA, 27 January 1999 and 10 October 1999. Kohima and Calcutta.
19. Watsu Mongdangi Inyaka Aruba Report, 5 May 1995. Unpublished Report, Mokokchung, Nagaland.
20. Interview with Merenla Jamir, member of Watsu Mongdung, 26 January 1999. Dimapur.
21. Election Office, Government of Manipur, *Electoral Roll 11th Parliamentary Elections*, Imphal, 1996.
22. M.S. Prabhakara, 2004. "Burdens of the Past", *Frontline*. September 10, p. 12.
23. Interview with Gina Shangkham, President MSR, 11 September 1999. Dhulikhel.
24. Ibid.
25. 1998. "A Brief Report of the Naga Women's Union, Manipur", *Raisurang*, no. 4, pp. 1–4.
26. Jayawardena, Kumari. 1986. *Feminism and Nationalism in the Third World*, p. 10. London: Zed Books.

11

MINORITIES, WOMEN AND PEACE: A SOUTH ASIAN PERSPECTIVE

Meghna Guhathakurta

> *Ekhaney tumi shonkhaloghu*
> *Okhaney tumi jomjomaat*
> *Ekhnaney tumi bostibashi*
> *Okhaney chosho raasta-ghat*
>
> *... Kothai jeno manush kandey*
> *Kothai jeno kandchey hai*
> *Manush boro bhoi peyechey*
> *Manush boro nishwahai.*
>
> *Here you are the minority*
> *There you are dominant*
> *Here you dwell in slums*
> *There you reign the highways*
>
> *... But somewhere humanity cries*
> *Somewhere you can feel the pain*
> *People have become fearful*
> *People are feeling helpless.*
>
> —Moushumi Bhowmik:
> singer, composer, lyricist

INTRODUCTION

The problem of minorities in South Asia has had its root in the history of the region. According to many scholars, the two-nation theory had created fissures between the two dominant religious communities in the subcontinent—Hindus and Muslims. The partition of 1947 had formalized this divide in the form of two distinct nation-states where one religious community dominates the other, that is, the Hindus in India and Muslims in Pakistan. The partition of the subcontinent along religious lines, with accompanying communal violence, produced a politics that gave rise to situations described in the songlines above.

However, it was not only colonial policy, which was responsible for the communalization of the subcontinent, but also the nature of nationalist movements in the region. The anti-colonial national movements in Asia have been mostly of an integrative type, that is, they embraced, at least in theory, all of the indigenous population subject to a single colonial state, regardless of ethnic differences. The notion of ethnicity was therefore suppressed in most discourses of nation building.

Even in the post-independent period of nation building, the newly independent modern nation-states of Asia, carved out of former colonial territories, adopted policies, which suppressed, used, or merely accommodated ethnic and cultural differences. This had left the problem of ethnic minorities un-resolved in contemporary statecraft as is to be noticed in the northeast of India or in the Chittagong Hill Tracts of Bangladesh.

The formalization of the new nation-states of South Asia was also accompanied by two other characteristics (a) unitary constitutions (with the exception of India, which technically was constituted as a union of states) and (b) centralized state policies. Both these characteristics, together and independently, helped to marginalize sections of the population, which historically have been removed from the centers of power on the basis of language (for example, the Bengalis within Pakistan) religion, (Muslims in India and Hindus in Bangladesh or Christians in Pakistan) and ethnicity (the Chakmas in Bangladesh or the Tamils in Sri Lanka).

Last but not the least, all states in South Asia are inherently patriarchal, a fact which often goes unnoticed in the mainstream political discourse. Male hegemony is apparent in any dominant power relations—personal, local, national or regional. It works to deprive and marginalize women from centres of power regardless of class, caste or ethnicity. However, oppression of vulnerable groups such as religious or ethnic minorities in recent years has specifically victimized minority women in a way that defies rationale and logic and compels one to understand the underlying patriarchal nature and the workings of our nation-states. It is from this perspective that I wish to look at the issue of minorities, women and peace. I will draw on experiences from Bangladesh since they are the ones closest to me, but the lessons learnt could no doubt contribute towards the understanding of similar phenomena within the South Asian context.

In order to understand the linkages between minorities, women and the prospect for peace-building in South Asia, one has first of all to understand the nature of the state from a feminist perspective. I first outline the nature of the Bangladesh state as a site where women contest the increasing influence of religious fundamentalists. I then look at the dynamics of a gendered power base, which victimizes minorities (and specifically minority women) almost as a systematic method of state induced terror. I conclude with some suggestions for a women's agenda for peace.

THE CHALLENGE OF FUNDAMENTALISM IN BANGLADESH

"Fundamentalism has been on the rise in Bangladesh ever since the Bangladesh state veered away from the post-independent ideology of socialism and secularism and underwent an Islamization process" (Kabeer 1991).[1] But it is quite ironical that, though fundamentalist forces have been systematically rehabilitated and encouraged through the two military governments, it is through their participation in the pro-democratic movement and the support which they gave to a democratically elected government of 1991, that they emerged stronger than before. In fact, all would have gone well for the fundamentalists if it had not been for the massive mobilization process generated by the *Gono Adalat* (the peoples tribunal) led by Jahanara Imam.[2] This brought back to the political forefront the demand to try leaders of *Jamaat-e-Islami*, (a party which gave all other orthodox religious parties a national support by virtue of being represented in Parliament) for committing war crimes during 1971 in collaboration with Pakistan. In the fight, which ensued between the people on the one hand and the establishment on the other, the establishment set itself the role to "maintain law and order."

This line fitted in well with the fundamentalists who spoke of control and maintaining a predominantly male-dominant status quo, a strategy similar to the one usually taken towards women in general! Religion came to be used as one of the primary means by which male-dominant values and existing gender-oppressive ideology were imposed and perpetuated. It created a division between the private and the public; separated the personal from the political. It thus became a weapon in the hands of the establishment to use time and again to demonstrate a semblance of order, stability and control in the face of growing unrest and dissatisfaction with the Government.

The current economic situation of Bangladesh also brought the woman question to the forefront. With donors emphasizing the incorporation of a Women in Development (WID) strategy in developmental thinking, and non-governmental organizations (NGOs) and garment factories drawing out women in ever increasing numbers into the work force, the growing visibility of women became an added threat to fundamentalist ideologies.

It was advantageous therefore for the fundamentalists to take women who step outside the bounds of social norms as their next target since they represented a potential threat to the male-dominant status quo. Their target has ranged from well-known public figures such as Jahanara Imam, women's rights activist Sufia Kamal, writer Taslima Nasrin to NGO workers or vulnerable village women. Recently, of course, this target has been enlarged to include progressive minded journalists who write to raise the consciousness of the people against these forces.

Responses of the Women's Movement in Bangladesh

The slogan that the personal is political may have been coined by women rights activists in the West, but it certainly became relevant for women in any society, where various repressive measures were followed in order to keep the personal from being political. In Bengal too, women had confronted the private/public divide from time immemorial. Rokeya Shakhawat Hossain (1880–1932), a forerunner of the women's rights movement for Muslim women had time and again reiterated that orthodox religious leaders had played a retrogressive role for women.

Men had used religion whenever women had tried to break from the shackles of society. Such awareness has historically led women to challenge and confront what they perceived to be an oppressive hierarchical order. Little of this is acknowledged among those in the women's movement, who subscribe to a more developmental outlook on the women's issue. Such an outlook therefore tends to bypass both micro-level resistance and challenge thrown by women at the grassroots as well as the more macro-level demands of the Women's movement, for example, legal reforms. However, grassroots pressure and the vulnerability of women in relation to social, legal and paralegal institutions have more recently created the need for legal literacy, leadership training and empowerment programmes, albeit within the conventional framework of development.

But the development discourse has not only avoided resistance on gender specific issues, it has also failed to take into account the various resistance movements at the national level. As such developmental interventions have remained not only apolitical but also ahistorical. This has accounted for much of the confusion as to what constitutes the culture of Bangladesh. Much of the "outsiders" view about this has been framed by a globalized discourse of a homogenous Muslim society. The fact that social and linguistic traditions play just an important role and had played the crucial role during the independence movement of the country seems to be largely ignored.

But this outlook has a much more serious repercussion on women's issues and how one deals with fundamentalism in Bangladesh. Whereas in the global framework, many Islamic movements in the Middle East have historically played an anti-imperialist role and have voiced protest over colonial oppression, the retrogade role played by the *Jamaat-e-Islami* as collaborators of war crimes in the Liberation War is acknowledged by Bengalis in general. But to many in the establishment, the politics of Liberation with its connotations of a linguistic cultural heritage and golden goals of self-sufficiency strikes a discordant note in today's world of free-market enterprise and labour migration. Such alternatives are thus not encouraged by any of the pro-establishment coterie: the donors (who seek a stable world order), the Government (who wishes to remain in power and hence sustain the existing power structure) or the fundamentalists (whose existence depends on the perpetration of a male-dominant patriarchal order)! Therefore, any form of resistance or challenge to the status quo, particularly if it comes from women, is trivialized, sidestepped or quelled as the case maybe.

KINSHIP AND POWER STRUCTURE

Kinship as an integral element of the power relations has been well researched in the context of Bangladesh village studies in the early seventies. What has not been so closely researched however has been the link of kinship to the more elitist power configurations at the core of national politics in Bangladesh. Since most of the political leadership in Bangladesh emerges from the expanding middle-class, it is not uncommon to find blood relatives among political personalities belonging to diverse ideological camps. Thus although, on one hand, competition at party level can become very violent and intolerant, the kinship factor provides a buffer zone where extreme views or positions are often negotiated. This has been a clever entry point used by Islamist parties who wanted to gain credibility in society. For example, in Rajshahi University, members of *Jamat-i-Islami* have been encouraged to marry into families in university administration so as to enhance their status within the campus. This is also the reason why even though there is political intransigence at the party level, members of rival parties are quite commonly seen together at social events and many at times purport to have common business interests. It is this feature in Bangladesh politics, which often enables one to bypass or even subvert political positions on the right or left, or political issues such as the trial of war criminals of 1971.

The kinship factor also brings into play a particular pattern of gendered politics, which is often invisibilized at the level of a political system. Since family and kinship ties are important in power configurations, women have become the means through which dominant power configurations may be made manifest. Hence abductions, forced marriages, rape of women belonging to marginalized groups, such as minorities or opposition party cadres, are often resorted to in the politics of domination and vendetta. A less violent but nevertheless effective method of inscripting women into the politics of class hegemony is through encouraging "political marriages" where a Member of Parliament (MP) or, better still, a minister as a father-in-law can help smooth out processes of obtaining licenses, securing jobs or ordering transfers of lucrative government posts. It is also this kinship factor, which serves to exclude to a large extent religious and ethnic minorities from the centres of power. Technically speaking, there is nothing to prevent minorities to participate in mainstream politics in Bangladesh and hence bring in their own kinship structures into play. However, the foregrounding of majoritarianism—inscribing Bengali as a state language and Islam as a state religion—automatically marginalizes religious and ethnic minorities from attaining a central role in determining class hegemony.

POST-ELECTION VIOLENCE AGAINST MINORITIES IN BANGLADESH

The post-election violence in Bangladesh (2001) specifically targetted the Hindu minority population though, in a broader frame, it also encompassed Awami League supporters and other progressive forces in the rural areas. The violence has largely been known to be initiated by supporters of the Bangladesh Nationalist Party supporters in various localities. The backlash after the elections was systematic and severe. Bangladeshi press has reported that attackers have entered Hindu homes, beaten family members and looted their property, and rape and abduction of women too were reported.

Among the atrocities committed were charging into households, attacking men, women and children with sharp knives and weapons, in certain cases threatening with guns, terrorizing women and children by beating and chasing them and, in certain cases, raping and attempting rape. Looting of Hindu households and sometimes Muslim households which sheltered Hindus took place throughout the night and in waves since most householders had fled in terror and their houses were left unguarded. No distinction was made between rich and poor households. Houses were left almost bare. As some of the victims said, even babies' clothes were stolen.

Although men were terrorized as well, it was women and children who had to bear the brunt of the attack. Once they saw the attackers, the women came out and begged for mercy or to have their husbands spared. The attackers then turned on the women, sometimes asking one woman to fetch another one by name, ("bring so and so to me") or else attempting to drag the women at hand. When a twelve year old girl refused to call her mother to the attackers she was raped herself.

A Case Study of a Village in Bhola

That night everyone had to hide in the rice fields fending off water-leeches from their hands and legs and that of their babies and children. Some women also had to climb trees in order to rescue themselves. But the fear of more attack prompted many to stay away from their own houses for more than a week, sometimes two weeks. In the second village we visited, a mother claimed that for 15 days her sons were forced to live in the betel nut orchards (*Supari Bagan*). Sometimes she would try to take food down to them, but the sons would hardly be able to eat at all due to sheer terror. In many houses, which could afford to do so, individual couples rented apartments in the nearest town for several months before returning to their homes, daughters-in-law were also sent away to their natal home districts if that area was safer. In the villages, it was poor women who were hit most hard, since they earned their living through labouring in the land and they could no longer do that due to physical insecurity. Often they had to send away their daughters to the homes of rich town people to be educated and kept safe. Among the Hindu community there were a few female-headed household where the men were working in India. Their security was especially endangered. One such woman who lived with relatives found security by cooking for the emergency police force, which was stationed there after the incident. People, who had some land but were looted of all their belongings, began to cut down trees in their homestead and orchards to provide emergency funding. No local NGOs had come to their rescue with programmes of relief. Only those organizations from Dhaka which had visited these villages to investigate the situation proved to be their only hope for salvation and relief.

There were some cases of exodus into India, but only for those households that already had someone living there. But in many cases the victims expressed that they were too poor to take that option. They did not have the minimum resources to make the move. In other cases, where families came from the landed class they still had too much at stake here to flee without preparation. Their exact words were: what shall we eat in India? We have to resort to begging.

The Aftermath

Although some steps were taken by the administration to arrest some of the more obvious culprits in one of the worst hit places and an emergency police force was stationed in the vicinity of *Annoda Prosad* village, the systematic denial of these incidents nationwide had prevented sterner measures to be taken by local administration. The villagers of *Annoda Prosad* felt somewhat relieved by the stationing of an emergency police camp in the vicinity. It is true that they also felt intimidated by the fact that some of the culprits were still roaming free and that those who had been arrested were being released on bail. Many culprits were reported as saying, "so what if they had to go to prison, it was temporary, almost like going to your in-laws" place for dinner'. They also intimidated that if the villagers mentioned their names to the police or administration then they would take it out on them. In the village of *Fatemabad* this threat was actualized when one Hindu boy was charged for being accessory to a so-called abduction of a Muslim girl. The incident was in fact one of an élopement, and some of the culprits of 2nd October incident at Fatemabad turned around the case to point the accusing finger to a Hindu boy and had him arrested. This was a way of showing their vengeance. The family of the boy was distraught. As it was, they had lost all their belongings and on top of it did not have the financial or moral strength to fight the legal proceedings. This was indeed a case for legal aid.

The Role of the Administration

The role of the administration from local to district level was at best hedgy about the incidents. Apart from the setting up of the police camp in the vicinity of *Annoda Prosad*, there was little indication that the administration was taking positive steps to file charges or find and bring the culprits to justice. The people in *Char Kumari* complained that the police had not filled in specific charge sheets for weeks after the incident. A few days had gone by even before they had come on the scene to investigate. There were also reports of attempts to cover up complaints, which have been made. For example, in the village of *Annoda Prosad*, a woman had wanted to file a case regarding her husband who was missing. But the local level leaders had tried to coax her into believing that he had gone to India and had even produced a letter which was read out to her since she was illiterate. But the odd thing was that the Officer-in-Charge (OC), when asked about this incident, repeated this story and he too gave the same excuse as to why a case cannot be lodged regarding this "disappearance". The District Commisioner on the other hand, seemed more sympathetic and was keen to maintain peace but also would not want to take any action that would displease local elites.

Locally, it was only the media, which had reported faithfully the incidents and followed it up regularly. The role of the politicians, however, has been wanting. Local MPs have either reportedly been inciting the attackers or indirectly supporting them by protecting the culprits from law enforcing agencies. The Minister for Religious Affairs elected from this area was sympathetic but was too far away in the capital to be able to monitor the day-to-day events.

THINGS TO BE DONE

From the above, it is clear that some steps need to be taken to cope with such incidents in the future. What is most important of course is the political will of the government to acknowledge the damage and to take measures to prevent further incidents like these. But NGOs also have a role to play, which was virtually absent during the 2 October 2001 incident. *Bhola* has traditionally been a natural disaster zone and local NGOs have effectively developed disaster management programmes over the years. But what needs to be acknowledged is that these incidents too are disasters, which leave people destitute and lost. Immediate relief, even shelters in some cases, are needed. Health care for those injured or raped are among some of the most immediate needs. The villagers told stories of the double trauma they faced when local hospitals declined to take rape cases or injury that legally should be handled by the police. But for most households it was the medium and long-term needs that claimed attention. Many households, which were affected, had candidates for the school certificate examinations, which were looming up and, since they were robbed of all their belongings, did not have the funds to buy books or enrol their children for the coming examinations. This was something that should have been looked into seriously by both government and non-government authorities. Monitoring cells could also be set up in such riot-prone area, which could help speedily take care of relief, medical and legal aid action in the aftermath of such events. Such cells could also be part of an early-warning system for anticipating future riots.

FUTURE LANDSCAPES: A REGIONAL PROBLEM

The villagers also feared future reprisals against the Hindu community, especially in response to violence regarding the Ayodha issue in India. They all expected a reprisal on the Hindu community around 15 March 1992 when the Hindu extremists had a plan to build a Hindu temple on the location of Babri Mosque, in UP, India. Rumours about a possible attack were ripe in both villages. Memories of the attack following the Babri Masjid incident in 1992 were still alive in their minds. This is a feature, which has been common in Bangladesh politics since the early nineties. The establishment of an independent Bangladesh on the basis of secular ideals had offered to the polity a sense of citizenship as opposed to that of religious sectarianism. Even though the word secularism had been omitted from the 1975 constitution, a non-sectarian concept of citizenship was something quite acceptable in the Bangladesh polity. As regional and global politics became more and more influenced by religious fundamentalism, sectarian identities of Hindu and Muslim re-emerged in the arena of politics. That by itself would not have unleashed the violence one saw on 2 October 2001. Rather, the incident was the result of machinations of a vested group of people who saw it to their advantage, both politically and economically, to foreground sectarianism as political vendetta against the Awami League.

The participation of religious minorities in mainstream politics has been largely marginalized with the establishment of a pro-Islamic ideology. Even so, because of the specific historical connection of the Awami League with the secularist notion, they have been identified as a substantive vote bank of Awami League. However, the existence of many structural discriminatory practices as well as the Vested Property Act, which for over three decades, until it was repealed by the previous Awami League government, had been responsible for a systematic and pervasive eviction of Hindus from their homesteads and a resultant exodus into India. Land, being a scarce commodity in overpopulated Bangladesh, was good enough a reason for local vested interests to be interested in the communalization of Bangladesh's politics. The nature of the party structure and leadership has contributed towards both the criminalization and communalization of this politics.

The centralization of power within the party structure has been paralleled by a geographic centralization in the capital. Thus, a large number of MPs who win seats in parliament are occasional visitors in their constituencies and normally reside only within the limits of the capital city. Hence much of their political control over their constituencies is handed over to their local henchmen, who in turn, exercise control over local administration as well (not unlike absentee landlordism of past eras). When the time comes to distribute the booties of an electoral victory, there are obviously more candidates to satisfy than there are resources, and hence leaders often turn a blind eye to consequent processes of extortion, which goes on in the localities. One of the characteristics of the recent assault is that most of them have taken place in rural areas. And in a politics characterized by techniques of *"char dokhol"* (forcibly occupying land in rural areas) or *"chandabaji"* (to collect contributions coercively), it is easier to justify extortion to their political leaders if the victims happen to be political opponents or their die-hard supporters or, in other words, those outside the purview of state power. Indeed, one may even stand the chance of being offered the post of a minister or state minister as a reward for it!

The issue of the assault on minorities is therefore enmeshed in a complex hub of power relation, which characterizes the current nature of politics in Bangladesh. Many say it is a careful plan to reduce the number of Hindu voters and create a separate electorate for them so that they no longer become a vote bank for the Awami League. Others mention that this is due to the machinations of a powerful circle allied to the ruling party whose own petty interests often override the concerns of a national government.

The counter to such trends must be found in the reassertion of the principle of a secular democratic practice in the political and social context of Bangladesh. Unlike many regions, the people of Bangladesh have memories of secular resistance politics, which it can draw upon. The advent of a global Islam and regional fundamentalism has challenged these tendencies. The mere existence of formal democracy is not enough to stave off the advances made by these forces. A reinvented and invigorated notion of a secular political culture, which is acceptable to the people of Bangladesh, given their rich cultural heritage, is now the need of the hour. Can we meet this challenge?

Notes and References

1. Kabeer, Naila. 1994. "The Quest for National Identity: Women, Islam and the State", in D. Kandiyoti (ed.), *Women, Islam and the State*. London: Macmillan.
2. Jahanara Imam, author of *Ekatorrer Dinguli* (Of Blood and Fire) and other books, mother of a martyred freedom fighter, gave courageous leadership to the movement against the fundamentalists and succeeded in mobilizing public opinion in favour of pro-Liberation forces at a critical juncture of Bangladesh's history. Suffering from cancer, she breathed her last on 26 June 1994.

Section III

Voices

Introduction

Anuradha Bhasin Jamwal

Identities can divide. Identities can unite. The crude irony of the fact was reflected in a personal incident. My lecture in Karachi on Kashmiri women in conflict—from victimhood to activism—prompted a man, visibly moved by the plight of the oppressed Kashmiri women, from the audience to gift me a documentary film CD *"Mera Ghar"* on the *Swara* practice. Despite my gratitude, the question on my mind, when he asked me to use it for my next presentation or lecture, was "What's the connection?". There were, on one side, the women of Jammu and Kashmir, who were from different ethnicities and religions, caught in the cross-fire between militants and soldiers at the borders between Pakistani and Indian forces, raped, molested and humiliated like in any conflict situation. On the other side is the Swara practice in the Pakhtoon area, where tribals have been pledging young girls to men against whom any crime has been committed as a way of easing tensions between two households. For a man's folly, his daughter or sister pays the price—bartered in the name of peace and in turn "dishonoured" and "stigmatized". What is the apparent difference in the Kashmir situation where women's bodies become tools of vengeance, barring the legitimacy that the Swara practice enjoys within the tribal system? None at all, except the backdrop of levels of violence in the two conflicts. "There is always a common thread running through women's stories—whether they are from violent conflicts, Dalit narratives or culturally conservative societies—where patriarchal set-ups tend to victimize women at two levels due to their multiple identities: first as members of a certain ethnic or religious group and then as women within that group." The gendered oppression, thus, has the potential to bring women from diverse backgrounds on a common platform.

It would be improper to put women exclusively in the hierarchy of victims and glamourize it. Yet, in both conflict and non-conflict situations, this victimhood, which is an apparent commonality exercised in wars, insurgencies and through unjust systems and practices, can enable women to transcend the traditional divides of language, caste and colour and form a distinct identity—a separate constituency of women. As Cynthia Cockburn puts in a following chapter, "feminism at its best is a way of thinking that transcends the contradiction of identity". Transcending this contradiction has lent greater clarity and strength to women's movements against oppression and violence around the globe. Two apt and somewhat successful examples within South Asia are the Naga and the Sri Lankan cases.

The Naga Mothers' Association in Nagaland made consistent efforts to broker peace between the two warring factions of the National Socialist Council of Nagalim and it also plays the monitoring role in the ongoing peace process and dialogue with New Delhi, though without questioning why women have not been brought to the negotiating table. The stories narrated by the Naga Mother activists about how they crossed the borders and risked their lives to seek a patch-up between the rival militant groups on humanitarian grounds is already well known. Equally inspiring, if not more, is the case of Sri Lanka. The efforts at brokering peace and bringing the Liberation Tigers of Tamil Eelam (LTTE) and the Sinhalese government to the negotiating table were narrated by Visaka Dharmadasa. Visaka, like several other Sri Lankan women, lost her son in the conflict but channelized her victimhood not into one of mourning and bitterness towards the "enemy" but one of compassion and understanding towards all sufferers.

Visaka's son serving in the Sri Lankan army, went missing in 1998. Not willing to plunge herself into endless grief, she used her energy to not just overcome grief but also bring peace and solace for other mothers and do her bit in preventing violence. Today, Visaka represents two women organizations—Parents of Servicemen Missing in Action and Association of War affected Women. These organizations ask the government to reciprocate the LTTE's actions of releazing soldiers and civilians. They also mobilize opinion, pressing both government and LTTE to respect the dead and make identification disks compulsory because the highest number of missing in Sri Lanka (about 12,000) are those who are often dead and their bodies go unidentified, often mutilated and disfigured after death.

Four years ago, Visaka and her colleagues realized that it was not only the Sri Lankan Sinhalese mothers who had losses to grieve, Tamil women too shared similar agonies. They found a common ground and decided to establish links with the women on the other side of the boundary. In 2002, the Sinhala and Tamil women joined hands publicly at a rally for the missing. Visaka says she does not feel angry at the LTTE for targeting her son as an individual; he was a warrior on the other side. Women like her believe that unless there is peace there will be more mothers like her, grieving for the dead or totally deprived of the luxury of grieving because their sons have not been declared dead and are bereft of ceremonial burial honours.

It was not easy getting the women on two sides together. But they were determined to trek it. They first established communication through letters and when they felt they would get a positive response, six of them, including Visaka whose younger son is still in the Sinhalese army, went to the north in the militancy entrenched area. They sought permission to go there on the pretext that they were going to offer prayers at an old historic church in the area and finally managed to meet their counterparts on the other side. That was the beginning of the ties. They felt that as women, who had so much at stake in wars and conflicts, they had a common ground and needed to wage a battle for peace—at least for a peaceful conflict minus the violence. Little did they realize at the moment of the first meeting that ties based on common tragedies can be so strong. But it did not take them very long. While they were still in the LTTE area, Sinhalese soldiers had shot dead some Tamil men in the same pocket. At first they feared that the Tamils may retaliate and make them victims of revenge. But so deep were the bonds of trust created in just those moments of meeting with the Tamil women that the Tamil men escorted these six women to safety that day. That was the beginning of the fine and lasting relationship. Today, women on both sides have managed to broker a cease-fire in Sri Lanka between the army and the LTTE. Though Norway facilitated peace talks may not have yielded results after they were snapped mid-way, violence has calmed down a bit and

Visaka and her colleagues are still struggling to do more—get women on the forefront as negotiators and ensure that talks proceed further, uninterrupted. Several other women activists working on different platforms nurture the same dream.

The dream of the Women's Action Forum (WAF) in Pakistan, for instance, is to fight against the *Shariat Act*, the *Qisas* and *Diyat Act*, the Law of Evidence, the *Hudood Ordinance* and especially the *Zina Ordinance*. In other words, the WAF would like to get all the retrogressive laws and the laws discriminating against women in Pakistan repealed. And the stories of women in Pakistan, at some point, unite with the stories of the so-called lower caste women in southern India.'

Their situation may be different, but their exclusion from "politics" binds them together somewhere. Or, for that matter, is the story of Kamalamma, a lady fighting for *Telangana* on behalf of the Communist Party, any way different from her counterparts elsewhere in the world? When the party finally decides to call off the struggle, Kamalamma simply returns to her ordinary life with hardly any means of livelihood. When she realizes that her life had not in any way changed through their struggle, way, she stopped going around singing that would have revived the movement. She did not feel strong enough any more. The life and times of women—be they in a situation of conflict between the Greek and Turkish Cypriots, be they in a situation of conflict between the Palestinians and Jews, or be they in a situation of the Balkan conflict—tend to remain the same, as unfair and inequitable as ever. In such a scenario, the sense of the self, in whatever way a person identifies herself/himself, leads us to "doing feminism" as Cynthia Cockburn would argue.

Such voices are inspiring and it is for this reason that they need to be heard—not only because women can be glamourized in the role of victims and their victimization politicized, but because they can create a change by struggling against, not only their own oppression, but against all that is unfair to humans, both men and women, including wars waged by the powerful against the powerless. It is commonly said that men make war and women make peace. Though, this may sound like a generalization, the use of word "men" and "women" is actually a connotation for masculine and feminist thought respectively, where war is a masculine notion and equated with oppression and machismo and peace is a feminist notion, a symbol of justice and pacifism. While some women can create more wars than some men do, some men can reinforce the feminist thought better than some women. It is in this context of feminist theme that women's voices need to be interpreted and heard, where the politics of humanity can shape new identities without its drawbacks of hate-soaked divisions.

The feminist struggles, in their true sense, have a strong advantage. History bears testimony to struggles for justice and against oppression the world over—year to year, decade to decade and century to century. The oppressive policies of the Nazi regime in Germany were replaced by the Russian terror against the Germans during the World War II. Incidentally, the Jews who faced the brunt of Nazi fascism started their own fascist regime against Palestinians. America's so-called liberation war in Vietnam, Afghanistan or Iraq has created greater oppression for the people in these countries. Can one kind of tyranny replace another? This is what the feminist notions of peace and justice can help put a check on because women have the capacity to build solidarities that can arrest the masculine trend of seeing people as us and them, the good and bad.

Borrowing from Maya Angelou's "Why the Caged Birds Sing", since women are at a greater disadvantage in violent or non-violent conflicts, they "stand on the grave of dreams", "wings clipped", "feet tied" and so open their "throats to sing":

> *The caged bird sings*
> *with a fearful trill*
> *of things unknown*
> *but longed for still*
> *and his tune is heard*
> *on the distant hill*
> *for the caged bird*
> *sings of freedom.*
>
> *(Maya Angelou)*

12

SHED NO MORE BLOOD: MOTHERS FOR PEACE*

Motto: "Human Integrity"

With the passing of decades, many lives have been lost and our tears of agony have mingled with the turbulent ripples of the streams that flow through the Naga Hills. The Naga Mothers' Association (NMA) has passed many agonizing years in its voluntary service for the cause of overall general welfare of the people and women in particular.

During our years of hard work, the organization had to undergo critical public attention as well as misconception about our basic aims and objectives.

Our agenda in 1994, at the NMA Fifth General Assembly, held at Zunheboto, brought into focus the agony and the cries of the people and, thus, resolved to set aside a day for mourning in memory of all those killed due to political turmoil in our land, irrespective of whether those killed were Nagas or non-Nagas.

The mourning day was observed on 5 August 1994, at Nagaland State Academy Hall, Kohima, starting with the tolls of church-bells of various denominations, in funeral tones early in the morning. Banners and posters in black background with messages like: "*Mothers anguished over tragic killings and deaths*", "*Forgive and unite*" were placed all over the capital town.

About three thousand mothers from different Naga tribes gathered together in tears and prayed for healing our society. Many public and church leaders were also present to share our grief.

---
* Previously published as a pamphlet by the Naga Mother's Association (NMA) printed in 1994 during the height of conflict among the different groups of Naga people.

In solidarity, the Kohima Chamber of Commerce and the Town Committee closed down their business establishments and shops till afternoon. The day was dedicated to the spirit of reconciliation and re-establishment of brotherhood and fraternity among our people.

As an outcome of the day, the following resolutions were unanimously adopted. It was resolved:

1. To form a team as *"NMA Peace Team"* under the theme *"Shed No More Blood"*.
2. That, the team shall appeal to all groups of Naga National Workers, our brothers and sisters to stop killing one another in the spirit of forgiveness. While appreciating the selfless sacrifice they have rendered for our people, we also appeal to them to remember that each drop of bloodshed is draining away the life-blood of our nation.
3. To restore our broken society, we resolved to first set our homes in order through setting up of family altar.

Since then, the same peace team has been engaged in the task of meeting the leaders of Naga National Workers, state politicians, tribal leaders and people in general, to create awareness and consciousness to *"shed no more blood"*.

A public peace rally was held on 22 November 1995, at Kohima, organized by NMA. Awareness on *"Human integrity and Consequences of killing"* was created by the speakers of the rally, which was described by the media as a *"historic event"*.

NMA sends its appeal to mothers all over our land, to work for peace in their respective areas. We are committed to the cause and, therefore, to the best of our ability and efforts, we will continue our mission for the sake of our future generations.

"LET COMPASSION REIGN"

(*NMA is grateful to each and every well wisher in our long drawn mission*).

God grant us the Serenity to accept the things we cannot change, courage to change the things we can and Wisdom to know the difference.

(Serenity Prayer)

13

WAF TO CONTINUE PROTEST AGAINST DISCRIMINATORY LAWS*

Women's Action Front (WAF) categorically reaffirmed its commitment to a just and peaceful society and to the separation of religion from the state and politics.[1]

Examining the status and effect of the discriminatory laws promulgated since 1977, WAF resolved to continue its protest against them. The *Shariat Act, the Qisas and Diyat Act, the Law of Evidence, the Hudood Ordinance* and, especially, *the Zina Ordinance* were singled out as the most dangerous for the nation and particularly for women. WAF continues to demand that all retrogressive and discriminatory laws be repealed.

The WAF convention took a very serious note of the growing number of new laws that are promoting bigotry and intolerance in the name of religion. Of these the following were listed as of immediate concern to WAF:

(i) The law against blasphemy included in the Penal Code of 1986 and the subsequent change in 1992.
(ii) Changes in the Penal Code under Section 123(a) which question the integrity and loyalty of all Pakistan citizens.
(iii) The including of a column in the ID card which identifies the religion of the holder and
(iv) The recent judgement of the *Shariat Bench* of the Supreme Court which seeks to declare sections of the Family Laws Ordinance of 1961 un-Islamic.

WAF agreed that the larger issue of violence against women had not been sufficiently highlighted. Apart from rape, women are

---
*Previously published as a pamphlet by Women's Action Forum, Pakistan.

made the target of crimes of "honour", domestic violence and sexual harassment. WAF resolved to coordinate an action campaign to raise awareness on these issues and to struggle against them.

Resolution

The following resolutions were passed at the convention:

1. WAF denounces the violence against women especially rape including custodial rape, rape for personal and political revenge and other forms of political and personal victimization.
2. It denounces the showing of rape victims receiving compensation from the prime minister on national TV. Instead the names, addresses, and pictures of the culprits should have been publicized.
3. It denounces the fact that, in the Noori Palejo case, the criminals were let off and, in the Veena Hayat and Khurshid Begum case, no serious attempt was made to apprehend the rapists.
4. It strongly condemns the singling out of women as targets of violence and rape in political conflicts, especially at this time of sufferings for the women of Kashmir and Bosnia.
5. WAF regards the struggle for human rights an integral part of the women's movement in Pakistan.
6. It denounces the arbitrary arrest and harassment of journalists and the violation of human rights, especially in the province of Sindh.
7. WAF deplores the enactment and enforcement of the law against blasphemy and changes in the Penal Code questioning the loyalty and patriotism of Pakistani citizens as well as the inclusion of the religion column in ID cards.
8. It deplores the attempt by the Shariat Appelate Court to declare the Family Laws Ordinance of 1961 (which at least provided a minimum of protection to women) un-Islamic.
9. It supports the Supreme Court, which overturned the decision of the Sindh High Court in connection with the Family Laws Ordinance.

10. WAF denounces the attacks on mandirs and churches and the minorities, especially the humiliation and suffering inflicted on the minority women in reaction to the destruction of the Babri Masjid in Ayodhya.
11. WAF also passed a resolution upholding the decision of the Sindh Assembly to denounce the inclusion of the religion column in the ID cards and urges other provincial assemblies and the National Assembly to follow its example.

NOTE

1. *Karachi*, 12 January 1992. The 8th National Convention of Women's Action Forum was held in Karachi in December 1992 wherein representatives from the Islamabad, Lahore and Karachi chapters reviewed the recent national and global changes and their impact on women in Pakistan.

14

THE WAY OF THE WORLD*

Josiane Racine and Jean Luc Racine

The Reddiar goes to Pondy on business very often and also, I think, for political business: he's won the elections twice. Don't ask me which party! I think it was the one with the spinning wheel. I don't understand very much about that.[1]

"Grandpa Gandhi, grandpa Gandhi, don't eat *bundi* ...". That's what I remember from school songs, slogans and men talking about Kamaraj the traitor, Uncle Nehru, Indira the chaste Mother, Annadurai our master, Karunanidhi the poet.

Apparently, this country was ruled by a white king in the past, the ruler of the Kingdom of Pondy who had heaped up lots of money and hid it under his bum. Everyone here says that: the Vittiar's father, the Gounder, my father-in-law as well. Gandhi appeared after my birth. They say he was a trembling old man who looked like an earthworm. But he had a great heart and he spoke well. Out of all those people his daughter Indira Gandhi did the most.[2] That chaste woman fought for us poor. When she arrived, things became better for us. She brought water to the *ceri*: she had wells dug, she told people with forty or fifty *kani* to give one or one and a half of them to the poor, so they could have enough to eat. She let it be known on the radio, and by sending out cars, that the government would distribute land near the pond and near the channels and that she was with us and was fighting for us. But the enemy party attacked her government. They say she went to prison.

---

*Previously published in a book written by Josiane Racine and Jean Luc Racine entitled *Viramma: Life of an Untouchable* (Verso, London, 1997), pp. 257–281.

The men were jealous of a woman in charge of the country. And in the end, she was killed by some juice drinkers, as I have told you. Poor Indira Gandhi! I loved her very much, even if I never saw her. The day she came to Pondy, I could not go even with the lorries that took us there. I had too much work that day, I had to collect groundnuts in the Little Reddiar's fields. But lots of people went to see her. They said she was as light as a white woman and her head was always covered. She was as beautiful as the moon. The chaste woman!

The blessed father Annadurai was one of the men who've governed the Tamil country. Apparently he fought for us a lot. But people who work for the poor do not live long. A widower from the enemy party cast a spell on him and that incarnation of the great gods died because of it. We cannot stay longer on this earth than we are given. It ruined my heart hearing he had gone. I quickly ran to Anjalai's, Kannima's and Araiyakka's and we sang a very long mourning song to pay homage to that man with a golden heart, the father of thousands of poor people. I began like this:

> *O Blessed!*
> *You were the light that shone for the poor of this earth!*
> *O man of dharma!*
> *O generous one, is it true you're leaving us?*
> *Here we are, orphans today.*

Our laments were so sad that the men started crying and they kept the songs going for a very long time. Later my husband took me to Madras by train. When I had gone there with my father, he would never have dared step a hair's breadth out of the Pariah quarter. In those days we did not visit anything. But everything is open to us today, even if we know where we have to stop! So I made the most of it by visiting everything: the college of the living, the college of the dead, the markets, and we went to see the *samadi* of Annadurai.[3] I laid a bunch of jasmine there. His tomb was covered with flowers and incense sticks. This earth is not just full of ingratitude!

That said, I never got anything personally from Indira Gandhi and Annadurai: not a scrap of land or one rupee. It's enough for me to know that some good souls are thinking of us, the poor. Now all the talk in the *ur* and the *ceri* is of parties, meetings and assemblies and our young are the first to get involved. The only thing I know is that it creates divisions, enemies, fights, revenge and murders. And it makes us women anxious because when our men and boys have been drinking, they stop joking and humming a tune. They start swearing at each other and fighting about their party stuff. Our young especially are becoming more and more violent: luckily the older generation are there to calm them down a bit. Anban is a master in all these party goings on, but if I was to ask him to explain them to me, I would not understand a word of it and I would not be able to tell you anything. When he comes back from work, you should talk to him or my husband and ask them anything you want. They will be able to tell you lots of things on that subject. I will listen along with you.

(*The next day Manikkam is with his wife and he comes to sit down*) "Well then Sinnamma! After Viramma's life, do you want me to tell mine?"

(*Viramma*) "Yes, yes! You are older than me! You've seen and done plenty of things: tell it all to Sinnamma! (*Viramma laughs.*) I've already told you what we want you to talk about—parties, politicians. And don't mess around with that equipment!" (*Viramma points to the tape recorder.*)

(*Manikkam laughing*) "Soon she'll have seen more things than me! She'll be more civilized than me!"

(*Viramma*) "We're not asking you that! Say what you know about the parties. Go on, give it all you've got!"

(*And Manikkam begins.*) In the beginning there was only Congress for us in India. I mean at the time of the war between India and the English.[4] There was a second party as well, which had come from Russia: the Communist Party. Political men who'd gone there had found that the same things could be done here for the workers. The elections began under the Whites: voting goes on for a whole day and the people choose such and such a party, which they like. The two parties both fight for the poor, but they've got nothing to do with each other. In the Communist Party it's the poor fighting for the poor, while in Congress, there are both: rich and poor, sincere and dishonest. Congress's ideas were good and they had some great souls: Indira, Kamaraj, Nehru, Gandhi. I think Gandhi was the first. He traveled a lot. He met people in each region, each town, each quarter, each street, and held meetings to teach them to imagine the future. He said to them, "It's by getting rid of ignorance that a country can evolve." Gandhi also fought against the English. He liberated

India. Yes, the Whites, the English set themselves up here saying that the country belonged to them. Gandhi said to them, "you have cheated everybody. You came as guests and you took over our India. Go back down the road that led you here!" And after fighting a lot, and planting the Congress flag over the whole country, he got independence.

Once I heard him. He spoke in simple words; "don't be afraid of anybody: neither the Reddiar nor the Gounder who put you to work. You must conquer your ignorance first of all. This *kaliyagam* will favour you, the Harijans. You should make the greatest efforts to conquer your ignorance. Ask the Reddiar and the Gounder if progress belongs just to them, if they're the only ones who have the right to grow rich?" That's what Gandhi said and he was the one who made us change caste, so we became Harijans and stopped being Untouchables. But even with his great heart and all this generosity, he was shot down. They say it was a Muslim, a nabob, who killed him.[5]

At the same time, or a little later, there was the war between the French and the Union. My father often told me that things were better in the time of the Whites. In those days, everything was a reasonable price. An anna or a fanon and a half was his pay. With that all the family ate properly. A penny's worth of aubergine, a penny's worth of spices: we'd find it by digging two feet down. We could easily irrigate aubergines, pumpkins, *ragi*, groundnuts and sesame and the poor made the most of it. Now you have to dig for more than a hundred feet to set up a pump and we can't afford it. The Whites also used to hire people to work for them in Pondy and the Gounder could hope to see their sons get an office job. And the Whites drank alcohol, like us; they ate beef, like us. We didn't want to get rid of them. But that wasn't what the Reddi thought.

The Reddi from different communes met up and brought together thousands of men. They armed them and sent them everywhere to cause fear. Their coup was well organized. Goubert Papa and the Reddi of Nilugarai, Cinnapalayam and Naliveli ran the whole thing.[6] They had everything they wanted: jeeps, lorries, men and the Madras police. Bahur fell first, then Nettappakkam and gradually they took the eighteen communes. Only ours was left. Apparently it wasn't easy to take Karmegam and Dakshnamurti Gounder did everything they could to resist, but of course Gundurayan Reddiar was on the side of the other

Reddi. He paid some guys to come with *mattai* and iron bars and he also appealed to the Madras police with their guns. Men were patrolling day and night in Karani, in the *ur* as well as the *ceri*, but the Gounder didn't get the help they were expecting from Pondy. One night when our men were asleep, some armed men came in a lorry. They went into the village firing into the air to frighten people and then, seeing that nothing was happening, they started firing all over the place. Everyone tried to run away, but where to? Tirulagam was already in Congress's hands. Only Sellipattu and Nellipet were left, but they heard gunshots coming from there as well. My parents-in-law put the children on their backs and went and hid with Muttuvel's family in the pandanus thickets, and they saw everything from there: blood, wounded, fires. The Reddi stepped in to stop the houses being burnt, because burning a house which hasn't been abandoned brings misfortune. But at the same time he gave the order that those who'd been captured should be thrown into a lorry and taken to Nettappakkam. At the same time other guys were wrecking the harvests. They mixed up all the grain they could find—paddy, *ragi*, foxtail, millet—poured petrol on and set them on fire. In the *ur* they stole money and burnt all the mortgage papers. When everything was over, the Reddi sent for rice from Mangappakkam and their men had a feast and planted the Congress flag.

The unrest lasted a good week and then, day after day, all the people who had got away started coming back. People, who'd gone far away, to their relatives in town, came back two or three months later. And then the ones who'd gone to prison in Nettappakkam came back as well and they told us about the beatings with gun butts, the urine they'd had to drink. Everyone here talks about it as if it happened yesterday, and the old tell it to the new generation, laughing wholeheartedly. That's what we got from supporting the Whites.

Now we've got all the parties in the village: the Communist Party, Congress, DMK, Anna DMK, the Vanniyar Party, Janata.[7] All of them fight for the poor, for the Harijans. They're all for us, but we can only put one of them in power. So we choose by who's leading the campaign. DMK, for example. That's a new party. They added an M to the old party of Periyar, the DK, the party of the Adi-Dravidar. Anna formed the DMK.[8] It fought for the poor and against the division into castes. In the *ur*, the great DK campaigner is Ananda Gounder and, in the *ceri*, it's Kaliyappa. DK used to be a strong party and that's why DMK caught on well here in Karani. Now there's nobody left in DK; it's become an old party. After the death of Anna, Karunanidhi and MGR argued and that led to two separate parties. Out of us Anban is DMK. Those two parties think the same, they want democracy and to do something for the poor, but once they're in power, they stop taking care of us. They're all dishonest like that. In the beginning, in Anna's time, the party had a conscience. Those people used to tell themselves they should work for the poor who'd elected them. They had programmes. But once they were in power and they'd discovered money, those representatives changed their mind and said to themselves, "Why give so many facilities to people who are under our orders? No! First we must fill our pockets and make the most of it to get rich!" And we've stayed the same as before, not being able to read or write. True enough, there's a Harijans' office in Pondy, but we don't know how to set about making a demand or signing. If you go in that office and know how to read and write, you're well received and you get what you want. But when we go and ask for something, they say, "Come back in twenty days!" or, "Wait three months!" What we understand is, "Build that dyke higher!", "Hoe the field!", "Irrigate there, put fertilizer here!" And we're given fifteen or twenty rupees a day for that.

Since we've been accepted into society and asked to vote, I've always voted for Gopala Gounder. He was a worker as well. He understands how difficult it is for us and, most of all, we can talk to him about our problems and ask him to get us a few plots of village or temple land. He understands things and at least he gives an answer. The Reddi live in the shade eating fruit and drinking milk. They don't receive us when we go and see them. We have to wait for hours before talking to them or we have to keep coming back, "Sir is asleep", or "Sir is taking his bath", "Sir's not free". Anyway they don't understand our worries. We work for them, but we sympathize with the Communist Party. The Communist Party is a party of the poor. Its goal is to fight for people who have got nothing to give them a better life. What the other parties want is to cream off money and land and make things better for the rich. When Anna was alive, his party was honest, but now everything is rotten.

One day there was a big drama with these parties. The Grand Reddi didn't know I was voting for the Communist Party. He thought we were all voting the way he told us to. One year, Gopala Gounder assembled all his people for a demonstration on the day before the election. But Kuppussami had gone to his daughter's and wasn't there to lead the march with the red flag that time, so Gopala Gounder asked me to take over. I was very unsure, because I knew the Grand Reddiar wouldn't take it well! But I ended up saying yes and the march went through the *ceri* shouting. "Long live Mr Subbaiah! Long live our party! Vote for the Communist Party, the true party of the people!"

Unfortunately the party with two levels had also decided to march the same day. And they yelled, "*Podungayya ottu irattaiyilaiyai patti!*" 'Vote with a clear cross next to the two leaves![9]

Both groups tried to shout louder than the others. When we got up to the temple of Draupadi the Anna DMK flat carrier tripped me up. I told him, "Innappa! Don't do that, or else there'll be a fight! You carry on with your demonstration and we'll carry on with ours!" But his group tore the flag out of my hands to hit me with the pole. We fought back and broke them up in the end. But the police had been told. One of the policemen marched forward pointing his gun at me. I clung to him and turned out of the way. The Gounder, who were there, defended me and everything calmed down. Even so the police arrested a few others and me and I was taken to Pondy. In court the Gounder spoke up for me again and, in the end, after a night in the station where we were beaten up a bit, we went back to the *ceri*.

After that, when K.S. was elected, I left the CP. That very evening I went to see Gopala Gounder and I said to him, 'Ayya! I have fought for the party for a long time and yesterday was the same. The party has good ideas, but I've got children to feed. I need work, my son does as well. All my family are serfs at the Reddiar's and we eat the *kuj* he gives us. I depend on him completely. I have to run to his house to borrow when we've got nothing to eat, or when we have to celebrate an important event. I don't want to provoke his anger and we must vote for him. Please understand and forgive me! Gopala Gounder told me he understood my reasons, and he added, "All I ask is that your family give me one vote, yours for example. All the rest can go to the Reddiar." That's how we voted and the whole *ceri* did the same.

Everyone thinks that Congress was very good in the past, with Gandhi, Nehru and Kamaraj. But we don't understand any more what's going on in the North. In the election for Parliament, people vote for Congress out of loyalty for Gandhi, who fought very hard for the poor. He defended us loyally and he was the one who raised us to the rank of Harijans. And then what would happen with a Tamil party like DMK in Parliament in Delhi? DMK is a party for people who speak Tamil, for problems in the Tamil country. People used to vote for the *dharmaraja*, but since his death, the Anna DMK hasn't managed to pick itself up and Karunanidhi is usually in power.[10] He has been in the party from the beginning too and he fights for us. Our Reddiar has voted for Anna DMK the last few years and the people followed him. A *kambattam* should know who to support and who not to. Since the death of M.G.R., he votes DMK and the people do as well. We say to ourselves, 'I'll do what he does. I am a worker, he is a *kambattam*. I am his serf. If he prospers, I get four or five measures of paddy thanks to him. Of course, I'm the one who works hard and my family wears themselves out for him, but the pay is there'. So we vote like him. And then we're looked after in our constituency: running water has been put in for the poor, the whole *ceri* has got electricity, we can collect tamarind fruits for three years, we have a rationing card, widows and disabled are given rice and clothes and children are fed at school. Even a girl like Shanti can study to go into the police.

But it's not enough to make everything all right! Communal land for instance. It was rented out to us, but when Congress got back into power, they took it back. Maybe the Congress Party fights for the poor, but the people in it have money. They're the sort of people who are offered tea or coffee when they go into shops. The sort of people who sit out in their armchairs on verandas in the cool of the evening and plan their move, make their decisions, which village head should be given two hundred or three hundred rupees under the counter, which accountant should be slipped some money to get the land register. They're the people who get the land we should be given. And if we fight to get that land, they'll come and tell the accountant, "Innappa! The Reddiar or the Gounder needs those fields. Cross out that name and this one. Make sure that disappears from the register: there'll be this much money in it for you." And the village head, the accountant and the *talaiyari* share it. The next day, there's an official there with a chain who's come to measure the communal land and he tells us, "Innappa! All this belongs to the Reddiar now. You mustn't come here any more, otherwise you'll end up in prison in handcuffs!" And if we refuse and stand up to them, they'll say, "You sons of whores, you've got a nerve to rebel against us!" and they'll have us beaten. But all of us have already come out in protest. All the heads of families who voted for the Communist Party were there and we shouted,

Long live the Communist Party! Long live India!
Long live Subbaiah! Long live Gopala Gounder!
Communal land for the poor!
Let us farm the communal land!
Down with the Government!

And we planted the red flag in the ground.

The policemen came to arrest us. They took us to the station with our flags and said to us, "Innappa! Why do you protest like this? You must hand a petition to the Governor, the Chief Minister, the people in government. You're protesting with the CP flags, 'Subbaiah! Subbaiah!' Do you think he's the one who's going to give you the commune's land?" "Yes," we told them, "He fights for us! He's the most honest and we trust him. The rest only help the rich!"

After that activists from the other parties came running to the station, particularly DMK party workers, "Let's go! We're going to get you all together to discuss this and make a quick decision. Let's see: how many households are there in the *ceri*: sixty, seventy-five? We'll give each family twenty *kuji*. No need to demonstrate! No need to protest! We look after you. Go on, go back to your homes. We will get in touch with you!"

That's what we hear each time we demonstrate, but we never see anything happen and the community land is still given to the people from the *ur* and not to us. Sometimes one or two people from the *ceri* get a little land to rent before the elections. It's the same with the ponds. In the past we ate mussels, snails, crabs from the paddy fields and fresh water fish. No one else used to eat them. Now even the Vanniyar have started to and they're the ones who get fishing permits. They fish with big nets and they sell us their fish! And if I tell my son to ask for a fishing permit for part of the pond, he tells me that he's ashamed! But we are the ones who are the poorest. We only eat if we've got work, otherwise our stomach stays empty. So why not rent us a few plots of land or a pond—us, the landless? This is the reign of the rich and they don't worry about the poor.

That was plain enough when I went to see the Reddiar about Anban's marriage. I said to him, "I have to marry my son. I'm going to look for a girl for him, Sami!"

"Hmm! You have to marry your son and find a girl for him? Han! How much will you need for that?"

"I need five hundred rupees and five sacks of paddy, Sami."

Still sitting comfortably in his armchair, kicking his feet, he said:

"Hmm! You need five hundred rupees and five sacks of paddy. That makes a thousand rupees! When are you going to pay me back?"

"Innanga! I wear myself out for you, my son too and my wife and my daughter. All four of us wear ourselves out for you and you think you won't be paid back?"

"Good, so you think you can pay me back! Anyway, I can't give you that much. Take two hundred rupees and a sack of paddy. I'll buy the marriage sari and the *tali*. That'll make an impressive marriage! You'll pay me back those two hundred rupees and the sack of paddy later by working for me."

"Sami, we've already done so much work for you! Won't you give us anything for that?"

"Dei! Your father died, I gave a hundred rupees. Your mother died, I gave another hundred rupees. When your brother died, I gave fifty. Every time there's a death or birth, you ask me for something!"

"It's true you give every time, Sami, but I always pay you back without fail. If you give me what I ask for now, it will come to fifteen hundred rupees with my savings. I'll be able to give my son an honourable marriage with that!"

"Ah no! I can't give you that: only two hundred rupees and a sack of paddy. Go and ask somewhere else!"

"How can I go and ask somewhere else, Sami? I'm a serf in your household. My oxen and my family work for you, and you're not going to do anything for that?"

"But I pay you a wage!"

"Yes, but a large measure of rice costs three rupees twenty. How can I live on that? If you'd give me a 2-quarter of a *kani* to farm, I could cope. I'd get three or four sacks, I could save what I didn't eat and I'd pay you back."

But it doesn't happen that way, for the simple reason that the Reddiar doesn't want us to cope. They say to themselves that if I managed to put two sacks aside from a 2 quarter of *kani*, I wouldn't respect them any more: "The next thing that one will do is cut his hair like us, put on a *soman* and a shirt, light a cigarette. But if we don't let him have that quarter of a *kani*, we'll keep him as a serf, with his loincloth and his turban".

Because they don't want their workers to be respectable and civilized here in the courty, Sinnamma. What they want is for us to stay backward and them to be advanced. We Pariahs are more supportive, we want what's best for the other, we help each other. If one of us is dying of hunger, a brother, a *pangali* will give him something to eat. If a woman comes to Viramma and says, "Sister-in-law, I've got nothing to eat this evening. Can you lend me a measure of rice? I'll give it back to you tomorrow when my son brings his pay", we'll lend straightaway. If someone visits us unexpectedly, we'll run to the neighbour's to borrow some money, which we give back the next day. We support each other in the *ceri*: we can't let people die of hunger!

But in your castes they want to bring Pariahs down. When you sweat, it's water. When we sweat, it's blood! Standing up under an umbrella making us work isn't tiring and you go and eat your meal, drink your coffee at the usual time. It's only about eight o'clock when I'm brought my first meal. At midday the Reddiar eats rice and lots of different vegetables on a beautiful banana leaf and I'm told, "Dei! Go and wash your hands!" and gruel is poured into them. In the evening I take off my loincloth, I wash it, I tie on a *soman*, I politely cross my arms and come and get my pay. I can only really rest after that. I buy myself a few lentils, aubergine or salted fish.

"And you don't forget two rupees' worth of palm wine!" (*Viramma laughs.*)

"That's my one pleasure of the whole day."

"OK, OK, carry on."

If the Reddiar let me go earlier, I could eat and go to sleep early as well, but, instead of that, I go to sleep late and get up early. And if I get to work a bit late, the Reddiar hears of it and tells me off, "Dei! Didn't your wife let you go? She squeezed you tight in her breasts, did she? You were well stuck in, were you?"

Why should they be the only ones who can sleep with their wife and talk to them? Have they got the right to make children and not us? We're men and women as well. We've got desires as well, and they take us to midnight. Whereas they wash their hands at six in the evening, their wife brings them food and then they go to bed to relax or play with their wife: they don't feel tiredness. After we've hoed all day, we eat in a rush and it's only then that we can speak, play, caress each other, and be man and woman. That's our happiness.

We work like that all our life for a Reddiar and then, when we need money for a very important matter, to light a lamp in a new household, he goes and gives us two hundred rupees and a sack of rice. How are you meant to manage with that? And the day after the marriage, if we don't go to work straightaway as normal, he'll say, "I gave money to that Pariah for that marriage and look, he hasn't come to work. He's got a nerve!"

So there you are: you're Reddiar, you've got the right to rest. You high caste, you can say, "That Pariah widower hasn't turned up yet!" But then who's that widower who called us that: Pariahs, Pariahs? And all the other widowers who call us Pariahs as well! We're not just poor, but on top of that, we've suffered the great wrong of being born Pariahs.

"Die! Get a move on with bringing in the cows or else you'll get the stick!" That's how the Reddiar threatened me when I was little. Now he wouldn't dare lift a hand against me, I'm the same age as him. And if ever he couldn't control himself, if he hit me, there'd always be someone around, a Gounder, a Naicker or even a Pariah to tell him, "Innayya! Even if he is a serf in your household, it's not good to hit a man your age. You're hitting him without so much as thinking: even his parents who brought him into this world, lulled him to sleep and fussed over him, cared for him and protected him, they wouldn't even dare do it." Now the Reddiar respects me, because I'm a reasonable man,

I'm fair, and I'm not extreme. I can stay in my place. But if someone picks a quarrel, I can defend myself, I can talk!

Six months ago my son Anban was hit. I got angry! It reminded me of the first time I was beaten very badly, when I was little. I was twelve maybe and I remember it very well. I had to graze a herd of about twenty and there were two oxen that were all stirred up and two cows that were always running off into the paddy fields. Impossible to graze them quietly. They'd hardly got out of the stable before those thieving cows were off grazing the Gounder's paddy field. He came up furious, saying, "Innada! May be you think that because you work for a Reddiar, a *kambattam*, anything goes? Does your Reddiar think that he can graze his cows in my paddy field? Wait while I go and ask him that question!"

"Innanga! I am his cowherd, but I can't get all these animals to graze quietly with these cows that run off the whole time!"

"Well then! One of their hooves has to be tied to their neck!"

I pointed out that I had tied up one of the cow's hooves, but even so they ran fast and they'd got away. But he didn't want to know any of it and he started giving me an earful.

"Innada! Son of a whore! You motherfucker! If you were a good caste, you wouldn't behave like this! You really are a Pariah, you widower!" And he hit me on the thigh with his stick. That hurt very much and I immediately insulted him myself, "You dirty Palli who's made it to Gounder! Son of a whore! You dare come here and hit me when my parents wouldn't dare touch me!"

Straightaway he ran to the Reddi's and said to him, "Innayya! Your Pariah boy insults me without even taking my caste into account, as if there wasn't difference any more between high castes and low castes! I am a Gounder and he's a Pariah and he tells me that I'm a son of a whore, that I fuck my sister! Is that any way to talk?"

I didn't go home at midday. I sent some other cowherds to the Reddiar's for my *kanji* while I kept an eye on their animals. When they got there, the Reddiar asked them, "Dei! Where is my Pariah?"

"Innanga! He's looking after all the cows. He can keep an eye on all them at one time and stop them running away. He wanted to say there and asked us to bring his food."

"OK, OK! There'll be a beating waiting for him tonight! Get on with it!"

When the boys told me that, I said to myself, "Why does he want to hit me when the other one's already done it?" That evening I took the animals back to the stable and tied them up: I fed the cows, the plough oxen and the calves, then I went up to the Reddiar's wife and asked for a half-measure of rice. While I was getting the rice in my *tundu*, the Reddiar came up behind me, without me seeing, and hit me hard with a rattan. I yelled, "Ayoyo! Why are you hitting me?"

Dei! What did you say to the Palli, the Padaiyatchi, ed?'

"Ayo, Sami! He's the one who called me a son of a whore and a motherfucker! That's why I swore at him!"

My father was working there and he came to defend me, "Sami! If that cow trampled the Palli's harvest, all he had to do was confiscate the cow or complain to you and ask for compensation. But with these unruly animals, how do you expect my son to cope? And how much do you pay him? Six little measures of rice a month, because we're your serfs and do all the work for you and bring you our children."

That was the first time the Reddiar hit me. He started again one other time. It was just before my marriage. Standing at the edge of the field he was overseeing the groundnut harvest: about fifty people were working on it. I was grazing a cow not far away. The Reddiar called me, "Manikkam! Manikkam!" But I didn't hear anything because of the wind blowing from the south and all the noise the people were making and I stayed sitting down next to the cow without answering him. He picked up a tamarind branch and coming up behind me, hit me hard on the head. I fainted, unconscious. Everyone came together and started saying, "What is this, a *kambattam* who hits a boy! A boy as strong as that, he could never have knocked him out: he got him from behind!" Everyone stopped work, leaving their tools and baskets where they were—women took advantage of it to fill the folds of their sari with groundnuts. They left taking me with them to hospital. The Reddiar had gone home and said what had happened: "I hit Manikkam with a tamarind branch. The workers gathered round and took him to hospital. Apparently he's in a bad way ...".

Then his mother bowled him out in Telugu, "How could you hit that boy who we've brought up as a son? If he recovers, he'll pay you back for what you've done to him. Maybe you think he'll be afraid of your money?"

They asked me at the hospital what had happened to me. I didn't tell them the truth because I didn't want it to get to the police and be told to lodge a complaint against the Reddiar: I have to work for him to live! And you have to be in court every time they ask you. I'm not rich enough to get involved in that. I'd rather die than have all that trouble. So I told the doctor that a trunk had fallen on my head. But he knew perfectly well that that wasn't true. He said to me, "Don't hide anything from me. Don't be afraid. You can tell me the truth. Did somebody hit you?" I told him again that a trunk had got me on the head.

The Reddiar's father came to see me in hospital, and he backed up what I'd said to the doctor. But people went up to him outside and complained about his son's behaviour. He answered them, "Yeppa! It wasn't me who told him to act like that! The harm has been done now. Tell Manikkam not to be angry." He handed out twenty-five rupees so I could be given good meals in the hospital and bought a little brandy or beer. But my father said to him, "I think of you as a father and you wouldn't have behaved like that. But how can money make up for what has been done?"

Meanwhile, I was saying to myself, "I'm not going to let this go, even if I have to stay there. He'll feel my fist! I'll get my revenge." Once I was better, I didn't want to work for that Reddiar any more, but my father forced me to.

One day the following season, when I was picking up groundnuts with my mother, the Grand Reddi called her, "Adi, Muniyamma Adi, Muniyamma! Come here, di!"

I said, 'Mother, Mother, he's calling you! Instead of saying "Muniyamma, come here!", he says, "Adi! Adi! Come here, di, vadi-podi![11]

Hearing that, he shouted at me, "Aye! son of a Pariah whore! Let me fuck your wife, you sister fucker!"

His son came and hit me with his umbrella. I seized the opportunity and hit him on the back and a thigh with my hoe. Immediately he went off to call the police, telling them that a Pariah boy working for his household had hit him, and the day workers in the field took fright and ran away. I went home as well. Everyone was afraid I'd be taken to the police station for a beating. I just had time to wash when an inspector and a policeman arrived on a motorbike. The inspector called me, "Dei! Come here!"

People gathered round immediately. I answered, "How do you expect me to come over there without any clothes? I'm in the middle of washing!"

"Dei, right then! You've got a nerve! Come here immediately or I'll count your bones!"

"Go and look somewhere else! I've already seen police like you. You're not going to intimidate me!"

'Dei! You hit the Reddi and still you come out with arguments? We're going to bang you up and give you a good beating, boy!'

"Ayo! Earn some respect and respect the law! Don't overstep the role of policeman and don't push it too far with me! You think I'm a colony man, a Pariah you can insult and who'll be afraid? I won't go to the police station with you! You say I hit the Reddi? Well then, take me to the main police station in Pondy. When the magistrate summons me, I'll be there."

"Aah, you're not coming! You want me to send people to Pondy! We're not going to get through with you till we've counted your bones!"

"Get going, ya! I've seen a bunch of people like you and they all wanted to count my bones too! Just try and touch me and you'll see. Go on, get out of here, instead of asking me for five or six rupees because I'm poor and the others for fifty or sixty. You're wasting your breath here!"

"And why's that? You are a Pariah boy and you hit a Reddiar instead of working!"

"They tell us, 'Come here' and we come; 'Go over there' and we go there; 'Sit down here' and we sit down. They can hit us but if we give them the same back, they send for the police, we're taken to the station and beaten up."

"What do you expect, ya! That's the way the world works! All you Pariah guys wear yourself out working and if you answer back, you've got to take the blows as well!"

"Yes, you take a backhander from the rich and then you beat us Pariahs!"

Sinnamma, if we talk to them straight, telling them what's what and slipping them a few notes, then they'll go and see the Reddiar and talk to him differently.

"Innayya! You make them work how you please, without having to follow any regulations or anything and then you beat them as well. Even if you've got all the police on your side, that's no reason to beat them. This boy wants to lodge a complaint. He wants to go over our heads. And if we beat him too hard, we'll be suspended as well. If you want, you can lodge a complaint as well!"

In the end they took me to the station and there I managed to give each of them ten rupees: you give what you can. They let me out after that and went to tell the Reddiar, "Innanga! He wasn't at home. He's gone and hidden somewhere. Wait a bit for us to find him: we'll put him in the hole and then count the pieces!"

Two days later the Reddiar went back to see them, "Well then, have you found him? Have you given him a beating, that delinquent?"

"Innanga! He's gone and lodged a complaint against you. You're going to be summoned the day after tomorrow for a confrontation!"

"Ah! That Pariah's got a nerve to take it as far as this! He can't have had the idea all on his own. Someone must have turned his head. I'm going to see how far this gentleman is going to go! Sir, thinks he's rich! All he can pawn is his grass hut: where's he going to find the money from?"

And he went and complained to everybody, "That Pariah has lodged a complaint against me and he's ready to pay for it"

The others—a neighbour, a friend, even an Untouchable like me said to him, "Innanga! A Pariah has dared argue with you. You hit him as a punishment and he's paid you back. Where are we heading if everyone fights like this? The matter's closed now, so where is the Reddiar, where's the Pariah in all this?"

But the people who support the Pariahs said, "What difference does it make if he's a Pariah? Does blood only flow in Reddiar's veins and not in Pariah's? It makes them laugh when we talk about Pariahs. But don't Pariahs have wives and children like everybody else? The Reddiar aren't the only ones with children. When it's a question of their children, they take great care. But the son of a Pariah is satisfied with very little: a little oil, a little *sikakai* to wash. The son of a Reddiar has that soap which smells good, what's it called? And he has meals with loads of dishes. The Pariah can't give his sons that. That's why he sends them to the Reddiar's to tend the cows, to be serfs and to get beaten up!"

And then there are other ones as well who go and say to the Reddiar, "No, no! He mustn't be allowed to get away with it! He must be given a good beating to bring him into line!"

After that business, I stopped working for the Reddiar and all my family did as well. The stable wasn't cleaned out, the cow dung wasn't collected, the cows didn't go out. The Reddiar hired other people but the work wasn't done well. I knew the customs of the house. The others couldn't do the work in the same way as me and the Reddiar didn't have the patience to teach them to do what he wanted. I could be trusted to take a thousand rupees to a *kambattam* in a neighbouring village, apart from doing agricultural work. A newcomer couldn't be asked to do that.

For six months I stood up to him and I didn't want any of my family to work at that Reddiar's. I became a day worker and my mother did too. I pruned trees, I ploughed, I worked the well. And at the end of six months, the Reddiar said to himself: it's not working at all without those Pariahs. I've tried other people but they don't work the way they should. So he told the Reddiar that Ambigai works for to send for me. He said to Pajani Gounder, "The Pariah from the Grand Reddi's has done this and he's done that. He hit him and hasn't come to work since. Tell him to come back!" And Murugaiya Gounder called me as well, "Innapa! Apparently you've stopped going to the Reddiar's over there. What's happening?"

"Yes, Sami, I don't want to work for him any more. He doesn't pay me well. He doesn't let me have a plot of land to farm and he hits me. Why should I go and work for him under those conditions?"

"OK, OK. All of that is not good. He should look after you like a mother looks after her child, and you should end your days in this Reddiar's household. You shouldn't go anywhere else."

'No, Ayya! Let him come and find me himself if he wants me. Otherwise he'll say to himself, "Oh, he's had a really hard time! That's why he's coming back now!" Let the Reddiar come and call me, "Come, da! Come, Manikkam!" Then I'll go. But I won't go back of my own accord!'

And the Reddiar came to call me. The people were around us. I said to them, "I got very little for my son's marriage. I was beaten and injured. The police arrested me. Is that an honourable way for a *kambattam* to behave? Does he look good coming to call me today? What's he doing with his reputation?"

An elder of the *ceri* added, "Yes! He always thinks Pariahs are afraid of the Reddiar and that they just have to be called to come running. He mustn't think that."

Sadayan said, "Dei! Let him go and look elsewhere. He's dropped you for six months! He beat you, he handed you over to the police, he lodged a complaint against you, and now he comes and says, 'Come, da, Manikkam!' like a prince."

Hearing that, the Reddiar understood that he really was in the wrong, that all the Pariahs had realized that and that they were saying it at the tops of their voices. So he said, "OK, OK! Come on! I won't do anything to you from now on! You will work honestly and with dignity and you will eat with dignity what I give you. You'll have a little land to farm. But I want my property to be well looked after!"

Then somebody else answered, "would you hit your son like that? He's the child of a rich man: he's entitled to be treated differently. We have no means of support. We're beaten. We're sent to court. You've got money and you can read! We're Untouchables, we're poor and we can only live by your side!"

"OK, OK!" the Reddiar answered, "you can ask for what you want, but Manikkam has to come and do his work!"

When all the elders of the *ceri* had finished talking, Murugaiya Gounder started, "OK! You've said what you had to say. But when a *kambattam* comes in person to find his worker, he has to go. You know the customs of the family, their stories, their way of living. They have to have you. Go there!"

And I went off to be a serf again ...

(*Viramma picks up the thread of her account.*) This year we got the ballot papers for the elections very early. My son and my nephew got them as well. There were lots of people at the Reddiar's and the *kabattam* of Ariyanallur and his wife came and stayed with him. There were visitors night and day. There was a big party, a meal for all the voters and loudspeakers playing music. It was like a wedding! The Reddiar called us, the Paratchi, to winnow the rice: there were four sacks to feed that many people! We didn't cook at home at all because we were given what was left over. There was a big *pandal* in the street and rows of narrow mats with banana leaves in front of them: they were for the Kudiyanar, the serving castes and the Pariahs. No one missed the meal, even though there was no meat. It's not often we get to eat as well as that! The important people, like the Gounder, the Naicher and the Udaiyar, came without their families. Their meal was served on the first floor of the house. Apparently there was brandy and chicken from a big restaurant in Pondy. Pakkiri, the cobbler's wife, told me: she picked up the dirty leaves at the end of the meal. There were masses of them! The Reddiar's wife was very generous, she gave her a very pretty sari, and underskirt and a blouse. But Pakkiri doesn't wear a blouse so she gave it to her sister-in-law. We only got five rupees each for winnowing the rice, but I'd rather earn less than do a degrading job.

Everyone handed out the ballot papers for their party for this election: the Reddiar for their side, the Gounder for theirs. We vote the way we want: I vote for the Reddiar who I work for, another woman will vote for her master, or we can also vote for who we like. Afterwards we can make things up and tell the others that we voted for them. But we take everybody's money! Because they've all got money. We had five parties at one time. The ploughmen's party gave twenty rupees and a bottle of brandy; the two leaves party twenty-five rupees and a very brightly coloured factory sari; the cow and the calf party twenty-five rupees and some groundnut oil; the spinning wheel party fifteen rupees, and another one gave fifteen as well.[12] We tell them all we'll vote for them and we take their money. But anyway, everybody's only got one vote and you have to vote for just one person. Everyone gives, but we can't vote for everybody who's given! You can't vote twice because you've got two hands!

Ayo, Sinnamma! There's lots of people at the place where we go and vote: a little bit like queuing for the cinema. There are two police trucks, policemen, inspectors, nurses. The policemen are standing there with their sticks and saying, "Go on! One by one! Through this door and go into that room!" We take what we're given and at last get to the man with the list, who calls out in the order of the list, "Manikkam", then "Wife of Manikkam: Viramma", then "Anban". When I got there I was asked, "What's your husband's name? Show me your card!" Someone old enters everything and checks it: "Look and see if her name's there. Her husband's name. Where's the ballot paper?" We form two queues: one for men, one for women. The ballot papers we get at home are not valid. We have to take one from there. When we get to the booth, we take the stamp and make a mark in front of the sign we want, and then all the ballot papers are put in a box.

Once I made a mistake: I should have stamped the rising sun and I put it on the hand. When I came out, my husband told me off, "Can't you tell the difference between a rising sun and a hand?" Of course I can, but when it's all drawn on paper, it's smudged and I can't make anything out. He was in a rage, the others too. I said to them, "Leave me alone! I'm trembling all over in front of all these men. How do you expect me to make something out? We'll see at the next election!"

Nowadays, just before each election, they do new works in the *ceri*. Look: the streets are well marked out and tarmacked in the new *ceri*. There's a tap on every corner and there's street lighting. It's really nice and we're not afraid any more going home at night, whereas before, in the dark, guys used to hide in the sugar-cane fields to come and pester us. Everything that was cramped in the old *ceri* is roomy now, on a bigger plot of land: it all depends on the size of the family. We got nothing because we already own our house and we've only got one child living with us. They told my husband, "You can stay where you are. Your family home is big enough for you. But your brother will be entitled to a plot in the new colony." That's how they do it. If brothers live together, then one out of two or two out of four get a new plot. And everyone builds their house as best as they can on the plot of land the government gives them.

Everyone in the *ceri* owns their house now. I have to redo my roof. I'm waiting for the sugar cane to be cut to hire a cart and go and collect the leaves. You have to allow for two full days of work. We take advantage of the harvest in Crittirai to redo the roof. In the past we'd also use *karudai samba* thatch and that would last for more than two years. But with the new types of rice we've got now, the thatch doesn't last like that. Yesterday I saw they were redoing the thatch on the house of Sinnappan, the *talaiyari*, who's living in Pondy now. He comes and spends a month here with his family each year for the festival of Draupadi.

All the people who've left the village keep a house like that to come back from time to time. The government has recognized his work. There's only me who works as the midwife for nothing or almost nothing. Sinnappan's wife is the president of the women's association here. She looks like you, Sinnamma. You'd think she was a woman from the *ur*, not at all like a Paratchi. The association has got a hall in the new colony now and Sinnappan's wife comes to talk there with other women from Pondy. I asked her about me being paid a wage for my work as the midwife and I asked Kaliyan, the *nattam*, as well. But neither of those sons of a widower did anything about it. No one wants to put in a request for me.

I talked about it as well to Murali, a boy from the *ceri*, who's well educated. He passed all his exams and now he's working in a government office in Pondy. He is in the rising sun party. He could say a word to the people in his party, but he always answers me, "What, aunt. Don't be in a rush: you'll be given notice to attend!"

"Yes, yes!" I tell him. "I'll get it when I'm in the cremation grounds!" (*Laughs*.) That boy is very helpful all the same. He puts in our requests to the office of Harijans. It's through him that I got a loan to buy a pair of oxen. I gave him twenty-five rupees and the *nattam* as well. Both of them go to the offices for all these requests and they slip two or three people some money to get the signature they need. If we don't pay, we never get anything!

Murali keeps our young ones up to date with what's happening in the parties. He gets them worked up and it ends in fights. "The Reddi doesn't pay you enough: you have to rebel!" This one's a traitor, that one's real thief!' That's what our young ones talk about! That's all that interests them. Our masters can't scold them any more because they react straightaway. That's exactly what the political parties preach. The cinema turns their heads as well and gives them ideas. One day I saw the son of Kannima go to Kuppussami's teashop and ask to be served. Kuppussami politely asked him to bring his glass, but that boy demanded to drink out of one of the shop's glasses and he started abusing Kuppussami. That really is some nerve! Just because at the cinema you see those misters drinking out of everybody's glasses doesn't mean that you have to do the same!

What will happen to Kuppussami's business if Pariahs start drinking out of his glasses? No one from the *ur* will go there any more!¹³

It comes from listening to all those politicians. Of course they don't have to worry now. By the grace of God, we, their parents, can still work. But there'll come a time when we can't any more. Then they'll have to go and ask our masters for help. You can't keep the stomach waiting. It's not their party or the men in government who are going to feed them. Thieves cannot live on what they've stolen forever. One day they have to go back to living a normal life. Well then, our young can't always live on politics either! They're brainless birds. They whistle noisily and end up drowning in the drinking trough. We've got to find a way to feed ourselves somehow. Can we pawn something to borrow money from the Marwari of Tirulagam? The only things we've got are our hands. The day we go without our *kuj*, we can run to the Reddiar's and he always ends up lending us a few measures of rice or a few rupees. That's why I always teach respect and obedience towards our masters. And that's also why I vote for the Reddiar myself.... My conscience always tells me to vote for him. I work for his household. He protects me and I should give him my protection as well. Everybody thinks the same as me: we're not dishonest towards the one who feeds us! The Gounder gives out lots more money than the Reddiar to get our votes. He tells all of us, "Don't vote for your Reddiar! Vote for us!" But the Reddiar has married off all our children! Even if I vote for the Gounder, they won't do anything for us. They think of us before the elections, but afterwards they don't even know where we live!

Three elections before this one, Sinnamma, there was a fight here. Our young ones had decided to stop voting for Perumal Gounder's party and vote instead for the new party of M.G.R. There were quarrels for days between the men of the two parties. One evening, Perumal Gounder's men came with sticks. One of the leaders was a Gounder called Vadivelu, who always comes and shows off round the *ceri*. That time he said, "Dei! You sister fuckers! Who gave you so many facilities here? It's got to be the man who governs Pondy, hasn't it?"

Every evening they came in a group like that, after going drinking, and that Vadivelu would shout at us, "Dei! You sluts, they say you're all high and mighty and that you're not going to vote for us? Eh! No one's forcing you, you know? Vote for us if you want to, or else hang on to your votes!"

We listened to them in silence, but there were always some young ones who shouted back, "It's all over now, you playing the wise guy! Nowadays you can't swing your dick like before or put a cap on our heads! You used to be able to trick us, but it doesn't work any more!"[14]

Luckily the elders calm them down. Next day we went to see the Reddiar and the elders of the *ur*. "Sami, our elders! We haven't done anything and yesterday evening Vadivelu the Gounder came to our *ceri*. He threatened to beat us. He insulted us crudely. We had difficulty restraining our boys!"

The Reddiar had the Gounder called straightaway and he gave him a severe telling off, "Innada! You went drinking yesterday and wanted to beat these people: terrified, poor people, hiding like animals in the forest!"

And the Gounder replied, "Innanga! It was because they took the money and then didn't want to vote for me. That's why I went to their homes!"

We left satisfied that the Reddiar had stepped in. That Vadivelu is really the only one who comes and swings his dick in the *ceri*!

Another time, long ago, it was much more serious. I still had my fifth daughter in my arms in those days and there was no water. Our stores of paddy were used up and we had to buy some in the market. I'd go every day to Naliveli, Mangappakkam or Nellipet to collect groundnuts. I couldn't work by day because I had the baby to feed and the owners wouldn't have put up with me stopping like that several times a day. I took the baby with me and simply went and picked up what the day workers had left: little shells or ones that were hard to pick. That would make me between one and three measures at the end of the day which I'd go and sell for three or four rupees. It hadn't rained for months, everything was baked and we were dying of hunger. My father was working in Madras and we decided to go to him to try and find work.

My husband left us there and he started working for a group who were smuggling for a nabob of Cuddalore.[15] They made bootleg alcohol in the villages out of palm sugar, bark, spices and mandarin peel and my husband transported it. He also dealt in cigarettes and gold for the nabob. He was paid twenty-five rupees a day, plus drinks and food. How else could we cope? We had to find something: a measure of rice was so expensive! But once he was caught and he went to prison, after we'd come back to Karani.

It was before an election and every day a car with a loudspeaker came to Karani telling us to vote for the Reddi of Naliveli who was standing against our Reddiar. No one in the *ceri* or the *ur* stopped to listen. The Reddi of Naliveli realized that he couldn't count on our votes and one day the car came to threaten us, demanding that we vote for him; but no one took it seriously, no one believed it. We said to ourselves, "What on earth can he do to our village, and who on earth would really vote for that monkey face?" The elections went off peacefully and we didn't see anybody for two days. And then, one disastrous morning, on the third day when everyone was still at home, we saw a lorry arrive full of good-sized *mattai*. The lorry stopped between the *ceri* and the *ur*. There were only two guys inside. A little later two other lorries drove up full of men. We'd just got up and we hadn't really taken in what was happening. And suddenly all the guys jumped out of their lorries, took the *mattai* and spread out in all directions.

They went into all the houses (*Viramma laughs*), and started beating everybody they came across, smashing the dishes and looting. We tried to flee. The Grand Reddiar and his family left by a car on the lane that goes behind the village. Some, like the Vattiyar's parents, managed to get on the bus and left for Pondy. Others hid in the pond and the trees. It was like an anthill that had been crushed. Everyone ran away. There were plenty of jewels stolen from the *ur*! Two lorries full of men to beat us or kill us! They took us out of the houses, "Dei! You didn't want to vote for us, this is for you!" Luckily my husband wasn't there, or else he would have been beaten as well. I had my daughter in my arms. I was sitting in the sun with the old cobbler, when three guys came up, as large as Bhima, and told him, "Dei, old man! Get up!"

But he said, "How do you expect me to get up, Sami? I'm trembling, I've got old legs!"

They kicked him over, then left for Pakkiam's and said to her, "Aye! Get out of there with your kid, you whore! So you didn't want to vote for us, eh?"

I don't know how I managed. Their punches had completely stunned me. I found myself on the road to Velpakkam without really being aware of it, I was so scared. They'd destroyed and wrecked everything and set fire to the registry office next to the Reddiar's. There wasn't anybody left in the village: not a soul, not a speck of dust. They could loot in peace. Only Rayappan had been seriously wounded. He was taken to Pondy hospital on a stretcher and he stayed there for days. When he came back he was like a Muslim corpse with bandages everywhere! (*Viramma laughs.*)

We came back little by little the next day. The registry office was still burning. Some animals had run away, others were dead. Loads of things were destroyed or stolen. In the *ceri*, all the dishes were broken, the food trampled on, the stores of grain either had holes in them or had been looted. Life was hard because we had to start again with almost nothing.

But, Sinnamma, that Reddi of Naliveli made a quick getaway!

"Where to?"

To *vaikundam*! (*Laughs.*) For two nights and three days, all you could hear was the poor cursing that dog: "I wish that cunt-licker would die! That demon fucker can die with his mouth open! May his line disappear! I hope someone takes off his wife's *tali*!"

And we said to ourselves, "Innanga! Is it just whores in this *ceri* and *ur*? Isn't there a single chaste woman so that at least her curse will be heard?"

Some time later we were working in the Little Reddiar's field and that's when we learned that that Naliveli dog had died of a heart attack! We dropped everything and set off with our children, the women in front. The men came afterwards. When that guy who screws Yama was dead, we wanted him still to hear us and our curses falling on him. They tried to push us back, but there were too many of us wanting to settle the score with him: "Rotten cunt! You sent your men to beat us, but God took care of you sooner than you expected! Make your journey, no one will miss you on this earth!"

Hmm! What a noble man! When he paid his workers, he didn't keep the money in a bag or in the fold of his *soman*: he put it on a spade and threw it on the ground so he could see the day workers knock each other over to pick it up! When he saw Paratchi walking past in the street, he'd shout at them, "Aye! You sister fucker! What are you hanging around here for?" Always words like that. He could afford to leave on a funeral stretcher covered in flowers, but those flowers wilted under our curses! Seeing our anger and all the unrest, the family and politicians decided not to keep the body very long. They brought forward the time of cremation. Everything was rushed and the rites were slapdash. He'll have to wait a long time in that cremation ground before being reborn seven times and ending up impaled: that's what Isvaran can give to creatures like that!

Something like that couldn't happen in this *kaliyagam*, Sinnamma. They come and find us and pay us to vote, and our young ones have put ignorance behind them. The government itself works for us. In the past, the owners made the poor work and gave them their food. They made the law. No one came and asked us what we wanted. And then they wanted us to vote and today, we Pariahs are becoming civilized. There's more people as well than there used to be, more poor, and they are making demands now. For my part, I work for a house which carries a lot of weight and everyone is well off. Thanks to their *dharma*, I live well too. My children are married. I've got grandchildren. I don't go without anything. I live without starving, Sinnamma.

NOTES AND REFERENCES

1. When Viramma or Manikkam say that the Reddiar or the Gounder won an election, they mean the candidate of the party they supported won, rather than that they did so personally. "Vote for a Reddiar" means voting the way he wants. Ballot papers in India contain the symbols of the different parties, the spinning wheel being for a long time the symbol of the Congress Party.
2. Gandhi and Grandpa Gandhi refer to Mahatma Gandhi who entered national politics in 1919—well before Viramma was born—and was assassinated in 1948. Jawaharlal Nehru was the first Prime Minister after Independence, from 1947 until his death in 1964. His daughter Indira Gandhi—no relation of Mahatma Gandhi—was Prime Minister from 1966 to 1977 and from 1980 to 1984, when she was assassinated. Kamaraj was the Congress leader of the state of Madras—subsequently the state of Tamil Nadu—from 1957 to

1963, and then the national President of the Congress Party. No doubt he is called "traitor" because of the split in the party in 1969 when Indira Gandhi broke away from him and his supporters. Annadurai—also known as Ann—founded the DMK, the regionalist Tamil party, in 1949, and in 1967 he became Chief Minister of the state of Madras until his death from cancer in 1969. M. Karunanidhi succeeded him until 1977 when the Anna DMK, founded by M.G. Ramachandran in 1972, won the elections for Legislative Assembly. M.G. Ramachandran's death in 1987 brought M. Karunanidhi back to power from 1989 to 1991, when Jayalalitha and the Anna DMK again won a sweeping victory. M. Karunanidhi and the DMK won again in 1996.

3. A *samadi* is the tomb or cenotaph of a famous person. The "college of the living" is the zoo, "the college of the dead" the museum.

4. Manikkam refers to the period before Independence dominated by the nationalist movement, which was led to a great extent by the Congress Party.

5. Gandhi in fact was assassinated by a Hindu extremist who accused him of having made too many concessions to Muslims and thus opened the way to Partition.

6. Goubert Papa is Edouard Goubert, the representative of French India at the National Assembly in Paris who, in 1953, supported the Congress Party in their demands that the French territories be returned. Chandernagor rejoined India in 1949 and the other trading posts—Pondicherry, Karikal, Mahe and Yanaon—were handed back, de facto, by the Mendes-France government in 1954. The transfer was confirmed *de jure* in 1962 and, despite violence of the sort Manikkam describes, the suggestion that there was a war between India and both France and Great Britain should be understood metaphorically.

7. Members of the Vanniyar caste, essentially farmers and peasants, go under numerous different names—Kudiyanar, Palli, Padaiyatchi, Gounder and even Naicker—and constitute the largest caste in the north of Tamil Nadu. They have formed various political parties: The Farmers and Toilers Party and Commonweal Party in the 1950s and 1960s and, at the 1989 elections, the Pattali Makkal Katchi. Janata was created in North India in 1977 out of the opposition to Indira Gandhi's Congress Party. Janata Dal defeated Rajiv Gandhi in the 1989 elections, and organized the large coalition which was called to power after the election in 1996.

8. P.V. Pariar (the Great) formed the anti Association Dravidians, in 1944: a social reform movement aimed at emancipating the south of India from the hegemony of the north and the higher castes. Members of the DK, led by Annadurai, formed the DMK, a political party with the same principles, in 1949. Etymologically, the Adi-Dravidar are the First Dravidians, perceived as the indigenous population of India, as distinct from the Aryans who settled North India in the third millennium BC, and Dravidians are taken to be the people of South India—the states of Tamil Nadu, Andhra Pradesh, Karnataka and Kerala—who speak one of the Dravidian family of languages. Adi-Dravidar can also be used to mean the Dalits of Tamil Nadu.

9. Mr Subbaiah led the Communist Party in the Territory of Pondicherry before and after the unification with India. The two leaves are the symbol of the Anna DMK.

10. A Union of states, India has two types of assembly; the Legislative Assembly at federal state level and the Parliament, Lok Sabha and Rajya Sabha, at national level. As Manikkam points out, Congress candidates are generally elected as Members of Parliament whilst the DMK and Anna DMK, reflecting their regionalist programme, dominate the Legislative Assembly of Tamil Nadu. The *dharmaraja*, the king of *dharma*, is M.G. Ramachandran, the founder of the Anna D.M.K.
11. The formulation "Adi! ... vadi-podi" conveys a sense of contempt.
12. The ploughmen's party is the Janata Party, whose symbol was once a plough. Two leaves are the symbol of the Anna DMK. The spinning which is the original symbol of the Congress Party which was kept by Old Congress or Congress Organization after the split engineered by Indira Gandhi in 1969. The breakaway party, New Congress or Congress-I, adopted the symbol of the hand. So, when Viramma goes on to describe stamping the hand instead of the rising sun, it means she voted for Congress-I instead of their main rival, the DMK.
13. Village teashops having two sets of glasses—one for the Dalits, another one for higher castes—is a typical example of persistent Untouchability practices. Less discreet is the ban on Dalits entering the temples in the *ur*.
14. "Put a cap on our heads" means to trick, from the popular story in which a traveling salesman falls asleep under a tree with his supply of caps besides him. A troupe of monkeys steal the caps and take them up into the trees. The salesman gets his merchandize back by making a great show of putting on the one cap they've left him. The monkeys then climb down to imitate him and put all the caps on his head.
15. The word "nabob" here means simply that the instigator of the smuggling business was a Muslim based in the town of Cuddalore, which is about twenty kilometers south of Pondicherry.

15

CHADUR AUR DIWARI*

FEHMIDA RIYAZ

Sire! What use is this black chadur to me?
A thousand mercies, why do you reward me with this?

I am not in mourning that I should wear this
To flag my grief to the world
I am not a disease that needs to be drowned in secret darkness.

I am not a sinner, nor a criminal
That I should stamp my forehead with its darkness
If you will not consider me too impudent
If you promise that you will spare my life
I beg to submit in all humility
O Master of Men!
In Your Highness' fragrant chambers
lies a dead body
who knows how long it has been rotting?
It seeks pity from you

Sire, do be so kind
Do not give me this black chadur
With this black chadur cover the shroudless body lying in your chamber
For the stench that emanates from this body
Walks buffed and breathless in every alleyway
Bangs her head on every doorframe
Covering her nakedness

---

*Previously published in a volume by the Pakistan India People's Forum for Peace and Democracy, 1995, entitled, *Other Voices From Pakistan: A Collection of Essays, News Reports and Literary Writings*, pp. 32–33. New Delhi, New Age International Limited.

Listen to her heartrending screams
Which raise strange spectres
That remain naked in spite of their chadurs.
Who are they? You must know them, Sir,
Your Highness must recognize them
These are the handmaidens
The hostages who are "balal" for the night
With the breath of morning they became homeless
They are the slaves who are above
the half-share of inheritance for Your Highness' off-spring

These are the Bibis
Who wait to fulfil their vows of marriage
In turn, as they stand, row upon row.
They are the maidens
On whose heads, when Your Highness laid a hand of paternal affection,
The blood of their innocent youth stained the whiteness of your beard with red
In your fragrant chamber, tears of blood, Life itself has shed
Where this carcass has lain
For long centuries this body spectacle of the murder of humanity

Bring this show to an end now
Sire, cover it up now
Not I, but you need this chadur now
For my person is not merely a symbol of your lust:
Across the highways of life sparkles my intelligence
If a bead of sweat sparkles on earth's brow it is my diligence.
These four walls, this chadur I wish upon the rotting carcass
In the open air, her sails flapping, races ahead my ship

I am the companion of the New Adam
Who has earned my self assured love

Translated by Rukhsana Ahmed

16

DRAWING LINES, ERASING LINES: FEMINISM AS A RESOURCE IN OPPOSING XENOPHOBIA AND SEPARATISM*

Cynthia Cockburn

In this chapter I have in mind those of you who study, teach about and take action within the field of "forced migration". I would like to try and bring a perspective from other places and other times on one factor that occurs in different ways in most conflicts and forced movements of people: and that is *the political manipulation of identity*. While many of you may address mainly the urgent humanitarian issues in the crisis that is "displacement", I shall be standing back to look more at certain political and social processes that lead up to displacement, and that flow from it.

I've called this chapter *Drawing Lines, Erasing Lines*. In forced migrations, people have been literally driven across a line of some kind, have they not—across a mountain range or a river that marks a tribal territory, across a national border, across the line that divides a rural area from a city, or through the wire that fences a camp.

But using the word "line" is also my way of inviting us to look at the lines we first draw in our imaginations, the ideas that later call those material lines into play. Partitions with their checkpoints, the walls of concrete going up in the West Bank today, come to being first in our minds. Refugees, before they were

---

* Based on a lecture delivered by Cynthia Cockburn during the 2004 valedictory session of Calcutta Research Group's Second Winter Course on Forced Migration.

uprooted, were first conceptually placed the wrong side of some social line (a category of persons not wanted, not belonging, dispensable and movable). They've been subject to a process of identification—of differentiation and exclusion from certain categories, the right ethnic group, the right religion, the right economic class—and will eventually have experienced connection and reinclusion into other identity categories labelled "refugee" and "Internationally Displaced Person (IDP)".

In the last few years I've been doing research in the little island of Cyprus, where a total of around 300,000 so-called Turkish and Greek Cypriots were identified, named, set against each other, and finally driven from their homes by force of arms or by fear, to go and live in an ethnically pure part of the island. No, I am wrong—to go and *constitute this*—since no such thing existed before. I've been told many personal stories that illustrate these identity processes in painful reality.

I'm going to argue, something that I learned in Cyprus and in other places, that a certain kind of feminist thinking can be very useful to us in addressing these issues of hatred and exclusion of others. This is because the process of the construction of ethnic difference and that of the construction of gender difference as perceived by feminist theory (I shall come to this in a moment) is similar. In both cases a politics identity is involved.

IDENTITY IN SOCIAL SCIENCE ... AND IN WOMEN'S ACTIVISM

There are a quite a few bodies of literature and learning, and quite a few practices and interventions, in which ideas about identity have been formulated. Each has developed its own particular language for talking about it. Psychologists have one "take" on the subject. Conciliators and conflict managers have another take on it. Philosophers have yet another. Psychologists and psychiatrists often address identity in the individual client. Conflict transformation specialists address identity in collectivities. Philosophers think in more abstract and general terms about personhood. All these, and a lot more, are valid and interesting ways of making sense of why people differentiate and categorize, define and separate themselves and others on the basis of collective "name".

My own take on the subject is grounded in sociology and political science. But much more to the point, it comes from empirical research. In the last ten years I have done a lot of listening to women, specifically women in women's groups in war-devastated regions, talking about themselves and each other: Who do they think they are? Where do they feel they belong? Who do they feel safe with? If they feel alienated—why? Who can they form alliances with—with other women? With men? Which women, which men? And, on what basis? Most of what I have learned about the drawing, crossing and erasing of lines, I have learned from them.

The Contradictory Nature of Identity

I think one reason why identity is such a rich and rewarding theme for study is that it contains inherent and terrible contradictions. Identity is irreducibly unavoidable in human society. Building a sense of self is a necessary part of every person's growing to maturity. A functional human being has to put together step-by-step an internal picture of where she stands, what makes her unique, what connects her to others. (Or him.) So identity is unavoidable—but it is also an *achievement*.

The trouble is, we cannot have identity without difference. And difference is both delight and danger. It is a huge source of pleasure. We fall in love with difference. But we also hate and kill for difference. We seem to have a deep need to belong. But there is no getting away from the fact that every time I say "I belong" I am liable to say someone else does not belong. For every self there's an "other", a non-self. In one sense the process is wonderful—after getting born at all, a baby's first success as a person is recognizing herself as not part of her mother—as a separate being. The contradiction lies in the fact that we are not also born with a guarantee that all identities are going to add up to some harmonious whole.

Some of you may see that I am paraphrasing William Connolly here. His book *Identity/Difference*—some of you may know it well—has been enormously important for me. Of course, I am drawing on a lot of thinkers and writers in this paper and will not burden you by mentioning them one by one. For Conolly, and a handful of other sources that are particularly reflected in this talk, I have given references.

Transcending the Contradiction: Thinking about "Process"

If that was a depressing start on identity, it is important to add right away: there does seem to be a way of transcending the contradictions. We can do it by shifting to a meta-level, above the dichotomy, and working at *process*. There is no avoiding making and marking difference between us. The key political question is *how* we do it, the process, the *mode of differentiation*. We can achieve transformative change in that. I know, because I've seen people doing it.

You do it yourselves, every one of you. Because you work with refugees. You daily confront a group of people with a pejorative label that's used to differentiate them from you. And for sure you have worked hard at the identity process, and learned to see the person in the refugee. You have seen the surprise with which he or she hears that name: me? a refugee? I never imagined I would be one of those! So you know the label is useful to tell you about circumstances, but not about selves.

Lines of differentiation vary in their rigidity. Think of ethnicity—it can be intransigent or relatively flexible, relatively permeable or impermeable. It may be sharply dichotomous, a matter of us and them, or involve pluralities so that one sees oneself as belonging to just one among many comparable communities. The other it separates from the self can be a little different or profoundly different, interestingly different or threateningly different, merely alien or a terrifying enemy.

We can define the other as a collectivity who must be reduced, annihilated, expelled, if we are going to survive. Or we can define them as a collectivity with whom dialogue and engagement is possible and necessary, who may be capable of adapting to our needs if we are capable of adapting to theirs, whose very survival and flowering is necessary if we ourselves are to be fulfilled. (I like to think that way about men and women.)

That calls for a special kind of political imagination, being able to envisage change. I worked for some time with women in Northern Ireland in an alliance of women across particular ethnic identities that have been politicized, fought over and killed for, for three centuries. I once asked Marie Mulholland, who still called herself an Irish nationalist and republican, how she could retain that identification and yet work constructively with women who called themselves Protestant Unionists. She said "it's because I can imagine a future when those names won't mean the same thing". She lived identity as provisional, not essential. As contingent necessity, not as truth.

Feminist Thought as a Tool: Gender and Other Kinds of "Other"

Feminism at its best is a way of thinking that transcends the contradiction of identity.

I realize that I need to be very clear here, that there is not only one kind of feminism. Unfortunately, the term "feminism" is applied to a lot of different theories and practices. For instance, essentialists who think women are all different from (and even superior to) men call themselves feminists. So do women who want to individually climb the career ladder, in business, the state or the armed services—to get equal with men, uncritical of the world they are aspiring to join and neglectful of the women they leave behind.

So I have to specify which feminism I'm talking about here. What I mean by it, very briefly, is: a collective feminism, with a project of transformative change, that perceives oppressively interlocking dimensions of power in all of which gender is implicated. It is a feminism that sees the world we live in as bad for men as well as women, and its institutions, not as things we want to get control of but, as things we want to dismantle and reshape. That is the sense in which I will be using the word "feminism".

From this perspective, gender differentiation, like ethnic differentiation, is a political project that involves drawing a line between people conceived of as types, reductive, inescapable categories. By "political" I mean that it involves power, purpose and collective action. The patriarchal gender order, like the ethnopolitical order, involves the exploitation of certain material facts together with stories from the past, to dichotomize men and women and to create privilege and dependency.

Feminism (defined this way) is a critique of the politics of gender identity—it perceives that *different modes* of gender differentiation are possible. We see it in everyday life: we see that different forms of masculinity and femininity exist within a given culture. One may be hegemonic—let's say the military man, or the successful entrepreneur, others are clearly subordinated or marginal—the "subaltern" masculinity of colonized people, disabled men.

Some masculinity/feminity dyads, couples, may be more dichotomous than others. A man may have a lot invested in a masculinity that is sharply differentiated from femininity. It could be he is proud of embodying, or trying to attain, qualities he and others in his culture admire as specifically masculine. On the other hand, he might startle traditional opinion by distancing himself from the cultural norm of masculinity. He might value some other qualities that he finds in himself. He may look on a woman not as someone complementary to himself but as, actually *like* him, a member of a category called "people" whose senses-of-self are infinitely varied and mostly do not fit the binary gender norm.

In our Women in Black (WiB) group in London, we were surprised to hear of other Women in Black groups that include men. But I understand this better, having just spent a week with Women in Black in Belgrade. In Serbia, from the start of the Yugoslav wars, there was a partnership between the women and some men who refused to fight in nationalist wars. They sheltered deserters and the men in turn helped them in a lot of ways. The men who were "let in" to the circle of WiB, so to speak, were admitted not on the basis of gender but of values—they were those who understood and supported feminism as well as antimilitarism. They saw the patriarchal system as implicated in the pressures on them, as men, to be soldiers, to be loyal to an exclusive masculine and nationalist identity.

Currently there is a young man living in a small room at the back of the WiB office in Belgrade. He is gay, as it happens. But I learned something important from him and the women he works with. Just as ethnicity, being Serb, Muslim, Croat is *not the point* in that space (what is the point is being anti-sexist, anti-xenophobic and antimilitarist), so in that space being gay or heterosexual is *not the point* (the point is being anti-homophobic). It is the values, not the identities, which count when you choose your allies. I will come back to this crucial point.

IDENTITY AND SENSE OF SELF

To think about identity in this way, at a political and social level, in relation to armed conflict, war and expulsions, calls for a particular way of conceiving of identity at the micro-level, the individual self. I need to say a little about this. I am sure you are familiar with this kind of thinking. Not so long ago the prevailing belief was that in each human being there is a pre-existing identity. The task of the child, the parent, the teacher, is to discover this kernel and nurture it. Today we are more inclined to use a metaphor that works better, to think of the self as a production, something composed like music, written like a book, always *in process*, never complete.

We (I mean in the social sciences) also emphasize more today that the way the person takes shape and changes over time is *relational*. There is no specification of selfhood we can even think of that does not have reference to other people, people we know or people we imagine. And since the world around us involves a lot of different kinds of relationship, the self is very *complex*, it is shaped through not one but a whole variety of attachments.

Selfhood also involves a tussle between the choice, the *agency*, of the individual and the demands and constraints of the social and political world around her. The state models the idea of the proper citizen, the military of a proper man, the church of a proper woman. "Models" is not strong enough: they project, propagandize these identities. The advertisers suggest a proper teenage identity, or a desirable middle class lifestyle. Your peers project a sense of what you should look like in order to be one of us. Your neighbours or compatriots or fellow churchgoers make clear what kind of a person is worthy of "our culture" or "our religion" or "our people".

In fact, I find it useful to keep the word "*identity*" for these projections, representations, voices and images, that address, call out to, persuade us from the social world. I prefer to think on the other hand of me or you having simply a "*sense of self*"—something painfully and provisionally achieved by negotiating, accepting, falling prey to, modifying, rewriting or refusing the names on offer. I do not think we can ever talk confidently about a *person's* identity. We cannot guess how many names and which names go to make up a real-life complicated person. Even less can we make an assumption about how any collective name is actually lived and felt.

How Freely Do We Constitute Ourselves?

Of course each of us exerts our agency partly free but partly bound. The factors that limit an individual's agency derive partly from the social formation she lives in. Before a gay rights movement has occurred and been named, a woman can hardly identify as a lesbian. If she calls herself anything it is likely to be a freak, a misfit, a discontent.

Likewise, where an ethnic group has not conceived of a national project, its members won't feel a national identification. In the Yugoslav republic of Bosnia before 1989, people who are today called Bosnian Muslims were much more likely to think of themselves as undifferentiated Yugoslavs. It was the upsurge of aggressive nationalism in Serbia and Croatia that evoked, at a certain definable moment, a responding Bosnian Muslim national project and a Bosniak identity that some, but not all, then took on as part of their changing sense of self. I remember a friend called Nudzjema telling me how it was only when she was being attacked as a Muslim she began to feel herself a Muslim.

The factors limiting agency are also a question of individual circumstance. Whether a person is born into wealth or poverty, count for a lot. So does her education and her work, how mobile she is, whether she has children or not (if she is not actually a "mother" she may be less prone to respond to appeals to identify with "motherhood"). Contingencies like this will suggest some identifications and rule out others.

The Manipulation of Identity in War

In studies of Forced Migration I imagine we are very often looking at wars, at armed conflict anyway. And I think maybe we need to think a bit about the extent of the role of identity processes in war. It is important not to overstate their importance. Especially it is important not to see identity always as a *cause* of war, as opposed to a manifestation of it.

First, some wars, or all wars to some extent, are about economic power and control—they are wars for valuable resources (like oil reserves) and for strategic territories—like vulnerable frontier regions. Other wars, maybe all wars to some extent, are about the power of certain elites who benefit from the political control they have, or hunger for the control they might gain. Identity may have relatively little to do with such wars — at the start anyway.

I think this may be the case in Colombia today. It is a country where women have begun to organize on an impressive scale to bring an end to violence. In that region there *is* ethnic difference—there are people of mainly Spanish origin, people mainly of African origin, and indigenous tribes of South America. But these are not the groups fighting each other. In fact, all three groups suffer. The violence the women are campaigning against is not ethnic, but a three-sided political conflict. There are left-oriented guerrilla forces that originated in a movement for social justice several decades ago but who have lost a lot of popular support due to the means they use. There are the paramilitaries, who fight the guerrillas. They are effectively private armies of the drug barons and serve the interests of the rich and the right-wing. And third, there is the state, backed by the USA's anti-narcotics policy. The Army is brutally repressive and punish the population for the sins of the guerrillas—while some of Army units are suspiciously close to the paramilitaries.

The effects of war on Colombian women are terrible. They say that war has deformed everyday life and is using women's bodies as booty. The slogans of the women's alliance *La Ruta Pacifica* are "Neither war that kills us nor peace that oppresses us" and "We won't bear sons or daughters for war."

But you don't have in Colombia collectivities of different cultures, different religions, different names who hate each other so much that they will wage war for their identity alone, for "history". Not at all. On the other hand, the Yugoslav wars do look on the face of it as if they were caused by ethnic identity. But I think even here stories about "ancient animosities", in Yugoslavia and in other places, when you look closer, does not hold up.

I learned a lot about this from a colleague Dubravka Zarkov. I remember being really surprised when I first heard her say "violence is productive". At first I could not accept it. Surely violence is essentially destructive? But of course! She showed me how the problem for the political elites in Serbia and Croatia had been that there was not *enough* ethnic difference in Yugoslavia in the 1980s to suit their ambitions—which were that each would control an undisputed nation-state inside unchallengeable borders. There was too much intermarriage going on! How could you create a Serbian state or a Croatian state out of people who not only could not tell an Orthodox church from a Catholic one, but did not bother to go to church at all? How could you make war against Muslims if they won't read the Koran and go to the mosque? We have to remind everyone "who they really are".

The war was designed to do just that. You do not forget who you are if you have seen your friends and relatives massacred in a given name, by people of another given name. The women of the Association of Mothers of Srebrenica and Zepa who are looking for the bodies of the 10,000 men and 600 women murdered there by extremist Serbs, are not in any doubt now that they are Bosnian Muslims. The war has been productive. War has produced ethnicity.

But what Dubravka and I went on to explore together was how war produces gender too—proper active warrior men, proper victimized submissive women. And how, in patriarchal terms, it is designed for that, it is productive in that way too. Simultaneously, while it is establishing proper ethnic lines, it is drawing proper gender lines too, through rape, for instance. It does not work smoothly. It runs into contradictions, because women sometimes have to take on "masculine" responsibilities when men leave to fight. But the effect of periods of militarization, overall, is to reinforce complementary and unequal gender relations.

So identities may not be the cause of a war but creating "otherness" is almost always among its tools and its products.

THE DANGERS OF IDENTITY POLITICS

Domination, whether it is imperialist domination, state authoritarianism, the systemic subordination of women in the patriarchal family, or heterosexism in society, has the tendency to call into being resistance movements that appeal to an identity: anticolonialist insurgencies in the name of a colonized people—let us say Palestine today; nationalist movements in the name of minorities that are not allowed to express their cultures within the state—like Cataluna in Spain; women in a movement of women's liberation; lesbians and gays, bisexuals and transsexuals protesting against the tyranny of compulsory heterosexuality. There is a logic and legitimacy to this because the ruling entity has spoken in a universalist language that claims the only truth and obliterates all other speech, a singular experience that is blind to all other realities.

The trouble with political movements based on the interests of an identity-group is two-fold. First, such groups tend to be themselves, exclusive of other groups. And second they tend to "paint themselves into a corner": their identity becomes fixed and essentialized, members of the category become that and only that. The actual fluidity, multiplicity, complexity and ambiguity that would describe our individual senses of ourselves is denied. This applies absolutely as much to the identity group "woman" as an identity group like "Irish Catholic" or "Croat" or "Jew".

It is just another expression of the contradiction of identity—we need it but it harms us. The challenge, some feminists would say, is to find ways of recognizing multiplicity within and without the named identity. Women come in a lot of different kinds: we differ in our relation to the family; in our class; in our sexuality; in our cultural attachments. We need to acknowledge this and, while not letting go of the name "woman", not take it for granted but rather take pains to work out what it may mean in any given circumstances.

The same applies in terms of ethnic name: "Palestinian" for instance. In Palestine there are both Muslims and Christians, there are more and less exclusive and rigid forms of both religions. There are Beduin and settled Arabs. Some "Palestinians" are "women", and women and men experience the Occupation in gender-specific ways. And there is not a straightforward dichotomy Israeli Jew v. Palestinian Muslim/Arab, as some might invoke. Because there are Palestinians living in Israel, there are Arab Jews (the Misrahim) and so on.

DEALING WITH IDENTITY IN OUR OPPOSITION TO WAR

The most effective kinds of movement then, have to be alliances of very varied people based, not on identity, but on political and moral values. And this is the practical issue for us, isn't it. How do we organize? Identity is a cause of a lot of suffering and struggle for each of us, and we can see it is playing a part in the conflicts all around us, and in the lives and chances of the displaced people you work with. So it matters quite a lot how we "do identity" and "think identity" in our political work, our organizations and our strategies for change.

I have learned most about this from women in Northern Ireland, who are among the most skilled I have met in negotiating identity in the midst of armed conflict. Women of Protestant Unionist and Catholic Republican backgrounds were working together by means of a group *process* that (as we mentioned earlier in this talk) transcends the contradiction, the trap, of identity. The process involved affirming identity—not denying it but acknowledging it. "Yes, I'm a Catholic. I am a Republican and believe in a united Ireland." But at the same time others of different identifications would be very careful not to make assumptions about it, not foreclose on it—instead waiting to see which of innumerable meanings this individual might ascribe to the name she acknowledges, the many ways she might live it, the many ways it might change.

They looked beneath the identity for the surer ground they might find for working together—political and moral values in common, a willingness to acknowledge past injustices. Being women gave them a certain commonality. But that needed deconstructing too. It was the values of equality, inclusion, nonviolence and justice in addressing both gender oppression and ethnicized conflict that could enable them to create a reliable alliance.

When I was with the women in Belgrade last month they were organizing a seminar between women living in Serbia and women of both Bosnian Serb and Bosnian Muslim communities living in Bosnia. A lot of their talk together hinged around distinguishing between "responsibility" and "guilt" for ethnicized aggression. Acknowledging that certain things were "done in my name", in my identity, facing up to them, asking what I might have done to prevent it, they were saying, is important. One woman said, with great honesty, for instance:

> Only when my *own* husband was to be called up, then I supported his refusal to serve and went out in the street myself to demonstrate

against the war. But I ask myself now, why only then, when I was *personally* affected? Why not before?

But at the same time it is not productive to take on collective guilt just because you bear a certain name. It is not easy to bear the identity of a people that do crimes. Another woman at this seminar said, "For years I have been ashamed of saying I am from Serbia, because of collective guilt." "Guilt" is terrible to bear and it often leads to more anger and more violence. What these women helped each other to see is that the single most important step out of the trap of collective guilt is to be clear about your values, about your responsibility and then to identify the actual criminals who committed atrocities and call for their prosecution.

WHY FEMINISM IS USEFUL IN COUNTERACTING XENOPHOBIA

The reason I think feminism (defined as I have defined it in this talk) is a useful resource in counteracting xenophobia, racism, and aggressive and exclusive versions of nationalism is like this....

In one way, many exclusions and oppressions have a certain similarity, in that they involve an identity process in which the collective self is constituted in opposition to an alien, inferior and dangerous "other". A line has been drawn between the self and that other. Over there, the other side of the line, it has to be contained and subordinated. At the same time, any reflections of the "other" remaining in the self have to be censored.

In this sense gender relations and ethnic relations are similar and connected. We see it in the way in which patriarchy defines women arbitrarily as (variously) weak, inferior, natural, emotional etc. and categorized as "not men", while the feminine qualities in men are punished. It is a parallel with the way Muslims in the Western world today, especially since 11 September 2001, are defined as dangerous, as an "other" civilization, and the Muslim minority within the state are repressively policed.

A feminist understanding of identity has a particular take on gender: we argue that it is socially constituted, that it is fluid and various, open to different interpretations, subject to strong pressures from outside the self and often problematic for the self. Anyone, any feminist, understanding this, surely understands that ethnic, cultural, religious or national identities are socially constituted too. There is nothing essential, given or fixed about them, any more than about masculinity or femininity. She is also likely to see that each person lives her gender in an ethnicized way—we are always not just a woman but a woman who has to deal one way or another with "being" a Serb, an English woman, or an Indian. And each person lives an ascribed ethnicity in a gendered way. Someone says "Turk", for instance. You may feel like asking: a Turkish man or a Turkish woman? Especially given what Turkish feminist Ayse Gul Altinay is telling us in her new book about how Turkish boys are brought up to be the soldier heroes of a military nation.

I learned a lot about this, studying the situation of women in Cyprus. I mentioned earlier how the Partition of Cyprus in 1974 produced huge forced migrations. They have lived a further three decades thinking of each other as the enemy and teaching their children to find their selfhood in the hatred of that dangerous "other". In 2002, a bi-communal women's group, called "Hands Across the Divide", got together, to call for an end to Partition. But people asked them: Why women? What have women got to say about this political (that is: men's) issue?

Well, for one thing, they could see that the partition process, which happened at a point in history when a line was drawn on a map, but continues to happen each and every day in the lines scored in people's heads, was the creation of elite men in twin communities that were not only ethnic hierarchies but gender hierarchies. Thinking as *women* they might have said (and indeed they did also say): "women suffer in a gender specific way in this interminable 'cold war' and we want change". But thinking as *feminists* they were able to say "there's something wrong here with the system of power". There is absolutely nothing illogical about women, as feminists, challenging a partition that's not a gender partition but an ethnicized one. Of course, there is a gender partititon too. The line between men and women runs through our parliament and political parties, our workplaces, our schools and our families. We challenge that. But the process that sustains ethnicized partition is the same *process* (feminists were saying) that sustains the gender partition. Political partition is a gendered phenomenon. What we want rid of is this power system and its whole mode of differentiation.

So the thrust of this talk has been that gender processes as well as ethnic and other identity processes, are at work in war and armed conflict, partition and separatism. A feminist gender analysis is relevant to war and peace in a way that war-makers and even peace-makers do not often recognize. I suggest that all of us, whether we identify as women or men, gay or straight, Hindu or Moslem—or whether quite precisely our sense of self resides in defying and reworking all such categories—will be more politically effective for "doing feminism".

REFERENCES

Afshar, Haleh and Mary Maynard (eds). 1994. *The Dynamics of "Race" and Gender: Some Feminist Interventions.* London: Taylor & Francis.

Brah, Avtar, Mary J. Hickman and Mairtin Mac an Ghaill (eds). 1999. *Thinking Identities: Ethnicity, Racism and Culture.* London: Macmillan Press.

Cockburn, Cynthia. 1998. *The Space Between US: Negotiating Gender and National Identities in Conflict.* London and New York: Zed Books.

Cockburn, Cynthia. 2004. *The Line: Women, Partition and the Gender Order in Cyprus.* London and New York: Zed Books.

Cockburn, Cynthia and Dubravka Zarkov. 2002. *The Postwar Moment: Militaries, Masculinities and International Peacekeeping.* London: Lawrence and Wishart.

Connolly, William E. 1991. *Identity/Difference: Democratic Negotiations of Political Paradox.* Ithaca and London: Cornell University Press.

Hall, Stuart and Paul du Gay (eds). 1996. *Questions of Cultural Identity.* London, Thousand Oaks, New Delhi: Sage Publications.

Rutherford, Jonathan (ed.). 1990. *Identity: Community, Culture, Difference.* London: Lawrence and Wishart.

Yuval-Davis, Nira. 1997. *Gender and Nation.* London, Thousand Oaks, New Delhi: Sage Publications.

17

IN CONVERSATION WITH DR HANAN ASHRAWI[1]

Aditi Bhaduri[2]

Tell me something about yourself.

I was born in Ramallah in Palestine, in a Christian family, just before the establishment of the state of Israel. My parents are originally from Ramallah but they went to Tiberias in 1948 and then moved to Jordan and then again came back to Ramallah. So they are refugees as well as people of the land. My education was in the American schools and then in the American University in Beirut and my PhD was from the University of Virginia in English Literature and in Comparative Literature. I lived a very sheltered life till I went to Beirut, where I saw the state of the refugees and then, in 1967, I became involved in the General Union of Palestine Students and I worked very hard for the elections in 1969 and in which I continue to be involved. I am married to Emile Ashrawi, a Muslim and I have two daughters. I have done a lot of work, much of which is academic.

I established the Department for English in Birzeit University. I was Dean for the Faculty for some time. Then I established the Legal Aid Programme as well as the Human Rights Information Campaign at the Birzeit University. I was quite an activist—I was arrested several times, detained, tried. I escaped many assassination attempts. (*Laughs*). When the first Intifadah started, we established the underground Political Committee, in the late 1980s and then we established the diplomatic committee to meet with international envoys. Then we launched the peace process, we negotiated. I was with Feisal Husseini, the negotiator with the Americans to launch the peace process. I was a member of the media committee

It was the peace process that made you known to the world. So what happened to it?

We fell into the Israeli trap of separating the territorial issues from the functional issues and so we took the functional approach, separating the people from the land and entered into a gradual approach, a gradualism that was not necessarily incremental and which allowed Israel to position itself in a way as to be the sole arbiter and, therefore, to place the Palestinians on probation all the time. There was a lot of foreign politics, an absence of mechanism for arbitration, for accountability for the Israelis and for protection of the Palestinians. It became a very primitive process, particularly given that there was a lot of ill-will on the part of Israel and a lack of impartial, even-handed commitment and involvement on the part of the US and the international community.

So has Oslo failed, is it dead, do you need to move on?

Well, let's say that the worst in the Declaration of Principles (DOP) and I don't even call it Oslo, has been exploited by Israel and its flaws have come back to haunt us and the worst has been exploited. You cannot say it failed entirely, it did fail in the major issues but realities were created on the basis of the DOP and you cannot undo those realities which (Ariel) Sharon is trying to do, he is trying to unravel the realities of the previous peace process and prevent the emergence of a new one.

By realities you mean...

Like the leadership coming back, the Palestinian Liberation Organisation (PLO) recognition, then the very limited and fragmented control over some of the Palestinian territories. But to implement that agreement we need a lot of goodwill and even-handedness that don't exist and so Israel exploited the flaws in order to avoid the necessary steps.

Many people I have spoken to—ordinary people—in different towns and villages in the West Bank—many told me that life under occupation had been easier than what life turned out to be under the Palestinian Authority (PA) rule.

Well, you can't compare apples and oranges. I think the difficulty now is that the occupation now has taken on a new phase, a new form. There is a buffer zone between us and the occupation—it's the Authority and the security systems and of course the Authority made many mistakes—especially violations of human rights and accountability and mis-management and I have always said that self-inflicted wounds are more painful. But at the same time a great deal of the pain is the fact that this occupation—the nature of the new Israeli occupation is much more brutal than the earlier one. Now you have multiple sieges, you have strangulation; you have the destruction of economy and massive settlement policy, an assassination policy, an assault against all Palestinian civilians regardless. So the occupation has become much worse. So, Palestinians feel doubly victimized now.

There have been charges of corruption against the PA. You yourself resigned as Minister of Higher Education....

I refused my re-appointment; let me put it that way. Questions of mis-management and corruption, of a lack of respect of the rule of law and violation of human rights. These are issues that are basic, there is no compromise on these issues, no justification. However, even given that, in comparison with other countries (in the Middle East) we are not that bad. But still we can do much better and I don't believe that anybody is above the law or above accountability. And it is up to us to create systems of accountability, and to prevent corruption from becoming the prevailing law.

So these things we have to work on and at the same time the signed agreements give rise to greater violations and corruption and that is something that has to be dealt with seriously because there has been a devaluation of Palestinian lives and rights as a result of the occupation and as a result of the adopting of the priorities of Israel in the peace process, where there is a total disregard for Palestinian rights and total commitment for Israeli security, leading to the distortion of internal realities.

And has it led to the compromise in the PA's credibility in the eyes of the world also?

That is right. That's extremely serious because these shortcomings and violations have tainted the Palestinian cause; our cause has its own integrity and should not be measured in accordance with the shortcomings of the individuals of the leadership. This is very unfair, this is undermining the cause, on the basis of the behaviour of the few. But what gives me hope in this situation is that there is a very strong sense of rectification, of reform amongst the people, a very strong drive not to accept this type of the behaviour. And this is a necessary step to begin with.

Many feel that the AL Aqsa Intifadah was directed more at the Palestinian Authority than at the Israeli occupation.

NO, I think the most direct part of it was at Israeli occupation, but part of the feelings of injustice, anger, frustration came as a result of the behaviour of the Authority.

But very few Palestinians are happy, the Al Aqsa Intifadah has actually not brought anything to them in concrete terms. We see that the main damage has been caused by the suicide bombers and we see that almost all of them (bombers) belong to depressed backgrounds, not the children of rich or qualified Palestinians. So many think that there are vested interests because the common man had nothing to gain and it's been over a year.

Since the signing of the DOP we lost more land, the Israelis confiscated more land, our economy went downhill and people lost more freedom. So, it's a very primitive and hateful peace process. But the Intifadah is part of it, you cannot look at it in isolation. Feelings of anger, desperation were building up. There were pent-up feelings of victimization which led to the reaction of Intifadah. Now, as always, I have advocated non-violence Intifadah. Frankly, I have never been not just comfortable or happy, but supportive of any type of violent actions because this is precisely what Israel wants. As a people under occupation, as I said, there is an integrity and moral dimension to our struggle for freedom and we cannot adopt the methods of the occupation. I have always said that if they have targeted our civilians it does not mean that we should target theirs. If we condemn what they do to us it does not give the license for us to do the same to them and in many ways the sense of frustration and anger came up in a combination of factors—economic, social as well as political. A feeling of being hunted, imprisoned, deprived, victimized. Its true—I don't want to discuss HAMAS or Islamic Jihad—but the suicide bombings have made the people doubly victimized, first of all the bombers themselves. I think of them as being victims, and I don't believe that they should have been ... persuaded, if you please, into doing that.

Brainwashed ... ??

(*Laughs.*) I don't believe extremist ideological arguments are conducive to any kind of constructive behaviour.

Once you start an absolutist argument—Jewish or Muslim or Christian—and then you invoke God and you feel you have absolute right and then you try to justify whatever you do. So extremism on the Israeli side certainly encouraged extremism on the Palestinian side. And I know that many people feel that it's their children who are suffering and not the children of the privileged. That's true. The Palestinian people as a whole have paid a big price. The Intifadah in itself has good points and bad points. Some advantages and disadvantages and its time we are honest enough and forthright enough to address and rectify the shortcomings of it.

We know about the disadvantages but what are the advantages you speak of?

For one it solidified the cohesive internal front. Next, it tried to at least expose the nature of the occupation and the fallacy of the Sharon plan that we can subdue a people by violence; that you can escalate repression and brutality and the Palestinian people will behave like sheep, will go to their death gladly. It sent a message that the Palestinian people will not accept subjugation and enslavement and at the same time the Intifadah to me is not only the violence. The Intifadah is the spirit of the people that refuses this subjugation and oppression.

Is there a rift forming between Christian Palestinians and Muslim Palestinians, again because many of the villages like Beit Jala, which have a predominantly Christian population, have been used as shields by Islamic militants to shoot and fire at Jewish settlements. At the same time, I have spoken to many Christian Palestinians who do not believe in these kinds of attacks and suicide bombings.

Certainly, no one will support this. But I do not believe this is a Christian–Muslim rift, it's a political decision. Addressing the suicide bombings, for example, it's not determined by religion. I know there are many Muslims who are against it as well, so it's not a Christian–Muslim divide. And Beit Jala has, of course, been targeted by the Israelis for a long time because, at one point, Israeli officials said we have to remove Beit Jala to make way for Gilo. So in many ways they try to impose a settlement on the land of Beit Jala and then they try to make life impossible for Beit Jala so that they can remove the whole town if possible in the service of illegal settlements.

That was used as an example, the people who shot from Beit Jala were certainly not Beit Jala people. But it does not mean that the divide is religious, it happened in Ramallah, it happened in other places where gunmen will start shooting from neighbourhoods, from inhabited areas and Israelis will use it as a pretext to shell the whole area. Israel has been trying for a long time to create this religious divide but I can assure you that historically this has never happened and this will not happen. Palestinian Christians view themselves as part and parcel of the Palestinian national identity and Christianity is one of the oldest and most authentic traditions and part of the authenticity of our identity.

We represent the oldest Christian tradition of the world and we have been Palestinian since day one and so there is no conflict between being a Palestinian and a Christian. And Palestinian society has always been pluralistic and tolerant. In times of conflict and crisis, of course, people start feeling that there are problems here and there, but it's nothing that cannot be solved. And I would not go so far as to say there is any kind of divide. Particularly, since it's a matter also not just of tradition and culture but of official policy. There should be no discrimination, no distinction.

What kind of a state would Palestine be?

It should be a democratic state, we are working on that. A state that is open, but that will adopt market economy but that, internally, has a constitution that is fair, modern, contemporary, global, that will be just to its people, that will respect pluralism, a tolerant state that will respect human rights and women's rights. A state that is democratic in practice, based on a system of governance and real active democracy. That will not happen by default, it's a challenge—very difficult but we have to keep working at it and lets say it will be a model in the region. It will be a state that will set a different tone.

It will not be an Islamic state?

Oh no, I don't believe any state should be defined and guided by religious principles.

You have a new responsibility now—spokesperson of the Arab League.

Well, I refuse to be a spokesperson. I opt for information and public policy and I limited my role to just preparing policy and so on.

But in your part of the world you are the only woman in Arab politics, who is known. I mean we see pictures of Queen Rania but she is not so active.

Well, I did not gain my position because I married somebody, or I am somebody's daughter. Actually, we have an active women's movement in Palestine. Yesterday I was having a meeting with the Women's Coalition for Peace. We have a long standing women's movement dating back to the 1920s, well before Israel was created. In the 1970s we formulated the gender agenda. We have different groups, I do not work alone—no woman can. We don't need only the support system but we need the collective input. The individual woman should not be used as an excuse to exclude other women; there should be empowerment of other women.

But Palestinian society is still a very patriarchal society, women having so many children and the population being small statistically the number of such women is big, but that of those active in public life is small.

We are a traditional society, largely patriarchal and male dominated society. But we also have a strong women's movement with a clear gender agenda. We don't have enough women in the Parliament or in the Government but we have very strong women in political movement, civil society, grass roots organisations. And we are working. I mean, during the earlier Intifadah, the women were at the forefront of the political struggle, national struggle, even the economic struggle. Now, because of the militarization of the Intifadah—it reflects the patriarchal system—there has been an attempt to exclude women. But we will not allow this and we are working with the empowerment of women. It does not mean that we have overcome all the traditional norms and patterns of behaviour and sources of power and authority but we are challenging them, that's the important thing. We are trying to provide alternatives and we are trying to legislate for parity and non-discrimination.

With reference to your new role in the Arab League, how effective has the League been with regard to the Palestinian issue?

Not very, I am afraid. The Arab League, when it has come to Arab issues, has certainly failed to meet the challenges historically. Even though it predates the European Union (EU), for example, and it's a regional organisation, which also predates the United Nations (UN). Unfortunately it always succumbs to internal Arab rivalries and rifts and does not have a will of its own. It reflects all the short comings and weaknesses of its member states and that's why it needs a qualitative shift in its attitudes, in its internal bylaws and the way it perceives itself, but it cannot, in a sense, move way ahead of the nature of Arab states themselves. And the problem with Arab states we all know—it's the nature of the regime, centralized systems, the people have not understood the imperatives of the transition to democracy and the will of law. And unfortunately, there has been no system of accountability, so people can fail, leaderships and regimes can fail time and time again and still maintain themselves in power. So, the Arab League has reflected the rivalries, the rifts, and the failures of the individual states.

I do believe that Amr Moussa is trying to make something new of it, but, frankly, I don't think it can fall back far away from the nature of the Arab system. So we do need to see major reform within the Arab world and it seriously needs democracy in order to empower the Arab League as the cohesive framework of the Arab world.

Do you see any major changes in the Arab world in the new future?

If the Arab world does not change by its own will, it will be changed. If there is no peaceful transition to democracy it will take place violently and I believe that there is a public opinion in the Arab world that is simmering, that is ready to boil over and it should be addressed. There's a new discourse, a new message is coming out from the Arab public opinion and there is a demand for serious reform and serious democratization. Again, it will not happen by default or by itself, there has to be an active movement, the political parties networking. The Arab world has to be part of the contemporary world; it cannot keep falling short, falling behind. There is no room in history for all those who fall by the wayside.

How would you be using your involvement with the Arab League to forward the Palestinian cause?

Well, it's not just a matter of public presentation, in terms of communication and media and public policy. There is also a matter of political decision-making and that's what makes the difference. You cannot have a public policy and a public discourse if you do not have any public debate or any policy and the decision-making that will make the presentation credible. Actually I have contributed to the Arab League rather than the Arab League having contributed to the Palestinian cause. I have prepared the policy, the plan with the objectives, with the work plan, the programmes with the agenda, the new structure, the budget, the message that should be adopted collectively by the Arabs. Now there has to be a political will and a real will to adopt this plan and implement it. That is the real test that remains to be seen. But I cannot contribute more than my time and know-how. So far I have not seen the political will, not just to adopt this plan, but to implement it.

And would you also be sending out any message to women in the Arab world?

We are doing that anyway. We do not need to be in the Arab League to do that. And I am not an employee of the League, all the work is voluntary. With the Arab women we are trying to create a gender network, with all the women's organisations that have a clear gender perspective and are feminist, if you wish, not in terms of a symbolic ritualistic thing like they have in the Arab women's summit where they invited the wives of the leaders. I don't see that as summit. A summit is of women who are themselves leaders and not somebody's wife or daughter. So that has to be done. We do networking and also try to work with Arab women, to empower Arab women to also extend the process to other women. To me the issue of women's rights is part and parcel of the human rights issue and the democracy issue. This is the way you gauge the accomplishment and participation of women in society. So we have to work within this comprehensive and integrated approach. Women's rights are not just the real test but the real requirement for a human rights and democratic agenda.

What does your organization MIFTAH aim to do?

WE work on two things simultaneously. Internally we work on democracy, human rights and law, democratization, reform, nation building, accountability but we also work on an agenda that is based on global engagement and networking with others. So we have an international dimension, a global dimension—networking with others, being part of this global agenda and trying to also present the Palestinian question and Palestinian realities in a way that will be honest and persuasive and to engage others while we are working internally on democratization and reform.

Do you network with any Indian organization?

Unfortunately, no. I have been invited several times to India but I have been trying to enter into a network, but we are beginning slowly and we are beginning with a ripple impact from Palestine to the Arab world. India, as the largest democracy and with its long-standing traditions, has to be engaged but we are presently working in concentric circles. We are starting with Palestinian-Arab and then moving. We do have more Western focus and networks and (are) working on the US because we believe that there have been serious moves to undermine Palestinian realities, particularly, given the nature of the peace process. So we focus on areas now that will affect and have a real impact on that.

When I talk to most of the Palestinians, I find that their perception of India is limited mostly to Indian films, and India's conflict with Pakistan. None of the people I know till now are aware that India was the first non-Arab state to recognize the PLO as the sole representative of the Palestinian people, way back in the 1960s. Also most Palestinians seem to be unaware of India's long-standing support for the Palestinian cause or the aid and cooperation rendered by India to the Palestinians.

We know that historically there have been great ties with India, even with the PLO, and which ever Government had been in power and not just Indira Gandhi's. We know there had been serious friendships and support and solidarity. I don't think Palestinians take stand on the basis of religion, Pakistan or otherwise. I think what has happened is that first, there is a lack of sufficient information available to the public. This is both a short coming of the Indian side as well as our side. I think the representative offices should be more active in terms of presenting the reality and nature of relations. Now everybody is talking on the basis of religious developments, everybody is seeing that there is a closer link between India and Israel and that the USA is trying to create a military cooperation like it did with Turkey. And now it is doing with India. That is apparent because it comes from Israel through Israel, so people tend to become suspicious of India without knowing the background and long history of solidarity and friendship.

So these things are not taught in schools, even as part of Palestinian history?

No, because we never started teaching Palestinian history. Under occupation all the days, when there were strong solidarity or ties, we were teaching either Egyptian history or Jordanian textbooks. We never had any Palestinian textbook, we had all our material in the press and the press was under Israeli censorship. So it is only now that we are beginning to have Palestinian texts. Nothing taught in the schools was Palestinian frankly, because under direct occupation by Israel we were not allowed to have our own text books, we were not allowed to use the term "Palestinian" that time, to have our own textbooks, or teachers on history or culture. This is all now beginning. But now people read the papers, they see what's happening, they judge only by the latest development that India is moving closer to the US and the US is trying to create links for Israel, particularly in military terms, with India and we heard some Indian voices talking about India should do to Pakistan what Israel is doing to Palestine. This created a negative backlash because you take this statement alone, you don't understand that our relations are different, even though there are now attempts to drive a wedge between us, but this is not the case. On the contrary, we have always advocated that India should be in the Security Council because we felt that that would be our safeguard as Palestinians. Instead of having the results of the Second World War super-imposed on the Security Council, India as the largest democracy and, we consider it as our part of the world, should represent us in the Security Council. So there are many misconceptions, misunderstandings, I agree. We should work on them together.

Anything in particular you would like to tell the Indian people?

Yes, I would like to say that not to lose heart, that we, the Palestinians in particular, do appreciate the long history of friendship and solidarity. But we need to have new ties and a new dialogue and that we need to reach out to each other. Palestinian-Indian friendship is something which is much more solid, much stronger than any of these later development or changes or attempts at distortion and driving wedges. So, we have a great hope for India and from India.

Notes

1. Extracts of the interview previously appeared in 2002, *The Sunday Statesman*, Kolkata and New Delhi, 26 March and in 2002, *The Telegraph*, Kolkata, 7 April.
2. This interview took place on Friday, 4 January 2002, in the office of MIFTAH in Beit Hanina, a suburb of Jerusalem, West Bank, Palestine. Hanan Ashrawi is the General Secretary of MIFTAH (Arabic: Key).

Further Readings on Themes in Peace Studies

Selected Readings: General

Aiyar, Swarna. 1995. "August Anarchy: The Partition Massacres in Punjab 1947", *South Asia: Journal of South Asian Studies*, Special Issue on "North India: Partition and Independence", XVIII: 13–36. Melbourne: South Asia Studies Association.

Ali, Salma. 2001. *Violence Against Women in Bangladesh-2000: A Report.* Dhaka: Bangladesh National Woman Lawyers' Association.

Alonso, Harriet Hyman. October 1997. "The Women's Peace Union and the Outlawry of War, 1921–1942" in Syracuse Studies on Peace and Conflict Resolution. Syracuse University Press: First Syracuse University Press edition.

———. 1993. *Peace as a Women's Issue: A History of the U.S. Movement for World Peace and Women's Rights.* New York: Syracuse University Press.

Amnesty International. 1995. *Bangladesh: Fundamental Rights of Women Violated with Virtual Impunity.* London, UK: Amnesty International.

Anthias, Floya and Nira Yuval Davis. 1989. *Women-Nation-State.* London: Macmillan.

Appadorai, Arjun, F.J. Korom and M.A. Mills (eds). 1991. *Gender, Genre and Power in South Asian Expressive Traditions.* Philadelphia: University of Pennsylvania Press.

Banerjee, Paula. 2005. "Peacekeeping and Conflict Management: South Asia," and "Peace Movements: South Asia," Encyclopedia of Women in Islamic Cultures, Volume 2. Netherlands: Brill Publications.

———. 2001. "Between Two Armed Patriarchies: Women in Assam and Nagaland," in Rita Manchanda (ed.), *Beyond Victimhood to Agency: Women, War and Peace in South Asia.* New Delhi: Sage Publications.

Banerjee, Paula, Sabyasachi Basu Raychoudhury and Samir Das. 2005. *Internal Displacement in South Asia.* New Delhi: Sage Publications.

Basu, Soumita. 2004. *Building Constituencies of Peace: A Women's Initiative in Kashmir, Documenting the Process.* WISCOMP.

Basu, Soumita and Sumona DasGupta. 2004. *Samanbal: Spaces for Reconciliation, Building Constituencies of Peace: Stakeholders in Dialogue III.* WISCOMP.

Berg, Ellen Ziskind. 1994. "Gendering Conflict Resolution", *Peace and Change*, 19(4): 325–48.

Bernice, Carrol. 1987. "Feminism and Pacificism: Historical and Theoretical connection", in Ruth Roach Pierson (ed.), *Women and Peace*. Sydney: Croom Helm.

Bhasin, Kamla, Smitu Kothari and Bindia Thapar (eds). 2001. *Voices of Sanity: Reaching Out For Peace*. New Delhi: Lokayan.

Bhasin, Kamla, Ritu Menon and Nighat Said Khan (eds). 1994. *Against all Odds: Essays on Women, Religion and Development from India and Pakistan*. New Delhi: Kali for Women.

Bhaumik, S., Meghna Guhathakurta and Sabyasachi Basu Ray Chaudhary 1998. *Living on the Edge: Essays on the Chittagong Hill Tracts*. Kathmandu: SAFHR.

Blackwell, Joyce. 2004. *No Peace Without Freedom: Race and the Women's International League for Peace and Freedom, 1915–1975*. Carbondale: Southern Illinois University Press.

Boulding, Elise. 1981. "Perspectives of Women Researchers on Disarmament, National Security, and World Order", *Women's Studies International Quarterly*, 4(1): 27–40.

Brock-Utne, Birgit. 1989a. *Feminine Perspectives on Peace and Peace Education*. New York: Pergamon Press.

Brown, Wilmette. 1984. *Black Women and the Peace Movement*. Bristol: Falling Wall Press.

Brown, Scott, Christine Cervenak and David Fairman. 1998. *Alternative Dispute Resolution Practitioners Guide*. Cambridge, MA: Conflict Management Group.

Burguires, M. 1990. "Feminist Approaches to Peace: Another Step for Peace Studies", *Millennium: Journal of International Studies*, 19(1).

Butalia, Urvashi. 1998. *The Other Side of Silence: Voices from the Partition of India*. New Delhi: Penguin Books.

Burguires, M. and Tanika Sarkar (eds). 1995. *Women and the Hindu Right: A Collection of Essays*. New Delhi: Kali for Women.

Cambridge Women's Peace Collective.1984. *My Country Is the Whole World: An Anthology of Women's Work on Peace and War*. Unwin Hyman.

Carroll, Berenice. 1987. "Feminism and Pacifism: Historical and Theoretical Connections", in Roach Pearson (ed.), *Women and Peace*, pp. 2–28. London: Croom Helm.

Carter, Susanne. 1993. *War and Peace through Women's Eyes*. New York: Greenwood Publishing Group. (Palestine): Gaza Centre for Rights and Law.

Chenoy, Anuradha M. 2002. *Militarism and Women in South Asia*. New Delhi: Kali for Women.

Chowdhury, Mahfuzul H. 1993. "Popular Attitudes, Legal Institutions, and Dispute Resolution in Contemporary Bangladesh", *Legal Studies Forum* 17(3): 291–300.

Cockburn, Cynthia. 1998. *The Space Between Us: Negotiating Gender and National Identities in Conflict*. London and New York: Zed Books.

Cynthia Cockburn and Dubravka Zarkov (eds). 2002. *The Postwar Moment: Militaries, Masculinities and International Peacekeeping-Bosnia and the Netherlands*. London: Lawrence and Wishart.

CIDA. 1998. "Gender Equality and Peacebuilding: A Draft Operational Framework". Ottawa: CIDA.

Collet, P. 1998. "Afghan Women in the Peace Process" in Lorentzen and Turpin (eds), *The Women and War Reader*. New York and London: New York University Press.

Cook, Alice and Gwyn Kirk Greenham. 1983. *Women Everywhere: Dreams, Ideas & Actions from the Women's Peace Movement*. London: Pluto Press.

Cook, R.J. (ed.). 1994. *Human Rights of Women: National and International Perspectives*. Philadelphia: Princeton University Press.

Corrin, Chris (ed.). 1996. *Women in a Violent World*. Edinburgh: Edinburgh University Press.

DasGupta, Sumona and Soumita Basu. 2005. *Athwaas: Expanding Parameters of Local Access, Building Constituencies of Peace: Stakeholders in Dialogue IV*.

Das, Samir. 2005. *South Asian Peace Studies*, Volume. II. New Delhi: Sage Publications.

De Alwis, Malathi. 1998. "Moral Mothers and Stalwart Sons: Reading Binaries in a Time of War", in Lois Lorentzen and Jennifer Turpin (eds), *The Women and War Reader*. New York: New York University Press.

Dunbar, Sia Regina. 1997. "Role of Women in Decision-Making in the Peace Process", in S. Wolte (ed.), *Human Rights Violations against Women during War and Conflict*, pp. 12–18.Geneva: Women's International League for Peace and Freedom.

Dutta, Madhusree, Flavia Agnes and Neera Adarkar (eds). 1996. *The Nation, The State and Indian Identity*. Calcutta: Samya Publication.

Eisenstein, Zillah. 1996. *Hatreds: Racialised and Sexualised Conflicts in the 21st Century*. New York, NY: Routledge.

Elshtain, Jean Bethke. 1995. *Women and War*. Chicago: University of Chicago Press.

Enloe, Cynthia. 2000. *Manoeuvres: The International Politics of Militarizing Women's Lives*. Berkeley. CA. University of California Press.

Enloe, Cynthia. 1983. *Does Khaki Become You: The Militarisation of Women's Lives*. London: South End Press.

Ferris, Elizabeth. 1993. *Women, War and Peace*, Research Report No. 14. Uppsala: Life and Peace Institute.

Galtung, J. 1975–1980. *Essays in Peace Research*, Vols 1–5. Copenhagen: Christian Ejlers.

Gardam, Judith Gail. 2000. "Protection of Women in Armed Conflict", *Human Rights Quarterly*, 22(1).

Gopinath, Meenakshi and Manjrika Sewak. 2004. *Transcending Conflict: A Resource Book on Conflict Transformation*. WISCOMP.

Guanadason, Aruna, Musimbi Kanyoro and Lucia Ann McSpadden (eds). 1996. *Women, Violence and Non-Violent Change*. Geneva: World Council of Churches.

Guhathakurta, M. 1999. Nari Obhiggota CHT: 1 (Women's Experience in CHT: 1) in Shongskriti, March.

———. 1986. "Gender Violence in Bangladesh: the Role of the State", *The Journal of Social Studies*, no. 30.

Hans, Asha. 2001. "Internally Displaced Women from Kashmir: The Role of UNCHR" in SARWATCH. Dacca.

Harrish, Adrienne and Ynestra King. 1989. *Rocking the Ship of State: Toward a Feminist Peace Politics*. Boulder: Westview Press.

Henderson, Michael. 1994. *All Her Paths Are Peace: Women Pioneers in Peacemaking*. New Jersey: Kumarian.
Hughes Nancy Scheper. 1998. "Maternal Thinking and the Politics of War", in Lois Ann Lorentzen and Jennifer Turpin (eds), *The Women and War Reader*, n. 21, pp. 227–33. New York University Press.
Jacobs, Susie, Ruth Jacobson and Jennifer Marchbank (eds). 2000. *States of Conflict: Gender, Violence and Resistance*. New York: Zed Books.
Jayawardane, Kumari. 1986. *Feminism and Nationalism in the Third World*. New Delhi: Kali for Women.
Jeffery, Patricia and Amrita Basu. 1999. *Resisting the Sacred and the Secular: Women's Activism and Politicized Religion in South Asia*. Delhi: Kali for Women.
(Note: This title was originally published by Routledge under the title *Appropriating Gender: Women's Activism and Politicized Religion in South Asia*.)
Kacic, Biljana (ed.). 1997. *Women and the Politics of Peace*. Zagreb: Centre for Women's Studies.
Kandiyoti, D. (ed). 1994. *Women, Islam and the State*. London: Macmillan.
Kaul, A. 2001. *Transcending Fault-lines: A Quest for a Culture of Peace*, Report on Kashmir. WISCOMP
Kearney, Mary-Louise (ed.). 1996. *Women and the University Curriculum: Towards Equality, Democracy and Peace*. Geneva: UNESCO Publications.
Krasniewicz, Louise. 1992. *Nuclear Summer: The Clash of Communities at the Seneca Women's Peace Encampment (Anthropology of Contemporary Issues)*. Cornell University Press.
Krishnatry, S.M. 1996. "The Return of Peace", *Northeast Sun*. 28 November.
Kuhlman A., Erika. 1997. *Petticoats and White Feathers: Gender Conformity, Race, the Progressive Peace Movement, and the Debate Over War, 1895–1919*. (Contributions in Women's Studies). Greenwood Press.
Lorentzen, Lois Ann and Jennifer Turpin (eds). 1998. *The Women and War Reader*. New York and London: New York University Press.
McCarthy, Coleman. 1995. "The Dalai Lama's Radical Non-Violence" in *His Holiness the Dalai Lama: Speeches, Statements, Articles, Interviews: 1987 to June 1995*, p. 136. Dharamsala: Department of Information and International Relations.
Maunaguru, Sitralega. 1995. "Gendering Tamil Nationalism: The Construction of 'Women' in Projects of Protest and Control", in Pradeep Jaganathan and Qadri Ismael (eds), *Unmaking the Nation: The Politics of Identity and History in Modern Sri Lanka*, pp. 158–175. Colombo: Social Scientists Association.
Manchanda, Rita (ed.). 2001. *Women, War and Peace in South Asia: Beyond Victimhood to Agency*. New Delhi: Sage Publications.
Martin, Susan Forbes. 1991. *Refugee Women*. London: Zed Books.
Melman, Billie (ed.). 1998. *Borderlines: Genders and Identities in War and Peace 1870–1930*. New York, London: Routledge.
Menon, Ritu and Kamla Bhasin. 1998. *Borders and Boundaries: Women in India's Partition*. New Delhi: Kali for Women.
Meinties, Sheila (ed.). 2002. *The Aftermath: Women in Post-Conflict Transformation*. London and New York: Zed Books.

Menon, Ritu and Kamla Bhasin. 1993. "Recovery, Rupture, Resistance: Three Perspectives on the Recovery Operation In Post Partition India", *Economic and Political Weekly*, 28(17).
Moghadam, V.M. (ed). 1994. *Gender and National Identity: Women And Politics in Muslim Societies*. London: Zed Books; Karachi: Oxford University Press.
Mohsin. 2003. *The Chittagong Hill Tracts, Bangladesh: On the Difficult Road to Peace*. USA: Lynne Rienner.
Morgan, V. 1995. "Peacemakers? Peacekeepers? Women in Northern Ireland 1996–1995", lecture given at the University of Ulster. Available online at http://cain.ulst.ac.uk/issues/women/paper3.htm
Pettman, J.J. 1996. *Worlding Women: A Feminist International Politics*. New York: Routledge.
Rathbone Irene. 1989. *We That Were Young (Women and Peace)*. The Feminist Press at CUNY.
Reardon, Betty A. 1993. "Women and Peace: Feminist Visions of Global Security", Suny Series, *Global Conflict and Peace Education*. State University of New York Press.
Reardon, Betty A., Ingeborg Breines and Dorota Gierycz. 1999. *Towards a Women's Agenda for a Culture of Peace*. Paris: UNESCO.
Rupp, Leila J. 1997. *Worlds of Women: The Making of an International Women's Movement*. Princeton, NJ: Princeton University Press.
Ridde, R. and H. Calaway (eds). 1987. *Women and Political Conflict: Portraits of Struggle in Times of Crisis*. New York: New York University Press.
Rooney, E. 1995. "Political Division, Practical Alliance: Problem for Women in Conflict", *Journal of Women's History*, 6(4) and 7(1): 42–48.
Ross, Dennis. 2005. *The Missing Peace: The Inside Story of the Fight for Middle East Peace*. Farrar. Straus and Giroux. Reprint edition.
Ruddick, S. 1989. *Maternal Thinking: Towards a Politics of Peace*. London: The Women's Press.
Ruddick, S. 1998. "'Women of Peace': A Feminist Construction', in L.A. Lorentzen and J. Turpin (eds), *The Women and War Reader*. New York and London: New York University Press.
Ruddick, Sara. 1983. "Pacifying the Forces: Drafting Women on the Interest of Peace", *Signs: Journal of Women in Culture and Society*, 8(3): 471–90.
Samaddar, Ranabir. 2005. *Politics of Autonomy*. New Delhi: Sage Publications.
———. 2004. *South Asian Peace Studies*, Volume I. New Delhi: Sage Publications.
———. 2003. *Refugees and the State*. New Delhi: Sage Publications.
Samuel, Kumuduni. 2000. "Women's Activism, Motherhood and the State in the context of Sri Lanka's Ethnic Conflict." Seventh National Convention on Women's Studies. Centre for Women's Research (CENWOR), Sri Lanka.
———. 2000. "Giving Peace a Chance-Women's activism and marginalisation in the peace process." OPTIONS, 1st Quarter, Colombo.
———. 1999. "Women's Rights Watch Year Report 1999". Colombo, Sri Lanka: Women and Media Collective.
Sangari, Kumkum and Sudesh Vaid (eds). *Recasting Women: Essays in Colonial History*. New Delhi: Kali for Women.

Sarkar, T. and Urvashi Butalia (eds). 1995. *Women and Hindu Right: A collection of Essays.* New Delhi: Kali for Women.
Shah Nafisa. 1997. *Women in the Crossfire.* Karachi/Lahore: Human Rights Commission of Pakistan.
Shaheed Fareeda and K. Mumtaz. 1987. *Women of Pakistan: Two Steps Forward, One Step Back?*, Other Voices of Pakistan. London: Zed Books.
Shiva, Vandana. 1994. *Minding Our Lives: Women from the South and North Reconnect Ecology and Health.* New Delhi: Kali for Women.
Sideries, T. 1995. "Rape in war and peace-Same category Different Experiences?", Paper presented at the Aftermath Conference, University of the Witwatersrand, Johannesburg, South Africa, 20–22 July.
Skjelsboek, Inger. 2001. *Gender, Peace and Conflict.* Oslo: International Peace Research Institute (PRIO), Sage Publications.
Smith, Dan. 1997b. *The State of War and Peace Atlas.* London: Penguin.
Smith, Lee Barbara. 1978. *Peace Corps/Nepal women in development action plan.* Trans Century Corporation.
Soley, M. 1996. "Teaching About International conflict and Peace", *Social Education*, 60(7): 432–38.
Swerdlow Amy. "Women Strike for Peace: Traditional Motherhood and Radical Politics in the 1960s", *Women in Culture and Society Series.*
Tickner, Ann J. 1994. "Feminist Perspectives on Peace an World Security in the Post-Cold War Era", in Michael T.Klare (ed.), *Peace and World Security Studies: A Curriculum Guide*, pp. 43–54. Boulder,Colorado: Lynne Rienner.
———. 1992. *Gender and International Relations.* New York: Columbia University Press.
Tinker, Irene. 1990. *Persistent Inequalities: Women and World Development.* New York: Oxford University Press.
Topmiller, Robert. 2002. *The Lotus Unleashed: The Buddhist Peace Movement in South Vietnam, 1964–1966.* University Press of Kentucky.
Trueblood, Benjamin Franklin. 1910. *Women in the peace movement.* American Peace Society.
Turpin, Jennifer and Lois Ann Lorentzen (eds). 1996. *The Gendered New World Order: Militarism, Development and the Environment.* New York and London: Zed Books.
United Nations. 1995. *Peace: Women in International Decision-making.* Report of the Secretary-General, E/CN.6/1995/12. New York: United Nations.
Wadley, Susan. 1991. *The Power of Tamil Women.* New Delhi: Manohar Publications.
Warnock, Kitty. 1995. "Arms to Fight, Arms to Protect: Women Speak Out about Conflict", unpublished paper presented at Oslo, 19 June, at a PANOS seminar on the project Arm to Fight-Arm to Protect.
West, L. (ed.). 1997. *Feminist Nationalism.* New York: Routledge.
Wieringa, Saskia (ed.). 1995. *Subversive Women: Women's Movements in Africa, Asia, Latin America and the Caribbean.* New Delhi: Kali for Women.
Winslow, Anne (ed.). 1995. *Women, Politics, and the United Nations.* Westport, CT: Greenwood Press.
Women in Black. 1994, 1997. *Women of Peace.* Belgrade: Women in Black.
Women's Feature Service. 1990. *The Power to Change: Women in the Third World redefine their Environment.* New Delhi: Kali for Women.

Yuval-Davis, Nira. 1997. *Gender and Nation.* London, Thousand Oaks, New Delhi: Sage Publications.

Zaman, H. 1999. "Violence against Women in Bangladesh: Issues and Responses", *Women's Studies International Forum*, 22(1): 37–48.

SELECTED READINGS ON NORTHEAST INDIA

Aleaz, Bonita. 2005. *Emergent Women: Mizo Women's Perspectives.* New Delhi: Mittal Publications.

Banerjee, Paula. 2005. "Assamese Women: Victims or Actors?", in Imdad Hussain (ed.), *The Guwahati Declaration and the Road to Peace in Assam*, pp. 119–32. New Delhi: Akansha.

Banerjee, Paula. 2004. "Women's Interventions for Peace in Northeast", in O.P. Mishra (ed.), *Forced Migration in the South Asian Region*, pp. 318–33. New Delhi: Manak.

Baruah, S.L. 1992. *Status of Women in Assam: With Special Reference to Non-Tribal Societies.* New Delhi: Omsons.

Brara, N. Vijaylakshmi. 1998. *Politics, society and cosmology in India's North-East.* Delhi: Oxford University Press.

Das, Samir. 2005. *Ethnicity, Nation and Security: Essays on Northeastern India.* New Delhi: South Asia Publishers.

Datta, Sreeradha. 2000. "Security of India's Northeast: External Linkages", *Strategic Analysis*, xxiv(8). New Delhi: IDSA. Available online at http: idsa-india.org/an-nov-co-8html.

Duarah, D.K. "Women's Movements in Arunachal Pradesh", *Resarun*, 22 (1 & 2): 39–42.

Fernandes, Walter and Sanjay Barbora. 2002a. *Changing Women's Status in India, Focus on the Northeast.* Guwahati: North Eastern Social Research Centre.

———. 2002b. *Modernisation and Women's Status in Northeastern India.* Guwahati: North Eastern Social Research Centre.

Ghosh, G.K. and Shukla Ghosh. 1997. *Women of Manipur.* New Delhi: A.P.H. Publishing Corporation.

Goswami, Roshmi, M.G. Sreekala and Meghna Goswami. 2005. *Women in Armed Conflict Situations.* Guwahati: North East Network.

Haksar, Nandita and Luithui Luingam. 1984. *Nagaland File: A Question of Human Rights.* New Delhi: Lancer.

Haksar, Nandita. 1990. *State Terrorism and its Repercussions*, Official Report, Naga People's Movement for Human Rights, Conference, Kohima, November 2–3.

Iralu, Easterine. 2001. *The Windhowver Collection.* Published by Steven Herlekar.

Kar, Bimal. 2002. *Women Population of North East India: A Study in Gender Geography.* New Delhi: Regency Publications.

Khala, Khatoli. 2003. *The Armed Forces (Special Powers) Act: Its Impact on Women in Nagaland.* New Delhi: WISCOMP.

Kikon, Dolly. 2004. *Experiences of Naga women in armed conflict situation: Narratives from a militarized society.* "WISCOMP Perspective" 11. New Delhi.

Mahanta, Aparna (ed.). 2002. *Human Rights and Women of Northeast India*. Dibrugarh: Centre for Women's Studies, Dibrugarh University.

Mishra, S. 1991. *Women in Tribal Community: A Study of Arunachal Pradesh*. New Delhi: Vikas Publishing House.

Nepram, Binalakshmi. 2002. *South Asia's fractured frontier: armed conflict, narcotics and small arms proliferation in India's north east*. New Delhi: Mittal Publications.

———. 2002. *North-East India: A Bibliography*. New Delhi: Nehru Memorial Museum and Library.

Pandey, B.B. (ed.). 1997. *Status of Women in Tribal Society: Arunachal Pradesh*. Itanagar: Directorate of Research, Government of Arunachal Pradesh.

People's Union for Democratic Rights, CRPF in Manipur: Findings of an Inquiry Commission on Firing in Imphal, October 1996, and Army in Nagaland: Findings of an Inquiry Commission, August 1996.

Rao, V.M. 2003. *Tribal Women of Arunachal Pradesh: Socio-Economic Status*. New Delhi: Mittal Publications.

Ruivah, K. 1993. *Social Changes among the Nagas: Tangkhul*. New Delhi: Cosmo Publications.

Sangkham, Gina. 2000. "Naga Women and Peace Process", *Kohima Newsletter*, pp. 1–8, 8 June.

Takhellambum, Bhabananda. 2003. *Women's Uprising in Manipur: A Legacy Continued*. WISCOMP Perspectives 2.

Veda, Gunjan. 2005. *Tailoring Peace: The Citizens' Roundtable on Manipur and Beyond*. Guwahati: North East Network.

Vitso, Adina. 2003. *Customary Law and Women: The Chakhesang Nagas*. New Delhi: Regency Publications.

SELECTED READINGS ON SRI LANKA

(Published with the permission of National Peace Council, Sri Lanka)

Abeysekera, Sunila. 1999. "Women and Peace in Sri Lanka: Some Observations", *Women in Action*, 3.

De Mel, Neloufer and Ramani Muttetuwegama. 1997. "Sisters in Arms: The Eksath Kantha Peramuna", *Pravada*, vol. 4(10 and 11).

Fernando, Nimalka. 2004. "Women and Politics-Challenges Ahead", *Options*, 33(1): 26–27.

———. 1998. "Women and Political Participation", *Lanka Guardian*, 20(2) June: 13–16.

Gomez, Mario. 1998. "A National List for Women?", *Lanka Guardian*, 21(6) October: 13–15.

Gomez, Mario and Shyamala Gomez. 2002. *Empowerment of Women in Regional/Local Governance*, Training Module, prepared by Kanthi Wijetunga, Additional Director.

———. 2001. *Gender and Politics in Sri Lanka-Preferring Women*. Colombo: CIDA.

———. 1997. "Reserving Quotas for Women", *Sunday Times*, 15 June.

Goonesekere, Savitri. 1990. "Women, Equality, Rights and the Constitution", *Thatched Patio*, Special Issue, 3(3) May/June: 28.
Gunasekara, Nandini. 2003. Policy on Reservation of Seats for Women in Urban Local Governance, prepared by Nandani Gunasekara Gunasekera T. Leitan and S. 1998. *Women in Rural Politics: A study of Women's Participation in Politics in Selected Rural Areas in Sri Lanka.*
Irriyagolla, Indrani. "Women of Sri Lanka: A Historical Perspective", reprint from the *Journal of the Royal Asiatic Society of Sri Lanka*, 1989/1990, n.s. vol. XXXIV.
Ismail, Jezima. 1995. "Can Women Lead Nations? A Muslim Perspective", *Lanka Guardian*, 18(6): 11 13.
Jayawardena, Kumari. 1998. "The Women's Movement in Sri Lanka 1985–95", *Options*, 2nd Quarter, Special 50th Anniversary, Celebrating Women, 14(2): 2–7.
Jayawardena, Kumari. 1974. "The Participation of Women in the Social Reform, Political and Labour Movements of Sri Lanka", *Logos*, 13(2), August: 17–25.
Jayawardene, Kishali and Chulani Kodikara. 1999. *Women and Governance in Sri Lanka, study conducted during the period 1998–2000*, Women and Governance Project, Final Report (Draft).
Kiribamune Sirima and Vidyamali Samarasinghe (eds). 1990. *Women At the Cross Road: A Sri Lankan Perspective*. Kandy: ICES.
Kuru-Utumpala, Jayanthi. 2004. "We need to step out (interview)", *Options*, 33(1): 20–22.
Liyanaarachchi, Deshini. 1999. Politics of Violence, *Options*, 4th Quarter, 20:25.
Liyanage Kamala. 2000. "Sri Lankan Women: Gender, Citizenship and Political Representation", in *Sambhavana* (Sinhala), *Journal of the University of Peradeniya*, 1 (July–December): 51–81.
———. 1999. "Women in Political Parties: 'The Sri Lankan Experience'", in Sirima Kiribamune (ed.), *Women and Politics in Sri Lanka: a Comparative Perspective*, pp. 101–42. Kandy: ICES.
———. 1996. "Party Women: Their Role in Sri Lankan Politics in Pakistan", *Journal of Women's Studies*, 3(1): 13–32.
Perera, Viola. 2004. "Women have no Political Voice (interview)", *Options*, 33(1): 17–19.
Samarasinghe, Vidyamali. 2000. "Subverting Patriarchy? Leadership and Participation of Women in Politics in South Asia", *Ethnic Studies Report*, 18(2) July: 193–228.
Samuel, Kumudini. 2002. "Include women in Negotiations for Peace", *Options*, 30 (2nd Quarter): 2–4.
———. 1998. "Celebrating Women 1948–1998: 'Pavithra Wanniarachchi'", *Options*, 14 (2nd Quarter): 1–4.
Senanayake, Kelly. 1997. "Women, the Revolution and the JVP", *Options*, 10 (2nd Quarter): 18–20.
Silva de Dulcy. 2002. "Women Trade Unionists", *Options,* 29 (1st quarter): 23–24.

Tambiah, Yasmin. 2003. 'The Impact of Gender Inequality on Governance', in *Essays on Gender and Governance*, pp. 59–95. India: UNDP.

———. (ed.). 2002. *Women and Governance in South Asia: Re-imagining the State*. Colombo: ICES.

Thiruchandran, Selvy. 1996. "The Feminist Challenges", *Lanka Guardian*, 18(22): 9–13.

Thiruchandran, Selvy (ed.). 1999. *Women, Narration and Nation: Collective Images and Multiple Identities*, New Delhi: Vikas Publishing House.

———. 1998. "The Politics of Practice and the Practice of Politics", *Nivedini*, 6(1), June and 2 December: 166–178.

———. 1997. *The Politics of Gender and Women's Agency in Post-Colonial Sri Lanka*. Colombo: WERC.

———. 1996. "The Feminist Challenges", *Lanka Guardian*, 18(22) 1 April: 9–13.

Vidyamali Samarasingha. 2004. "'Situating Women' From Conflict To Peace: Perspectives on Women's Role in Sri Lanka", Paper presented at a workshop on "The Toolkit On Conflict and Peace" organised by ICES, Kandy in collaboration with AED and USAID, 11 March.

———. 2000. "Subverting Patriarchy? Leadership and Participation of Women in Politics in South Asia", *Ethnic Studies Report* (ICES), 18(2) July: 193–228.

Women's Concerns and the Peace Process: Findings and Recommendations. International Women's Mission to the North East of Sri Lanka, 12–17 October 2002.

"Women's Concerns and the Peace Process: Recommendations of the International Women's Mission to the North East of Sri Lanka", 12–17 October 2002, *Pravada*, 8(4): 40–41.

"Women and the Peace Process", *Pravada*, 7(8 and 9): 22.

About the Editor and Contributors

The Editor

Paula Banerjee is a member of the Calcutta Research Group (CRG). She specializes in issues of conflict and peace in South Asia. She has published extensively on issues of gender and forced displacement and autonomy. She has co-edited a number of books of which the most recent ones are *Internal Displacement in South Asia* (2005) and *Autonomy Beyond Kant and Hermeneutics* (2007). She has also been working on themes related to women, borders and democracy in South Asia. She is on the editorial board of a number of international journals such as *Prachya* and *Forced Migration Review*. She is currently teaching and is the Chair of the Department of South and Southeast Asian Studies, University of Calcutta.

The Contributors

Malathi de Alwis is a feminist scholar and activist at the International Centre for Ethnic Studies, Colombo, Sri Lanka. She was Visiting Professor at the New School for Social Research, New York.

Aditi Bhaduri is a gender consultant and a freelance journalist based in India. She is currently working on Kashmiri Pandit women.

Cynthia Cockburn is a feminist researcher and writer working at the intersection of Gender studies and Peace/Conflict Studies. She is a Visiting Professor in the Department of Sociology at City University, London. Since 1995, she has been working closely with women peace activists in conflict zones such as Cyprus, doing qualitative action-research.

312 About the Editor and Contributors

Samir Kumar Das is a research coordinator of the Calcutta Research Group (CRG). Presently, he is a Professor in the Department of Political Science, University of Calcutta. His researches on the society and politics of the Northeast and Assam in particular, are widely known.

Sumona DasGupta is the Assistant Director of WISCOMP. Her thesis on the Trends of Militarization in Indian Politics in the 1980s is widely read.

Fauzia Gardezi has worked as a research associate at the University of Toronto. She is associated with the Élisabeth Bruyère Research Institute, Ottawa, Ontario.

Meghna Guhathakurta is currently working in Research Initiative Bangladesh. Formerly, she was a Professor in the Department of International Relations, University of Dhaka. She is a well-known human rights and gender activist in Bangladesh.

Rada Ivecovic is a Professor of Philosophy in France. Since 2004, she is the Program Director at Collège International de Philosophie at Paris. Among her numerous research interests, the most prominent are Feminist Theory and Feminist Philosophy as well as Political Philosophy.

Anuradha Bhasin Jamwal is Executive Editor of the *Kashmir Times*. She has worked and written extensively on the Kashmir conflict, focusing on the need for intra-state dialogue between India, Pakistan and the people of Jammu and Kashmir. Her work has also focused on issues of displaced people in Jammu and Kashmir.

Kalpana Kannabiran is Professor of Sociology at NALSAR University of Law, India and founder member of a women's collective, Asmita Resource Centre for Women where she coordinates legal outreach for women. She is the current Chair of RC32 (Women in Society) of the International Sociological Association. Her areas of specialization are Sociology of Law, Jurisprudence and Gender Studies.

About the Editor and Contributors

Vasantha Kannabiran is the Founder of Asmita, which brings diverse groups of women into networks that address a range of issues spanning conflict, peace, survival, women's rights and secularism. For over 30 years now, Vasantha has been closely involved with the questions of armed militancy, civil liberties and the meaning of peace for women in Andhra Pradesh.

Jean Luc Racine is a CNRS Senior Fellow, Centre for the Study of India and South Asia at the School for Advanced Studies in Social Sciences (EHESS), Paris. He is also the Director of the International Programme for Advanced Studies, run by the Fondation Maison des Sciences de l'Homme, Paris, in cooperation with Columbia University.

Josiane Racine is co-author of the celebrated volume, *Viramma: Life of an Untouchable.*

Fehmida Riyaz is a celebrated poetess who started the first women's publishing house in Pakistan. She launched a magazine, *Awaz,* which criticized the government. She was exiled from Pakistan by Zia ul-Haq for her liberal views regarding Muslim women, and has since lived in India.

Ranabir Samaddar is the Director of the Calcutta Research Group (CRG) and the Editor of its journal, *Refugee Watch.* He is known for his work on cross border migration, autonomy and dialogue as an instrument of politics and social justice.

Nirekha De Silva is involved in monitoring and protecting the Rights of Sri Lankan IDPs through various research projects and advocacy work. She was a Researcher at the Disaster Relief Monitoring Unit of the Human Rights Commission and at the National Peace Council of Sri Lanka.

Stree Shakti Sanghatana After the Emergency was lifted in 1977, a group of women came together to form Stree Shakti Sanghatana. Historically rooted in Telangana, with headquarters in Hyderabad it brought many women from various backgrounds together. It is a small articulate group set out to politicize women's issues.

Saro Thiruppathy is a researcher and a feminist activist in Sri Lanka.

Volga is the Founder Member of Asmita Resource Centre for Women. She has written the lyrics for *War and Peace*, and *Lakshmana Rekha*—Kuchipudi ballets on the effect of war and domestic violence which have been performed across the state.

Index

abduction, recovery and rejection, 134–35
activism, 36, 176, 275–76
Adikari, Rani, 160
agency spectrum, 35
AHIMSA, 141
AIDS Care Hospice, 62
Akashi, Yasushi, 142
alcoholism, 60–61
Alfred, Monica, 141–42
All India Garo Union, 61
All-Manipur Social Reformation and Development Samaj, 67
All-Tribal Women's Organization (ATWO), 64
Angami, Neidonuo, 61, 62, 63
Annadurai, 243, 244, 247–48, 250
Annan, Kofi, 46
antimilitarism, 279
Apunba Lup, 212
Arab Jews, 284
Arab League, 296–97
Aristotle, 121
armed conflicts, 37, 43, 135, 285, 288. *See also* war
arms proliferation, 30, 38
army and paramilitary forces, brutality and savagery in India, 66–68
Ashrawi, Hanan, 289*ff*
Assam Human Rights Commission, 58
Assam Rifles, 33, 65, 67, 68, 69, 211–12
Association of Mothers of Srebrenica and Zepa, 283
Association of Parents of Disappeared Persons (APDP), 58
Association of War-Affected Women, 142, 143, 234

Athwaas, 43, 65
authoritarianism, 283
autonomy, 6, 7, 18
Awami League, Bangladesh, 229

Babri Mosque demolition, 228, 242
backwardness of women, 83, 84
Balkans, 6, 119, 125
Bandaranaike, Sirimavo, 140, 159, 164
Bangladesh: challenge of fundamentalism, 220–21; Vested Property Act, 229, women, 9, 12, 136, 137; response of women's movement, 221–23
Bangladesh National Party (BNP), 224–25
Bargi dam, 36
Baruah, Paresh, 58
Beijing Platform for Action, 143
Bharatiya Mahila Mandali Club, 95
Bhola, Bangladesh: post-election violence against minorities, 225–27
bio-diversity, 26
biological determinism, 119–20
biological differences, 27
biology as destiny, 153
birth control, 86–87, 89, 125
Birzeit University, 289
blasphemy, 240
Border Security Force (BSF), 10, 213
Bosnia-Herzegovina, 118, 125
British suffragist movement, 112
brotherhood, 115–17, 124
bureaucracies, 107

capital-centric systems of security, 25
care and resistance, 65–71

316 Index

caste barriers, 32, 37, 41, 219. *See also* class
Central Reserve Police Force (CRPF), 61
Centre for Women's Research (CENWOR), 144
Chakmas in Bangladesh, 219
chastity, 79
child marriage, 90
Chisi, Khesilie, 61
Chittagong Hill Tracts of Bangladesh, 219
Chittaranjan, Pebam, 72–73
Civil Rights Movement, Sri Lanka, 141
civil society, 21, 142, 211–12, 296; role in armed conflicts, 41–42; women's organizations, 138, 140, 143–44
civil wars, 113, 117
class, 32, 41, 144, 219; domination in Sri Lanka, 165–67; hierarchies, 153; oppression, 105
Cold War, 25, 287; post-Cold War, 20, 22, 127
collective action, 97
collective security, 46
colonialism and neo-colonialism, 26, 117
Co-Madres in El Salvador, 57
communal discrimination, 17
communal violence, 219
communalization, 219, 229
Communist Party (CP), 245, 247–49, 251; women's participation, 81–95
Communist Party of India–Marxist-Leninist (CPI-ML), 73
Communist Party of Nepal (Maoist), 34
community, communities, 58, 122, 133, 136–37; predicament in times of conflict, 134
conflict prevention, 20, 21–24, 30–32, 41–47
conflict transformation, 21–22, 275
Congress, 175–76, 245–47, 250
consciousness of woman, 5, 18, 37, 83, 84, 104, 141

content, context and structure of relationships, 22
Convention on the Elimination of All Forms of Discrimination Against Women (CEDAW), 148
Coomaraswamy, Radhika, 140, 141, 146
corruption, 291
criminalization of economy, 38
Croatia, 127, 281
cultural factors, 17, 26, 31, 103–04, 107, 133

decision-making, representation of women, 27, 43, 45, 138
Declaration of Principles (DOP), 290, 292
Deka, Pranati, 58
democracy, democratic, 40, 54*ff*, 216, 298; crisis in India, 176; resistance, 54
democratization, 216
Deva Kannalawwa, 160–61
development, 43; globalization and gender: through the lens pf security in South Asia, 31, 36–37; interventions in Bangladesh, 222
Dharmadasa, Visaka, 142, 234
differentiation, mode, 277, 288
discrimination against women, 87–88, 146
displacement, 30, 274; and instability, 137; of women, 5, 37
Disturbed Areas, 67
division of work, 91–92
divorce, 90
domestic labour, 79–80, 87
domestic violence, 11, 135, 241
domesticity, 93
dowry, 13
Dravida Kazhagam (DK), 247–48
Dravida Munnetra Kazhagam (DMK), 247–51
drug addiction, 60–61
Drug Rehabilitation Centre, 61–62

Eelam Peoples' Revolutionary Front (EPRLF), 167

early warning and early response, 22, 45
ecological disasters and migration, 17
economic: dependence of women, 106; development, 22–23; globalization and democratization, 30; inequality, 36; insecurity, 25; reforms, 42
economy, 105
educational deprivation, 25, 36
electoral politics, 213, 245–69
empowerment of women, 33–34, 296
Enloe, Cynthia, 32
environmental degradation, 24, 36
equality and social equity, 26, 34, 42, 82–83, 91–92, 117
ethnic: conflicts/differences, 22, 30, 32–33, 43, 64, 219;—in Yugoslavia, 283; identities, 153, 277–78; minorities in Bangladesh, 224; movements, 56, 57
ethnicity, 41, 54*ff*, 144, 219, 233, 279
European Union (EU), 21, 296
exploitation and oppression, 26, 84, 87–90, 97, 100–101, 103, 104, 109

factional killings, 62
family, 79, 84, 90, 91, 93, 100; predicament in times of conflict, 134
farmer's resistance movement in Pakistani Punjab, 36
father-symbol, 122–23, 126
federalism, 141
Federation of South African Women, 57
female lineage, 126
femininity, 124, 287
feminization of poverty, 44
feminism, feminist, 32, 34, 57, 113, 144, 214, 234; formulations of security, 45; interventions in International Relations, 27–30; from within Islam, 101–4; politics, 136; public activity, 113; as a resource in opposing xenophobia and separatism, 274*ff*; thought, as a tool, gender and other kinds of other, 278–79; western, 99

flesh trade, 16
forced marriage, 134
formal masculine worldview politics, 7
fratricidal wars, 117–18
fundamentalism, challenge in Bangladesh, 220–21

Gam Udawa (village reawakening), 159
Gandhi, Indira, 243, 244, 245, 299
Gandhi, M.K., 243, 245–46, 280
Garo Students' Union, 61
gender, gender issues, gender relations, 4–6, 31, 41, 106, 149, 222, 284, 295, 297; audit, 7; and conflict prevention, 20*ff*; and development and forced migration, 37; differentiation, 278; dimensions in labour migration, 15–18; division of labour, 5, 62; identities, 31, 39, 56; ideologies, 31, 39; inequality, 115–17, 124–25, 129, 153; justice, 6–8, 27, 36; and maternal politics, 73; movements in Northeast India, 55–65; oppression, 105–06, 233; and other kinds of other, 278–79; partition, 287–88; and peace-building, through the lens of security in South Asia, 38–41; roles, 31, 34, 147; and security, 21, 29–32, 42, 45
Ghali, Boutrous Boutrous Ghali, 38
Global Partnership for the Prevention of Armed Conflicts (GPPAC), 41–43, 45–46
globalization, 25, 41
Gono Adalat, 220
Gounder, Gounder, 246–50, 254–55, 265–66
Gounder, Murugaiya, 260–62
Gramsci, Antonio, 100
Greek Cypriots, 275
Grupo Apoyo Mutuo (GAM) in Guatemala, 57
Gujarat riots, 176

Habermas, 59

HAMAS, 292
Hands Across the Divide, 287
Haokip, M. Hechin, 64
healthcare, 25, 36
hegemonic discourses, 104
Herath, Renuka, 158
heterosexuality, 284
hierarchy, 27, 29; of conflicts, 4
Hindus, 58, 218–19
Hossain, Rokeya Shakhawat, 221
human rights, 36, 39, 58, 101, 113, 114, 166, 176, 298; discourse of victimhood, 35; gendered discourse, 153; organizations in Pakistan, 13; violations;—in Israel, 291;—in Pakistan, 241;—in Sri Lanka, 152, 162
Human Rights Commission, Sri Lanka, 140
human security, 20, 24–26, 30, 37, 42, 45; ecological context, 25–26
humanitarian intervention, 46–47, 274

identity formation, identity, 30, 39–40, 43, 112, 113, 116, 118–19, 122–23, 233, 234, 277–78, 287–88, 294; contradictory nature, 276; manipulation in war, 281–83; politics, dangers of, 283–84; and sense of self, 280–81; in social science and women's activism, 275–76
ideological barriers, 79
ideological resistance, 32
illiteracy, 25
Imam, Jahanara, 220, 221
imperial domination, 283
Imroz, Pervez, 58
India: Armed Forces (Special Powers) Act (AFSPA), 1958, 61, 66–68, 72–73, 211–12, 215; Christian Marriage and Adoption Bill, 56; Constitution, 66; National Security Act, 212
Indian Peace Keeping Force (IPKF), 139–40, 168
Indo-Naga peace process, 61, 63

inequality, 105, 166; in South Asian societies, 42
infrastructure development, 36
inheritance, women's entitlement to, 56
injustices, 21–22
insecurities, 36
institutional barriers, 43
institutional capacity, 25
intellectual rights, 37
Inter Group Dialogue and Mediation Skills, 64
internal and external forces, 26
international borders, 213
International Center for Ethnic Studies (ICES), 141, 143–44
international community, 128, 166
international political economy, 25–26
International Relations (IR), 3–4, 24, 27–30, 47; women's perspective, 27–30
international trafficking networks, 13
Internationally Displaced Person (IDP), 275
interstate relations, 3–4
Intifadah, 292–93, 296
Islam, feminism, and the women's movement in Pakistan: 1981–91, 7, 97*ff*
Iswari Devi, 211

Jamaat-e-Islami, 102, 222, 223
Janata Party, India, 247
Janatha Vimukhthi Peramuna (JVP), Sri Lanka, 139, 152, 157, 159
Japan: aid to Sri Lanka to fight Tamil separatists, 44–45
judicial activism, 41
justice and equality, 113

Kalashnikovs, 34
Kamal, Sufia, 221
Kamalamma, 236
Kamaraj, K., 243, 245, 250
Kant, Immanuel, 4
Kantha Handa (Voice of Women), 143
Karunanidhi, M., 248, 250

Kashmir Mother's Front (Associations of the Persons of the Disappeared), 35
Kashmiri women in conflict, 35, 233
kinship and power structure in Bangladesh, 17, 223–24
Kiriammawarunge Dane (The Feeding Milk Mothers), 160
knowledge creation, 29
Kripa Foundation, 61
Krishnan, Kavita, 73
Kukis, 64–65; women, 213
Kumaratunge, Chandrika Banadaranaike, 140, 150, 164, 170

land rights, 36
language controversy in Assam, 71–72
Law of Evidence, 101, 240
Legal Aid Programme, Birzeit University, 289
legal reforms, 23
Liberation Tigers of Tamil Eelam (LTTE), 6, 40, 44, 138, 139–40, 142, 148, 157, 168, 234; women cadres, 6, 34, 144–46
livelihood, 11, 23, 37; rights, 36; security, 25–26, 30
lobbying, 138
lumpenization, 11

Madres de la Plaza de Mayo in Argentina, 57
Maheshwar dam, 36
majoritarian state systems, 41
male bias, 30
male control over women's lives, 106
male dominance, 27, 106, 116, 119, 219, 221; in Sri Lanka, 163–67
male nationalism, 124
Mangsatabam, Annie, 211
Manipur Students Federation (MSF), 72
Manipur, gendered atrocities, 33
Manorama, Thangjam, 66–69, 211–12
Maoist rebels in Andhra Pradesh, 175

Marikkar, Neela, 142
marketization, 26
markets, 37
Marx, 158
masculine appropriation of female sexuality, 136
masculine culture of militaries, 144
masculine discontinuity, 126
masculinity, 135, 287
masculinity, cultural noms, 279
masculinity/femininity dyads, 279
material factors, 104
material resistance, 32
maternal care and the politics of resistance, 54
McCann-Erickson Worldwide, USA, 142
Meira Peibis, 33, 67, 211–12, 214
Meiteis, 64; women, 56
migrant labour from Bangladesh, 17
migrant women in Bangladesh, 18
migrants from Bangladesh, 16
migration, 16, 25, 30; autonomous female, 17; forced, 281; gender dimensions, 15–18; illegal, 11–12
Militarization of civil society, 146
militarization of women in Sri Lanka, 144–50
Militarization, 283
militarism and gender: through the lens of security in South Asia, 32–35
militarism and militarization: of state and society, 26, 31, 38; military, symbol of masculinity and domination, 135
militarism, 144
military power of the state, 37
military women in post-conflict situation in Sri Lanka, 147
military, 37
minorities, 41
minorities, women and peace, a South Asian perspective, 218*ff*
Mizo customary laws, 56
Mizo Women's Federation (MWF), 56

monotheism, 126
moral imperatives, 4
morality, 84, 88
Morgenthau, Hans, 28
Mother Courage, 60
Mother's Union of Meghalaya, 60–61
mother–child relationship, 63, 65
motherhood, 201
motherhood, 6, 39, 54, 63–64, 65, 69–70, 74, 133, 136; and democratic politics, 55–59; as space of protest in Sri Lanka, 139, 152*ff*
motherland, 72–73, 126
Mothers' Front, 51n^{52}, 57, 139–40, 152–64; and the state, interplay, 161
Mothers' Union of Tura (Meghalaya), 58, 60, 61
Moulana, Alavi, 159
Moyon Naga Council, 213
Moyon Sanuw Ruwrkheh (MSR), 212–13
Mulholland, Marie, 277–78
Multiculturalism, 141
Muslims, 58, 218–19

Naga Hoho, 62
Naga Mothers' Association (NMA), 56, 60–63, 215, 234, 238–39
Naga Peoples' Movement for Human Rights (NPMHR), 68
Naga women, 55, 62, 212–14
Naga Women's Union Manipur (NWUM), 60, 62–64, 213, 214
Namasudra community, 16
Narmada Bachao Andolan (NBA), 37
Nasrin, Taslima, 221
nation, identification: with male figure, 124–26; with women, 126–27
National Human Rights Commission (NHRC), 61
national security practices, 29
national security, 26
National Security Studies, US, 24
National Socialist Council Nagalim (NSCN), 234

nationalism, 113*ff*, 214; in Serbia and Croatia, 281
Nationalist Socialist Council of Nagaland–Isaac Muivah faction (NSCN [I-M]), 62, 213; Khaplang faction, 62, 213
Navaratne, Gamini, 167
Naxalites in Andhra Pradesh, 176–77
Nazism, 117, 237
Nehru, Jawaharlal, 243, 245, 250
new social movements, 37
non-governmental organizations (NGOs): in Bangladesh, 221, 225, 227; in Sri Lanka, 169, 171
non-violence, 26
North Atlantic Treaty Organization (NATO), 46
North East, 136, 137
Northeast India, 6, 33; women's politics for peace, 54, 55–56, 211–16
nuclear deterrence, 3
nupi lan in Manipur, 7
Nupi Marups, 67

organ trade, 12
Organization for the Disappeared Soldiers, 165
Organization of Parents and Families of Disappeared, 165
Oslo peace negotiations, 147–48
overpopulation, 24

Pakistan: Bangladesh women immigrants, 12; DIYAT, 101, 2236, 240; Family Laws Ordinance (1961), 240, 241; Hudood Ordinances, 100, 101, 236, 240; inter-community tensions, 41; Penal Code (1986 and 1992), 240; QISAS, 101, 236, 240; *Shariat* Bill, 97, 108, 236, 240; Zina Ordinance, 236, 240
Palestinian Authority (PA), 290, 291–92
Palestinian Liberation Organization (PLO), 290, 299
Palestinians, 237, 283–84, 289–300; Christians-Muslims, 293–94
Parents of Servicemen Missing in Action, 234

Partition of Indian subcontinent, 134–35, 218–19
passive revolution, 100
patriarchy, 6, 27, 32, 34, 41, 44, 54–56, 63, 68, 69, 70, 72, 105–07, 109, 115, 124, 133, 135–37, 156, 220, 223, 296
peace process in Andhra Pradesh, 178–80
peasant women, 79–80, 82
People's Liberation Army (PLA), 33, 66, 211
Periyar, P.V., 247
personal identity, 26
policy options, 22
political domination, 116
political movement in Israel, 296
political partition, 287
political representation, 124
political socialization, 138
politicization of motherhood, 62
politics, 7, 26, 37, 54, 62, 95–96, 216; in Bangladesh, 228–30; of gender identity, 278; of gratitude, 71–74
polygamy, 11
post conflict situations, 6, 25; reconstruction and peace-building processes, 31
post-election violence against minorities in Bangladesh, 224–26; role of administration, 226–27
poverty, 17, 40, 80
power balance, 3
Power relations, 223, 229
power relations, 40, 46, 94, 115
Premadasa, Ranasinghe, 139, 156, 157, 160
Prevention of Terrorist Activities (POTA), 73
price of women, 15
private domain of family, domestic labour and sexuality, 79–80, 87, 90, 93
proletarianization of women of immigrant families, 17
property rights, 216
prostitution, forced, 12
Protestant Unionist Women, 278

public humiliation of women, 134
public participation in peace process, 44
public sphere of production, politics and war, 79, 81–93, 107, 216
purdah, 79

race, 41, 144
Rajapakse, Mahinda, 154, 165
Ramachandran, M.G., 248, 250
rape, 61, 66, 80, 83, 88, 90, 101, 224, 240–41; being used as an instrument of subjugation, 33
Razakars, 80, 83
Reddi, 246–47, 249, 258, 268
Reddiar, Gundurayan, 246, 250–62, 265–67
refugees, 274–75
regressive identification, 122
rehabilitation, 156
religion, religious, 41, 43, 133, 158, 233; diversity, 43; divide, 293–94; rituals as resistance in Sri Lanka, 157–60;—counter-rituals, 160–61
repression, 80, 91
reservation for women, 6
resistance struggles, 35, 37, 135–37
rights of women, 4, 99, 101–02, 106, 297
Rongpi, Jayanta, 73
Rwanda, 47, 118

sale of women, 10; consent to be sold, 11–15
Samaraveera, Mangala, 154, 165, 167, 168
Samuel, Kumudini, 141
Saravanamuttu, Manorani, 165–66, 168, 169
Sardar Sarovar project, 37
secularism, secular ideology in the women's movement, 7, 108, 220
security, 4, 11–12, 31, 36, 37; changing discourses, lens of human security, 24–26; gender and conflict prevention, perceptions from South Asia, 20*ff*
Seelawathi, D.G., 168

322 Index

self, sense of, and identity, 280–81
self-determination, 33, 128
self-empowerment, 17
selfhood, 280–81
self-identity, 119
self-representation, 122
separatism, 288
Serbian women, 279, 281, 283, 285–86
sex-related crimes, sexual exploitation, 5, 16, 32, 61, 80, 105, 134, 145, 241
sexual relationships, 85, 87–89
sexuality, 34, 125; and reproduction, 90; of mothers, 69–70
Shangnu, T., 64
Sharma, Rubul, 73
Sharmila, Irom, 212
Sinhala Mothers Front of the South, 139
sisterhood, 115, 116
slave trade, 12, 13
social: acceptance, 34; change, 108; evils, 60–63; movements, 214; norms, 84, 85; processes, 274; relationships, 17, 27, 115
socialism, 113, 114, 117, 220
socialization, 6, 73
societal institutions, 107
socio-economic and environmental sources, 25
socio-economic problems of women, 99
Somalia, 47
sovereignty of the state, 24
Sri Lanka, 41, 136, 137; counter rallies, 157–58; counter rhetoric, 156–57; mothers' tears and curses, 161; Sub-Committee on Gender Issues, 148–49; Tamil separatists, 44–45, 139, 219; women in peace politics, 40, 138*ff*; political participation, 152*ff*; Women's Manifesto, 149–50
Sri Lanka Freedom Party (SLFP), 139, 154–55, 157–59, 161, 166, 167, 169–70;—and male orchestration, 163–67

Sri Lanka Women's NGO Forum (SLWNGOF), 143
state, state power, 37, 137; and society, relationship, 138
status of women in East European countries, 114
Strategic Studies in UK, 24
Stree Shakthi Sangathana, 5, 78*ff*
structural causes of conflict, 23, 42
subordination of women, 283
Sujeewardhanam, S., 168
surplus, 7
survival migration, 17
Swara practice, 233

Tamil Eelam Liberation Organization (TELO), 168
Tamil separatists in Sri Lanka, 44–45, 139, 219. *See also* Liberation Tigers of Tamil Eelam (LTTE)
Tamil Women's Agency in Sri Lanka, 167
Telangana movement, 5–6, 7, 78, 80–81, 92, 236
Telugu Desam Party (TDP), 175–76
territorial integrity, 24, 46, 53n^{67}
terrorism, 30, 32
Terrorist Acts, 37
Thiranagama, Ranjini, 141
Tilakawardane, Justice Shiranee, 142–43
toolkit approach to prevention, 23
traditional roles, 96
trafficking in women: in Bangladesh, 12–15; in Nepal, 12; in Pakistan, 15
transcending the contradiction, 277–78
transnational conflicts, 114, 25
Turkish Cypriots, 275
Tushimi, Amita, 64

Udugampola, Premadasa, 159, 162
underdevelopment, 24
unemployment, 11
United Legislative Front, 211
United Liberation Front of Assam (ULFA), 58–59